Table of Contents

Free Gift

In order to thank you for buying my book I am glad to present you
- 1000 Bestseller Recipes Cookbook -

Please follow this link to get instant access to your Free Cookbook:
http://www.bookbuying.top/

Introduction

Why should you opt for a Mediterranean diet?
Why is this diet so popular all over the world and why should it become a way of living for you?
We are here to answer all these questions and to help you start a fresh new chapter in your life!
Let's find out all there is to know about the Mediterranean diet!

The most important thing you need to know about the Mediterranean diet is that in fact, it's just a healthy way of living. It's strongly related to living and eating habits of people from countries next to the Mediterranean sea like Greece, Spain, Italy and so on.

The Mediterranean diet also means you should include in your daily diet ingredients like bread, pasta, fruits, rice, potatoes, veggies, fish, clean meat, healthy oils, etc.
It also means you get to consume more fish, seafood, beans, eggs and a lot of milk and of course, natural yogurts.
All these foods will improve your overall health; they will provide the necessary intake of calcium, proteins and other vitamins and important nutrients.
A Mediterranean diet will help you lose some extra weight if you are in need of something like this.

Isn't this great?
What more could you ask? Where else can you find something like this? Which other diet allows you to eat some of the most unbelievably tasty dishes in the world and stay healthy at the same time?
Make a choice!
Decide to follow a Mediterranean diet today and get all the recipes you need from this great cookbook.
Start your new life today and enjoy the Mediterranean taste!

Mediterranean Diet Breakfast Recipes

Tasty Scrambled Eggs

Preparation time: 5 minutes
Cooking time: 5 minutes
Servings: 2

Ingredients:

- 1 tomato, chopped
- 1 tablespoon vegetable oil
- 1 cup baby spinach
- ½ cup feta cheese, cubed
- Salt and black pepper to the taste
- 3 eggs

Directions:

Heat up a pan with the oil over medium heat, add spinach and tomatoes, stir and cook for a few minutes. Add eggs, mix to scramble and cook for 30 seconds. Add cheese, salt and pepper, stir, cook for 20 seconds more, divide between plates and serve. Enjoy!

Nutrition: calories 150, fat 2, fiber 0, carbs 2, protein 10

Delicious Egg Salad

Preparation time: 10 minutes
Cooking time: 0 minutes
Servings: 4

Ingredients:

- ½ cup sun-dried tomatoes, chopped
- 8 eggs, hard-boiled, peeled and chopped
- ¼ cup olives, pitted and chopped
- 1 small cucumber, chopped
- 1 small red onion, finely chopped
- ½ cup Greek yogurt
- ¼ teaspoon cumin
- A splash of lemon juice
- Salt and black pepper to the taste
- 1 and ½ teaspoon oregano

Directions:

In a bowl, mix eggs with onion, olives, cucumber and tomatoes. Add salt, pepper, lemon juice, Greek yogurt, cumin and oregano, stir well and keep in the fridge until you serve it. Enjoy!

Nutrition: calories 230, fat 1, fiber 2, carbs 1.4, protein 7

Mediterranean Breakfast Bowl

Preparation time: 10 minutes
Cooking time: 20 minutes
Servings: 6

Ingredients:

- 1 teaspoon onion powder
- ¼ cup Greek yogurt
- 12 eggs
- 1 teaspoon granulated garlic
- Salt and black pepper to the taste
- 1 teaspoon extra virgin olive oil
- 1-pint cherry tomatoes cut in halves
- 2 cups quinoa, already cooked
- 5 ounces baby spinach leaves
- 1 cup feta cheese, crumbled

Directions:

In a bowl, mix eggs with salt, pepper, onion powder, granulated garlic and yogurt, whisk well and leave aside for now. Heat up a pan with the oil over medium high heat, add spinach, stir and cook for 3 minutes. Add tomatoes, stir and cook 3 more minutes. Add eggs mix, cook for 9 minutes and stir them to scramble. Add quinoa and cheese, stir, cook for 2 minutes more, transfer to bowls and serve hot. Enjoy!

Nutrition: calories 357, fat 20, fiber 2, carbs 20, protein 23

Mediterranean Oats

Preparation time: 5 minutes
Cooking time: 0 minutes
Servings: 1

Ingredients:

- 2 tablespoons walnuts, chopped
- ½ cup oats
- ¾ cup almond milk
- 1 date, chopped
- 1 tablespoon chia seeds
- 1 tablespoon vanilla powder
- ½ teaspoon cinnamon

Directions:

In a bowl, mix milk with walnuts, oats, date, chia seeds, vanilla powder and cinnamon. Stir well, keep in the fridge overnight and serve the next day cold. Enjoy!

Nutrition: calories 345, fat 18, fiber 3, carbs 38, protein 16

Delightful Figs And Yogurt

Preparation time: 10 minutes
Cooking time: 5 minutes
Servings: 4

Ingredients:

- 8 ounces figs cut in halves
- 2 cups Greek yogurt
- 1 tablespoon honey
- A pinch of cinnamon
- ¼ cup pistachios, chopped

Directions:

Heat up a pan over medium heat, add honey and heat it up. Add figs, stir and caramelize them for 5 minutes. Divide yogurt into bowls, add caramelized figs on top, sprinkle cinnamon and pistachios and serve. Enjoy!

Nutrition: calories 200, fat 5, fiber 2, carbs 24, protein 5

Tasty Mediterranean Frittata

Preparation time: 10 minutes
Cooking time: 20 minutes
Servings: 6

Ingredients:

- ¼ cup kalamata olives, pitted and chopped
- 6 eggs
- ½ cup milk
- ½ cup tomatoes, chopped
- ¼ cup black olives, pitted and chopped
- ¼ cup feta cheese, crumbled
- 1 cup spinach
- Salt and black pepper to the taste
- 1 teaspoon oregano, dried
- A drizzle of olive oil

Directions:

Grease a baking dish with a drizzle of oil. In a bowl, mix eggs with milk, salt, pepper, tomatoes, black olives, kalamata olives, spinach, cheese and oregano and whisk well. Pour this into the pan, spread, introduce in the oven at 400 degrees F and bake for 20 minutes. Serve hot. Enjoy!

Nutrition: calories 176, fat 3, fiber 7, carbs 21, protein 16

Delicious Poached Eggs Dish

Preparation time: 10 minutes
Cooking time: 20 minutes
Servings: 6

Ingredients:

- 2 green bell peppers, chopped
- 2 garlic cloves, minced
- 3 tablespoons olive oil
- 1 yellow onion, chopped
- 1 teaspoon sweet paprika
- 1 teaspoon coriander, ground
- Salt and black pepper to the taste
- A pinch of red pepper flakes
- ½ cup tomato sauce
- 6 tomatoes, chopped
- 1 teaspoon sugar
- 6 eggs
- ¼ cup parsley, chopped
- ¼ cup mint, chopped

Directions:

Heat up a pan with the oil over medium heat, add bell peppers, onion, garlic, salt, pepper, paprika, coriander, pepper flakes and cumin, stir and cook for 10 minutes. Add sugar, tomatoes and tomato sauce, stir and simmer for 10 minutes. Add more salt and pepper to the taste and make 6 holes in the mix. Crack an egg into each, cover pan, reduce heat and cook until eggs are done. Sprinkle parsley and mint all over and serve. Enjoy!

Nutrition: calories 300, fat 18, fiber 4, carbs 23, protein 15

Simple Mediterranean Breakfast Strata

Preparation time: 10 minutes
Cooking time: 1 hour
Servings: 4

Ingredients:

- 2 garlic cloves, minced
- 3 tablespoons butter
- 1 cup mushrooms, sliced
- 2 shallots, chopped
- 6 cups white bread, cubed
- 1 teaspoon marjoram, dried
- ½ cup artichoke hearts, chopped
- ¼ cup kalamata olives, pitted and cut in quarters
- 4 ounces mozzarella cheese balls, cut in halves
- 1/5 cup sun-dried tomatoes, marinated and chopped
- ¼ cup parmesan, grated
- 6 eggs
- 1 and ½ cups half and half
- Salt to the taste
- ¼ cup basil, chopped

Directions:

Heat up a small pan over medium heat, add 1 tablespoon butter, melt it and use to brush 4 baking cups. Heat up the same pan with the rest of the butter over medium heat, add shallot and garlic, stir and cook for 2 minutes. Add mushrooms and marjoram, stir, cook for 4 minutes and transfer to a bowl. Add artichoke pieces, bread cubes, olives, tomatoes, salt, mozzarella and parmesan and toss everything well. Divide this mix into greased baking cups. In a bowl, mix eggs with half and a half and whisk well. Divide this over mushroom mix from the cups, sprinkle basil at the end, introduce in the oven at 325 degrees F and bake for 50 minutes. Leave cups aside to cool down for 5 minutes before serving. Enjoy!

Nutrition: calories 300, fat 6, fiber 8, carbs 20, protein 15

Mediterranean Breakfast Pancakes

Preparation time: 10 minutes
Cooking time: 5 minutes
Servings: 2

Ingredients:
- 6 ounces Greek yogurt
- ½ cup flour
- 1 egg
- 1 teaspoon baking soda

Directions:

Put yogurt in a bowl and whisk it well. Add the egg and stir well again. In another bowl, mix baking soda with flour and stir. Combine the 2 mixtures and stir well. Heat up a pan over medium high heat, spoon some of the batter into the pan, spread, cook until it turns golden, flip and cook on the other side as well and transfer pancake to a plate. Repeat with the rest of the batter and serve your pancakes with some maple syrup on top. Enjoy!

Nutrition: calories 111, fat 1.4, fiber 2, carbs 15, protein 10

Mediterranean Baked Eggs

Preparation time: 10 minutes
Cooking time: 50 minutes
Servings: 4

Ingredients:
- 2 yellow onions, cut into medium wedges
- 2 red bell peppers, cut into thin strips
- 1 teaspoon coriander
- 1 teaspoon cumin
- Salt and black pepper to the taste
- Some thyme leaves
- 6 tablespoons olive oil
- A handful cilantro, chopped
- A handful parsley, chopped
- 1 puff pastry sheet
- 1 egg, whisked
- 6 eggs
- 12 teaspoons sour cream

Directions:

In a bowl, mix onions with bell pepper, thyme, salt, pepper, oil, cumin and coriander and toss to coat. Spread into a baking dish, introduce in the oven at 400 degrees F and bake for 30 minutes. Take veggies out of the oven, add half of the cilantro and parsley, toss to coat and leave aside. Roll out puff pastry, cut into 6 squares, place them on a lined baking sheet, prick them with a fork and keep in the fridge for 30 minutes. Take pastry squares out of the fridge, brush with whisked egg, spread 3 teaspoons sour cream on each, divide veggie mix and also spread, lift square edges a bit, introduce them in the oven at 425 degrees F and bake for 10 minutes. Take galettes out of the oven, crack an egg in each, introduce in the oven again and bake for 10 minutes. Take galettes out of the oven, sprinkle salt, pepper to the taste, the rest of the cilantro and parsley, drizzle some oil over them if you want and serve. Enjoy!

Nutrition: calories 340, fat 20, fiber 3, carbs 20, protein 11

Arugula And Roasted Peppers Frittata

Preparation time: 10 minutes
Cooking time: 45 minutes
Servings: 12

Ingredients:

- 3 garlic cloves, minced
- 1 tablespoon olive oil
- 1 cup white onion, chopped
- 8 eggs, whisked
- 12 ounces canned roasted bell peppers, chopped
- 2 handfuls arugula, chopped
- Salt and black pepper to the taste
- ¼ cup basil pesto
- 1 cup mozzarella cheese, shredded
- Cooking spray

Directions:

Heat up a pan with the olive oil over medium high heat, add onion, stir and cook for 5 minutes. Add garlic, stir and cook 2 minutes more and take off heat. In a bowl, whisk well eggs with arugula, red peppers, salt, pepper, cheese and pesto. Add onions mix and stir well again. Pour this into a baking dish which you've sprayed with some cooking spray, introduce in the oven at 350 degrees F and bake for 45 minutes. Take frittata out of the oven, slice and serve hot. Enjoy!

Nutrition: calories 200, fat 12, fiber 1, carbs 0, protein 10

Incredible Banana Toast

Preparation time: 10 minutes
Cooking time: 20 minutes
Servings: 6

Ingredients:

- 2 eggs
- ½ cup milk
- 6 bread slices
- 1 teaspoon vanilla extract
- ½ teaspoon cinnamon, ground
- A pinch of salt
- 3 tablespoons sugar
- 2 tablespoons butter
- For the banana syrup:
- 3 tablespoons whipping cream
- ¼ cup butter
- ¾ cup brown sugar
- 1 teaspoon vanilla extract
- ¼ teaspoon cinnamon, ground
- 2 bananas, chopped
- 4 tablespoons rum

Directions:

In a bowl, mix milk with eggs, salt, vanilla, ½ teaspoon cinnamon and 3 tablespoons sugar and stir well. Heat up a pan with 2 tablespoons butter over medium high heat, dip bread slices in this eggs mix, place them in the pan, fry for 2 minutes on each side and transfer to a plate. Heat up a pan with ¼ cup butter over medium high heat and melt it. Add brown sugar, stir until it dissolves, cook for 2 minutes and take off heat. Add whipping cream, 1 teaspoon vanilla and ¼ teaspoon cinnamon and stir well. Spoon this sauce over toasted slices, top with sliced banana and serve. Enjoy!

Nutrition: calories 180, fat 7, fiber 4, carbs 32, protein 5

Creamy Breakfast Oatmeal

Preparation time: 15 minutes
Cooking time: 20 minutes
Servings: 3

Ingredients:
- 1 cup rolled oats
- A pinch of salt
- 2 cups boiling water
- 2 teaspoons butter
- ½ teaspoon cinnamon, ground
- Fresh berries for serving
- Honey for serving
- Your favorite nuts for serving

Directions:
Put boiling water in a pan, add oats, bring to a boil over medium heat, cook for 5 minutes, reduce heat and cook for 10 more minutes string all the time. Take pot off the heat, add cinnamon and butter, cover and leave aside for 5 minutes. Stir oats again, divide into bowls, top with berries, honey and nuts and serve. Enjoy!

Nutrition: calories 160, fat 3, fiber 4, carbs 30, protein 6

Breakfast Egg Casserole

Preparation time: 10 minutes
Cooking time: 45 minutes
Servings: 6

Ingredients:
- 1 cup red bell pepper, chopped
- 2 tablespoons butter
- 1 yellow onion, chopped
- 1 and ½ cups spinach
- ½ cup milk
- Salt and black pepper the taste
- 8 eggs
- 1 teaspoon olive oil
- 2 ounces feta cheese, crumbled
- 1 cup tomato, chopped
- 1 tablespoon basil, chopped

Directions:
Heat up a pan with the butter over medium high heat, add onion and bell pepper, stir and cook for 6 minutes. Add spinach, stir and cook for 2 minutes. Meanwhile, in a bowl, mix eggs with salt, pepper and cheese and stir well. Add cooked onions mix and stir well again. Heat up another pan with the olive oil over medium heat, add eggs mix and spread evenly. Introduce the pan in the oven at 350 degrees F and bake for 35 minutes. Take out of the oven, spread tomatoes and basil all over, leave aside to cool down for 5 minutes, cut and serve. Enjoy!

Nutrition: calories 250, fat 13, fiber 0, carbs 12, protein 17

Bagel And Eggs

n time: 10 minutes

ime: 2 minutes

Servings: 4

Ingredients:

- 6 hard-boiled eggs, peeled and chopped
- 1 tablespoon green onion, chopped
- 1/3 cup ham, chopped
- ½ cup mayonnaise
- Salt and black pepper to the taste
- 4 whole grain bagels
- ½ cup cheddar cheese, grated

Directions:

In a bowl, mix eggs with salt, pepper, onion, ham and mayo and stir well. Cut bagels in half, spread eggs mix on each half, sprinkle cheese, place everything in preheated broiler and broil until cheese melts. Enjoy!

Nutrition: calories 250, fat 2.2, fiber 2.4, carbs 22, protein 12

Delicious Stuffed Baguette

Preparation time: 10 minutes

Cooking time: 15 minutes

Servings: 6

Ingredients:

- 1 tablespoons dill, chopped
- 5 eggs
- 1 tablespoon cream cheese
- 1 zucchini, grated
- ½ cup jarred roasted peppers
- 1 tablespoon kalamata olives, pitted and chopped
- 1 whole wheat baguette
- Cooking spray
- Salt and pepper to the taste

Directions:

In a bowl, mix eggs with salt, pepper and dill and stir well. Heat up a pan over medium high heat, add cooking spray and zucchinis, stir and cook for 3 minutes. Add eggs mix, spread, reduce heat and cook until eggs are done for 5-6 minutes. Add cream cheese, peppers and olives, stir, take off heat and leave aside for 2 minutes. Cut baguette in half, spread eggs mix on one-half and top with the other. Divide this into 6 pieces and serve. Enjoy!

Nutrition: calories 160, fat 12, fiber 2, carbs 15, protein 17

Ham And Egg Pitas

Preparation time: 10 minutes
Cooking time: 10 minutes
Servings: 4

Ingredients:

- 6 eggs
- 2 shallots, chopped
- 1 teaspoon vegetable oil
- 1/3 cup smoked ham, chopped
- 1/3 cup sweet green pepper, chopped
- ¼ cup brie cheese
- Salt and black pepper to the taste
- 4 lettuce leaves
- 2 whole wheat pita bread

Directions:

Heat up a pan with the oil over medium heat, add green pepper and shallots, stir and cook for 5 minutes. In a bowl, whisk eggs with salt and pepper. Pour this into the pan, add cheese and ham, stir gently and cook until eggs thicken. Cut pitas in half, open pockets, spread 1 teaspoon mustard in each pocket, add 1 lettuce leaf, spread eggs mix and serve. Enjoy!

Nutrition: calories 350, fat 7, fiber 2.3, carbs 24, protein 20

Avocado And Feta Cheese Breakfast

Preparation time: 10 minutes
Cooking time: 0 minutes
Servings: 3

Ingredients:

- 1 avocado, pitted and mashed
- 3 whole grain bread slices, toasted
- Juice of ½ lemon
- Salt and black pepper to the taste
- 2 tablespoons feta cheese
- ¼ teaspoon paprika
- 4 cherry tomatoes, cut in halves

Directions:

In a bowl, mix avocado with salt, pepper, lemon juice, paprika and stir well. Spread this mix on toasted bread slices, top with cherry tomatoes and feta cheese on them and serve. Enjoy!

Nutrition: calories 249, fat 18, fiber 3, carbs 18, protein 9

Breakfast Couscous

Preparation time: 15 minutes
Cooking time: 5 minutes
Servings: 4

Ingredients:
- 3 cups low fat milk
- 1 cinnamon stick
- ½ cup apricots, dried and chopped
- 1 cup couscous, uncooked
- ¼ cup currants, dried
- A pinch of salt
- 6 teaspoons brown sugar
- 4 teaspoons butter, melted

Directions:

Heat up a pan with the milk and cinnamon over medium high heat for 3 minutes and take off heat. Add couscous, currants, apricots, salt and sugar, stir, cover and leave aside for 15 minutes. Discard cinnamon stick, divide into bowls, sprinkle some brown sugar on top of each and serve. Enjoy!

Nutrition: calories 250, fat 6.5, fiber 4, carbs 24, protein 10

Breakfast Chickpeas Hash

Preparation time: 10 minutes
Cooking time: 10 minutes
Servings: 4

Ingredients:
- 2 cups baby spinach
- 4 cups frozen hash brown potatoes
- 1 tablespoon ginger, grated
- ½ cup yellow onion, chopped
- Salt and black pepper to the taste
- 1 tablespoon curry powder
- 15 ounces canned chickpeas, drained
- ¼ cup olive oil
- 1 cup zucchini, grated
- 4 eggs

Ingredients:

In a bowl, mix spinach with potatoes, curry powder, salt, pepper, ginger and onion and stir. Heat up a pan with the oil over medium high heat, add potatoes mix and spread on the bottom and cook for 5 minutes. Reduce heat to medium, add chickpeas and zucchini and stir a bit. Make 4 wells in this mix, crack an egg in each, cover pan and cook for 5 minutes. Divide between plates and serve. Enjoy!

Nutrition: calories 110, fat 6, fiber 3, carbs 14, protein 2

Mediterranean Diet Soups And Stews Recipes

Lamb And Oyster Stew
Preparation time: 10 minutes
Cooking time: 1 hour and 10 minutes
Servings: 6
Ingredients:

For the sofrito:
- 2 cups sweet onion, chopped
- 3 dried chilies, chopped
- 2 cups red bell pepper, chopped
- Salt and black pepper to the taste
- 2 teaspoons rosemary, chopped
- ¼ cup olive oil
- ½ teaspoon red pepper flakes
- 1 cup dry sherry
- 2 cups water
- 29 ounces canned tomatoes, chopped
- 6 garlic cloves, minced
- For the stew:
- 2 garlic cloves, minced
- ¼ cup jarred roasted red peppers
- 2 teaspoons oregano, chopped
- 1 pound lamb, ground
- 1 tablespoon red wine vinegar
- Salt to the paste
- 1 teaspoon red pepper flakes
- 2 tablespoons olive oil
- 1 cup dry sherry
- 36 oysters, shucked
- 1 and ½ cups canned black-eyed peas, drained

Directions:

Heat up a pan over medium high heat, add 3 dried chilies, toast for 2 minutes, transfer to a cutting board and cool them down. Put the water in a pot, bring to a boil, add toasted chilies, stir and simmer for 20 minutes. Take chilies out of the pot and cut them in half. Heat up a pot with ¼ cup oil over medium high heat, add chilies, bell pepper, salt, pepper, rosemary and ½ teaspoon pepper flakes, stir and cook for 10 minutes. Add tomatoes, 6 garlic cloves and 1 cup sherry, stir, reduce heat to medium-low and simmer for 30 minutes. Meanwhile, in a bowl, mix lamb with jarred roasted peppers, 2 garlic cloves, vinegar, oregano and salt and stir well. Heat up a pot with 2 tablespoons olive oil over medium high heat, add lamb mix, stir and cook for 4 minutes. Add 1 teaspoons pepper flakes and 1 cup dry sherry, stir and cook for 2 minutes. Add oysters, peas and more salt if needed, stir and cook for 5 minutes. Transfer sofrito to bowls, top with lamb and oysters stew and serve.

Nutrition: calories 340, fat 16, fiber 3, carbs 21, protein 19

Delicious Lentils Stew
Preparation time: 10 minutes
Cooking time: 35 minutes
Servings: 4
Ingredients:

- 4 cups water
- 1 cup carrots, sliced
- 1 yellow onion, chopped
- 1 tablespoon extra-virgin olive oil
- ¾ cup celery, chopped
- 1 and ½ teaspoon garlic, minced
- 1 and ½ pounds gold potatoes, roughly chopped
- 7 ounces chorizo, cut in half lengthwise and thinly sliced
- 1 and ½ cup lentils
- ½ teaspoon smoked paprika
- ½ teaspoon oregano
- Salt and black pepper to the taste
- 14 ounces canned tomatoes, chopped
- ½ cup cilantro, chopped

Directions:

Heat up a pot with the oil over medium high heat, add onion, garlic, celery and carrots, stir and cook for 4 minutes. Add oregano, potato, chorizo, paprika, salt and pepper, stir and cook for 1 minute. Add lentils and water, stir, bring to a boil, reduce heat to medium-low and simmer for 25 minutes. Add tomatoes, more salt and pepper and cilantro, stir, cook for 5 minutes, divide into bowls and serve. Enjoy!

Nutrition: calories 400, fat 16, fiber 13, carbs 58, protein 24

mb Stew

me: 10 minutes

: 2 hours

Servings: 4

Ingredients:

- 2 and ½ pounds lamb shoulder, boneless and cut in small pieces
- Salt and black pepper to the taste
- 1 yellow onion, chopped
- 3 tablespoons extra virgin olive oil
- 3 tomatoes, grated
- 1 and ½ cups chicken stock
- ½ cup dry white wine
- 1 bay leaf
- 2 and ½ pounds gold potatoes, cut into medium cubes
- ¾ cup green olives

Directions:

Season lamb with salt and pepper and put in a bowl. Heat up a pot with the oil over medium high heat, add lamb, brown for 10 minutes, transfer to a platter and keep warm for now. Heat up the pot again, add onion, stir and cook for 4 minutes. Add tomatoes, stir, reduce heat to low and cook for 15 minutes. Return lamb meat to pot, add wine, stir and cook for 1 minute. Add bay leaf and stock, stir, increase heat to medium high, bring to a boil, reduce heat again, cover pot and simmer for 30 minutes. Add salt and pepper to the taste, potatoes and olives, stir and cook for 1 more hour. Divide into bowls and serve. Enjoy!

Nutrition: calories 450, fat 12, fiber 4, carbs 33, protein 39

Smokey Mediterranean Soup

Preparation time: 10 minutes

Cooking time: 40 minutes

Servings: 4

Ingredients:

- 12 ounces pork meat, ground
- 12 ounces veal, ground
- Salt and black pepper to the taste
- 1garlic clove, minced
- 2 garlic cloves, sliced
- 2 teaspoons thyme, chopped
- 1 egg, whisked
- 3 ounces Manchego, grated
- 2 tablespoons extra virgin olive oil
- 1/3 cup panko
- 4 cups chicken stock
- A pinch of saffron
- 15 ounces canned tomatoes, crushed
- 1 tablespoons parsley, chopped
- 8 ounces pasta

Directions:

In a bowl, mix veal with pork, 1 garlic clove, 1 teaspoon thyme, ¼ teaspoon paprika, salt, pepper to the taste, egg, manchego a panko and stir very well. Shape 20 meatballs from this mix using your wet hands and put them on a plate. Heat up a pan with 1 and ½ tablespoons oil over medium high heat, add half of the meatballs, cook for 2 minutes on each side, transfer to paper towels, drain grease and put on a plate. Repeat this with the rest of the meatballs. Heat up the pot with the rest of the oil, add sliced garlic, stir and cook for 1 minute. Add the rest of the thyme, the rest of the paprika, saffron, stock and tomatoes, stir and cook for 2 minutes. Add meatballs, stir, reduce heat to medium low, cook for 25 minutes and season with salt and pepper. Cook pasta is accruing to instructions, drain them, put into a bowl and mix with ½ cup soup. Divide pasta into soup bowls, add soup and meatballs on top, sprinkle parsley all over and serve. Enjoy!

Nutrition: calories 380, fat 17, fiber 2, carbs 28, protein 26

Delicious Egg Soup

Preparation time: 10 minutes
Cooking time: 10 minutes
Servings: 4

Ingredients:

- 1 teaspoon shallot, chopped
- 1 tablespoon butter
- 1-quart chicken stock
- 2 eggs
- 3 tablespoons lemon juice
- 2 cups peas
- 2 tablespoons parmesan, grated
- Salt and black pepper to the taste

Directions:

Heat up a pot with the butter over medium high heat, add shallot, stir and cook for 2 minutes. Add stock, lemon juice, some salt and pepper, stir and bring to a boil. In a bowl, mix eggs with salt and pepper and whisk well. Add eggs to soup, more salt and pepper to the taste, peas and parmesan cheese, stir, cook for 3 minutes. Divide into bowls and serve. Enjoy!

Nutrition: calories 180, fat 39, fiber 4, carbs 10, protein 14

Lamb Stew With Mint And Apricots

Preparation time: 10 minutes
Cooking time: 1 hour and 45 minutes
Servings: 4

Ingredients:

- 3 cups orange juice
- ½ cup mint tea
- Salt and black pepper to the taste
- 2 pounds lamb shoulder chops
- 1 tablespoon mustard, dry
- 3 tablespoons canola oil
- 1 tablespoon ras el hanout
- 1 carrot, chopped
- 1 yellow onion, chopped
- 1 celery rib, chopped
- 1 tablespoon ginger, grated
- 28 ounces canned tomatoes, crushed
- 1 tablespoon garlic, minced
- 2-star anise
- 1 cup apricots, dried and cut in halves
- 1 cinnamon stick
- ½ cup mint, chopped
- 15 ounces canned chickpeas, drained
- 6 tablespoons yogurt

Directions:

Put orange juice in a pot, bring to a boil over medium heat, take off heat, add tea leaves, cover and leave aside for 3 minutes, strain this and leave aside. Season meat with salt and pepper, add mustard and rasel hanout and toss to coat. Heat up a pot with 2 tablespoons oil over medium high heat, add lamb chops, brown for 3 minutes on each side and transfer to a plate. Add the rest of the oil to the pot and heat it up. Add ginger, onion, carrot, garlic and celery, stir and cook for 5 minutes. Add orange juice, star anise, tomatoes, cinnamon stick, lamb, apricots, stir and cook for 1 hour and 30 minutes. Transfer lamb chops to a cutting board, discard bones and chop. Bring sauce from the pot to a boil, add chickpeas, stir and cook for 10 minutes. Discard cinnamon and star anise, add mint, stir and divide into bowls. Serve with yogurt on top. Enjoy!

Nutrition: calories 560, fat 24, fiber 11, carbs 35, protein 33

Tasty Orzo Soup

Preparation time: 10 minutes
Cooking time: 10 minutes
Servings: 4

Ingredients:

- ½ cup orzo
- 6 cups chicken soup
- 1 and ½ cups parmesan, grated
- Salt and black pepper to the taste
- 1 and ½ teaspoon oregano, dried
- ¼ cup yellow onion, finely chopped
- 3 cups baby spinach
- 2 tablespoons lemon juice
- ½ cup peas, frozen

Directions:

Heat up a pot with the stock over high heat. Add oregano, orzo, salt and pepper, stir, bring to a boil, cover and cook for 2-3 minutes. Add onion, reduce heat to medium and simmer for 3 minutes. Take soup off the heat, add salt and pepper to the taste, parmesan, peas, spinach and lemon juice, stir well and divide into soup bowls. Serve right away. Enjoy!

Nutrition: calories 201, fat 5, fiber 3, carbs 28, protein 17

Rhubarb And Lentils Soup

Preparation time: 10 minutes
Cooking time: 40 minutes
Servings: 6

Ingredients:

- 2 tablespoons coconut butter
- 3 chard leaves, stems removed and leaves chopped
- 1 teaspoon coriander seeds
- 1 teaspoon cumin seeds
- 2 teaspoons mustard seeds
- 2 teaspoons garlic, minced
- 1 tablespoon ginger, grated
- ¼ teaspoon cardamom, ground
- ¼ teaspoon turmeric, ground
- 1 jalapeno pepper, chopped
- 1 yellow onion, chopped
- ¾ cup rhubarb, sliced
- 1 teaspoon brown sugar
- Salt and black pepper to the taste
- ¾ cup green lentils
- 5 cups water
- 3 tablespoons cilantro, chopped
- 6 tablespoons yogurt

Directions:

Heat up a pan with the butter over medium high heat, add cumin, mustard and coriander seeds, stir and toast for 1 minute. Reduce heat to medium-low, add turmeric, garlic, ginger and cardamom, stir and cook for 2 minutes. Add chard, jalapeno and onion, stir and cook for 5 minutes. Add rhubarb, sugar, lentils, salt, pepper and 5 cups water, stir, bring to a boil and simmer for 30 minutes. Divide soup into bowls, top with cilantro and yogurt and serve. Enjoy!

Nutrition: calories 170, fat 7, fiber 6, carbs 22, protein 8

Chicken Stew

Preparation time: 10 minutes
Cooking time: 2 hours and 10 minutes
Servings: 4
Ingredients:

- 3 garlic cloves, minced
- 1 tablespoon parsley, chopped
- 20 saffron threads
- 3 tablespoons cilantro, chopped
- Salt and black pepper to the taste
- 1 teaspoon ginger, ground
- 2 tablespoons olive oil
- 3 red onions, thinly sliced
- 4 chicken drumsticks
- 5 ounces apricots, dried
- 2 tablespoons butter
- ¼ cup honey
- 2/3 cup walnut, chopped
- ½ cinnamon stick

Directions:

Heat up a pan over medium high heat, add saffron threads, toast them for 2 minutes, transfer to a bowl, cool down and crush. Add 1 tablespoon cilantro, parsley, garlic, ginger, salt, pepper, oil and 2 tablespoons water and stir well. Add chicken pieces, toss to coat and keep in the fridge for 30 minutes. Spread onion on the bottom of a pot. Add chicken, drizzle the marinade, add 1 tablespoon butter, place on stove over medium high heat and cook for 15 minutes. Add ¼ cup water, stir, cover pot, reduce heat to medium-low and simmer for 45 minutes. Heat up a pan over medium heat, add 2 tablespoons honey, cinnamon stick, apricots and ¾ cup water, stir, bring to a boil, reduce to low and simmer for 15 minutes. Take off heat, discard cinnamon and leave to cool down. Heat up a pan with the rest of the butter over medium heat, add the rest of the honey and walnuts, stir and cook for 5 minutes. Transfer this to a plate, spread and leave aside. Add chicken to apricots sauce, stir and cook for 10 minutes. Add salt and pepper to the taste, the rest of the cilantro, stir and serve on top of walnuts. Enjoy!

Nutrition: calories 560, fat 10, fiber 4, carbs 34, protein 44

Simple Fish Stew

Preparation time: 10 minutes
Cooking time: 1 hour and 30 minutes
Servings: 4
Ingredients:

- 6 lemon wedges, pulp separated and chopped and some of the peel reserved
- 2 tablespoons parsley, chopped
- 2 tomatoes, cut in halves, peeled and grated
- 2 tablespoons cilantro, chopped
- 2 garlic cloves, minced
- ½ teaspoon paprika
- 2 tablespoons water
- ½ cup water
- ½ teaspoon cumin, ground
- Salt and black pepper to the taste
- 4 black bass fillets
- ¼ cup olive oil
- 3 carrots, sliced
- 1 red bell pepper, sliced lengthwise and thinly cut in strips
- 1 and ¼ pounds potatoes, peeled and sliced
- ½ cup olives
- 1 red onion, thinly sliced

Directions:

In a bowl, mix tomatoes with lemon pulp, cilantro, parsley, cumin, garlic, paprika, salt and pepper and stir. Add 2 tablespoons water and 2 tablespoons oil and stir again. Add fish fillets, toss to coat, cover and keep in the fridge for 30 minutes. Heat up a pot with the water and some salt over medium high heat, add potatoes and carrots, stir, cook for 10 minutes and drain. Heat up a pan over medium heat, add bell pepper and ¼ cup water, cover, cook for 5 minutes and take off heat. Coat a pot with the rest of the oil, spread potatoes and carrots, add ¼ cup water, onion slices, fish and its marinade, bell pepper strips, olives, some salt and pepper, heat up over medium-low heat, cover and cook for 45 minutes. Divide into bowls and serve. Enjoy!

Nutrition: calories 440, fat 18, fiber 8, carbs 43, protein 30

Gazpacho

Preparation time: 60 minutes
Cooking time: 2 minutes
Servings: 4

Ingredients:

- ½ green bell pepper, chopped
- ½ red bell pepper, chopped
- 1 and ¾ pounds tomatoes, chopped
- ¼ cup bread, torn
- 9 tablespoons extra virgin olive oil
-
- 1 garlic clove, minced
- 2 teaspoons sherry vinegar
- Salt and black pepper to the taste
- 1 tablespoon cilantro, chopped
- A pinch of cumin, ground

Directions:

In your blender, mix green and red bell peppers with tomatoes, salt, pepper, 6 tablespoons oil, vinegar, garlic and cumin and pulse well for 5 minutes. Keep this in the fridge for 1 hour. Meanwhile, heat up a pan with the rest of the oil over medium high heat add bread pieces, cook for 1 minute and transfer them to paper towels. Divide cold soup into bowls, top with bread cubes and cilantro and serve. Enjoy!

Nutrition: calories 260, fat 23, fiber 2, carbs 11, protein 2

Chickpea And Kale Soup

Preparation time: 10 minutes
Cooking time: 35 minutes
Servings: 4

Ingredients:

- 1 bunch kale, leaves torn
- Salt and black pepper to the taste
- 3 tablespoons olive oil
- 1 celery stalk, chopped
- 1 yellow onion, chopped
- 1 carrot, chopped
- 30 ounces canned chickpeas, drained
- 14 ounces canned tomatoes, chopped
- 1 bay leaf
- 3 rosemary sprigs
- 4 cups veggie stock

Directions:

In a bowl, mix kale with 1 and ½ tablespoons oil, salt and pepper and toss to coat. Spread this on a lined baking sheet, introduce in the oven at 425 degrees F, bake for 12 minutes, take out of the oven and leave aside for now. Heat up a pot with the rest of the oil over medium high heat, add carrot, celery, onion, some salt and pepper, stir and cook for 5 minutes. Add tomatoes and chickpeas, stir and cook for 1 minute. Add bay leaf and rosemary, stock and more salt if needed, stir and simmer for 20 minutes. Discard rosemary and bay leaf, puree using your blender and divide into soup bowls. Top with roasted kale and serve. Enjoy!

Nutrition: calories 360, fat 14, fiber 11, carbs 53, protein 14

Delicious Bouillabaisse

Preparation time: 10 minutes
Cooking time: 35 minutes
Servings: 6

Ingredients:

- 2 garlic cloves, minced
- 2 tablespoons olive oil
- 1 fennel bulb, sliced
- 1 yellow onion, chopped
- 1 pinch saffron, soaked in some orange juice for 10 minutes and drained
- 14 ounces canned tomatoes, peeled
- 1 strip orange zest
- 6 cups seafood stock
- 10 halibut fillet, cut into big pieces
- 20 shrimp, peeled and deveined
- 1 bunch parsley, chopped
- Salt and white pepper to the taste

Directions:

Heat up a pot with the oil over medium high heat, add onion, garlic and fennel, stir and cook for 10 minutes. Add saffron, tomatoes, orange zest and stock, stir, bring to a boil and simmer for 20 minutes. Reduce heat to medium-low, add fish pieces, stir and cook for 2 minutes. Add shrimp and simmer for 4 minutes more. Sprinkle parsley, salt and pepper, divide into bowls and serve. Enjoy!

Nutrition: calories 340, fat 20, fiber 3, carbs 23, protein 45

Watermelon Gazpacho

Preparation time: 4 hours
Cooking time: 5 minutes
Servings: 4

Ingredients:

- 3 pounds watermelon, sliced
- ½ teaspoon chipotle chili powder
- 2 tablespoons olive oil
- Salt to the taste
- 1 tomato, chopped
- 1 tablespoon shallot, chopped
- ¼ cup cilantro, chopped
- 1 small cucumber, chopped
- 1 small Serrano chili pepper, chopped
- 3 and ½ tablespoons lime juice
- ¼ cup crème Fraiche
- ½ tablespoon red wine vinegar

Directions:

In a bowl, mix 1 tablespoon oil with chipotle powder. Brush watermelon slices with this mix, sprinkle salt, place them on preheated grill over medium high heat, grill for 1 minute on each side, transfer to a cutting board, leave aside to cool down, chop and put in a blender. Add cucumber, tomato, shallot, cilantro, chili pepper, salt and the rest of the oil and pulse very well. Transfer to bowls, top with lime juice and vinegar, keep in the fridge for 4 hours and then serve. Enjoy!

Nutrition: calories 115, fat 0, fiber 2, carbs 18, protein 2

Red Pepper And Shrimp Soup

Preparation time: 30 minutes
Cooking time: 5 minutes
Servings: 6

Ingredients:

- 1 English cucumber, chopped
- 3 cups tomato juice
- 3 jarred roasted red peppers, chopped
- ½ cup olive oil
- 2 tablespoons sherry vinegar
- 1 teaspoon sherry vinegar
- 1 garlic clove, mashed
- 2 baguette slices, cut into cubes and toasted
- Salt and black pepper to the taste
- ½ teaspoon cumin, ground
- ¾ pounds shrimp, peeled and deveined
- 1 teaspoon thyme, chopped

Directions:

In your blender, mix cucumber with tomato juice and red peppers and pulse well. Add bread, 6 tablespoons oil, 2 tablespoons vinegar, cumin, salt, pepper and garlic and blend again well. Add more salt and pepper, transfer to a bowl and keep in the fridge for 30 minutes. Heat up a pot with 1 tablespoon oil over high heat, add shrimp, stir and cook for 2 minutes. Add thyme, salt and pepper, cook for 1 minute and transfer to a plate. Add 1 teaspoon vinegar and some salt and stir well. Divide cold soup into bowls, top with shrimp and serve. Enjoy!

Nutrition: calories 230, fat 7, fiber 10, carbs 24, protein 13

Mussels Stew

Preparation time: 10 minutes
Cooking time: 50 minutes
Servings: 4

Ingredients:

- 1 yellow onion, chopped
- 2 tablespoons oil
- 1 fennel bulb, stalks removed, sliced and roughly chopped
- 1 carrot, thinly sliced crosswise
- 1 red bell pepper, chopped
- 2 garlic cloves, minced
- 3 tablespoons tomato paste
- 16 ounces canned chickpeas, drained
- ½ cup dry white wine
- 1 teaspoon thyme, chopped
- A pinch of smoked paprika
- Salt and black pepper to the taste
- 1 bay leaf
- 2 pinches saffron
- 4 baguette slices, toasted
- 3 and ½ cups water
- 13 mussels, debearded
- 11 ounces halibut fillets, skinless and cut into chunks

Directions:

Heat up a pot with the oil over medium high heat, add fennel, onion, bell pepper and carrot, stir and cook for 5 minutes. Add garlic and tomato paste, stir and cook for 1 minute. Add wine, stir and cook for 2 minutes. Add water, thyme, paprika, chickpeas, bay leaf and saffron, stir, bring to a boil, cover and boil for 25 minutes. Add salt and pepper to the taste, halibut and mussels, cover and simmer for 6 minutes more. Discard unopened mussels, ladle into bowls and serve with toasted bread on the side. Enjoy!

Nutrition: calories 450, fat 12, fiber 13, carbs 47, protein 34

White Gazpacho

Preparation time: 10 minutes
Cooking time: 6 minutes
Servings: 4

Ingredients:

- 3 bread slices
- ¼ cup almonds
- 4 teaspoons almonds
- 3 cucumbers, peeled and chopped
- 3 garlic cloves, minced
- ½ cup warm water
- 6 scallions, thinly sliced
- ¼ cup white wine vinegar
- 3 tablespoons olive oil
- Salt to the taste
- 1 teaspoon lemon juice
- ½ cup green grapes, cut in halves

Directions:

Heat up a pan over medium high heat, add almonds, stir, toast for 5 minutes, transfer to a plate and leave aside. Soak the bread in warm water for 2 minutes and transfer it to your blender. Add cucumber but reserve some for serving, salt, oil, garlic, almost all the scallions, lemon juice, ¼ cup almonds and vinegar and pulse well. Ladle soup into bowls, top with reserved cucumber, the rest of the scallions, the rest of the almonds and 2 tablespoons grapes. Enjoy!

Nutrition: calories 200, fat 12, fiber 3, carbs 20, protein 6

Vegetable Stew

Preparation time: 10 minutes
Cooking time: 30 minutes
Servings: 4

Ingredients:

- 1 yellow onion, chopped
- 1 tablespoon extra-virgin olive oil
- 2 cups sweet potatoes, peeled and chopped
- 1 and ½ teaspoon cumin, ground
- 4-inch cinnamon stick
- 14 ounces canned tomatoes, chopped
- 14 ounces canned chickpeas, drained
- 1 and ½ teaspoon honey
- 6 tablespoons orange juice
- 1 cup water
- Salt and black pepper to the taste
- ½ cup green olives, pitted
- 2 cups kale leaves, chopped

Directions:

Heat up a pot with the oil over medium high heat, add onion, stir and cook for 5 minutes. Add cumin and cinnamon stick, stir and cook for 1 minute. Add potatoes, tomatoes, chickpeas, olives, honey, orange juice and the water, stir, cover, reduce heat to medium-low and cook for 15 minutes. Add kale, salt and pepper, stir, cover again and cook for 10 minutes more. Divide into bowls and serve. Enjoy!

Nutrition: calories 280, fat 6, fiber 9, carbs 53, protein 10

cken Soup

Ingredients:

- ½ cup water
- Salt and black pepper to the taste
- 6 cups chicken stock
- ¼ cup lemon juice
- 1 chicken breast, boneless, skinless and cut into thin strips
- ½ cup white rice
- 6 tablespoons mint, chopped

Directions:

Put the water in a pot, add salt, ½ cup stock, stir, bring to a boil over medium heat, add rice, stir, reduce temperature to low, cover and simmer for 20 minutes. Take off heat and leave aside. Put the rest of the stock in another pot, bring to a boil over medium heat, add chicken and cook for 5 minutes. Add rice, salt and pepper to the taste, lemon juice and mint, stir, cook for 4 minutes more, divide into bowls and serve. Enjoy!

Nutrition: calories 180, fat 2, fiber 1, carbs 21, protein 20

Eggplant Stew

Preparation time: 10 minutes
Cooking time: 50 minutes
Servings: 4

Ingredients:

- 3 eggplants, chopped
- Salt and black pepper to the taste
- 6 zucchinis, chopped
- 2 yellow onions, chopped
- 3 red bell peppers, chopped
- 56 ounces canned tomatoes, chopped
- A handful black olives, pitted and chopped
- A pinch of allspice, ground
- A pinch of cinnamon, ground
- 1 teaspoon oregano, dried
- A drizzle of honey
- 1 tablespoon garbanzo bean flour mixed with 1 tablespoon water
- A drizzle of olive oil
- A pinch of red chili flakes
- 3 tablespoons Greek yogurt

Directions:

Heat up a pot with the oil over medium high heat, add bell peppers, onions, some salt and pepper, stir and sauté for 4 minutes. Add eggplant and zucchini pieces, more salt and pepper, allspice, cinnamon, oregano, tomatoes and honey, stir, bring to a boil, cover, reduce heat to medium-low and cook for 45 minutes. Add flour mix, olives and chili flakes, stir, cook for 1 minute, divide into bowls and serve with some Greek yogurt on top. Enjoy!

Nutrition: calories 80, fat 2, fiber 4, carbs 12, protein 3

Marvelous Vegetable Omelet

Preparation time: 10 minutes
Cooking time: 10 minutes
Servings: 4

Ingredients:

- 6 eggs
- 2 cups fennel, chopped
- 1 tablespoon olive oil
- ¼ cup green olives, pitted and chopped
- 1 plum tomato, chopped
- 2 tablespoons parsley, chopped
- ¼ cup artichoke hearts, chopped
- Salt and black pepper to the taste
- ½ cup goat cheese, crumbled

Directions:

Heat up a pan with the oil over medium heat, add fennel, stir and cook for about 5 minutes. Add artichokes, tomato and olives, stir and cook for 3 more minutes. In a bowl, mix eggs with salt and pepper, whisk well, add to the pan, stir gently and cook for a couple more minutes. Sprinkle cheese all over, introduce in the oven at 325 degrees F and bake for 5 minutes. Sprinkle parsley on top at the end, cut omelet into medium wedges, arrange on plates and serve. Enjoy!

Nutrition: calories 210, fat 2, fiber 1, carbs 3, protein 5

Bean Breakfast

Preparation time: 10 minutes
Cooking time: 15 minutes
Servings: 4

Ingredients:

- 1 and ½ tablespoons olive oil
- 1 tomato, chopped
- 1 garlic clove, minced
- 1 yellow onion, chopped
- ¼ cup parsley, chopped
- 1 teaspoon cumin, ground
- 15 ounces canned fava beans
- ¼ cup lemon juice
- A pinch of red pepper flakes
- Salt and black pepper to the taste
- 4 warm whole wheat pita bread pockets

Directions:

Heat up a pan with the oil over medium heat, add onion, stir and cook for 5 minutes. Add garlic and tomato, stir and cook for 3 more minutes. Add beans, cumin, lemon juice, parsley, red pepper flakes, salt and pepper, stir well, bring to a simmer and cook for 5 minutes. Fill pita pockets with fava bean mix, divide between plates and serve. Enjoy!

Nutrition: calories 150, fat 3, fiber 1, carbs 5, protein 5

Interesting Breakfast Quinoa

Preparation time: 10 minutes
Cooking time: 0 minutes
Servings: 4

Ingredients:

- 2 cups low fat milk
- 1 vanilla bean, seeds scraped out
- 2 cups quinoa, already cooked
- ½ teaspoon cinnamon powder
- 1 tablespoon honey
- 1 cup blueberries
- ¼ cup almonds sliced

Directions:

In a bowl, mix milk with vanilla bean and cinnamon and whisk well. Divide quinoa into breakfast bowls and mix with vanilla and cinnamon milk. Divide blueberries and almonds in each bowl, drizzle honey at the end and serve.
Enjoy!

Nutrition: calories 110, fat 1, fiber 2, carbs 4, protein 5

Delicious Breakfast Fennel Salad

Preparation time: 20 minutes
Cooking time: 0 minutes
Servings: 4

Ingredients:

- 1 tablespoon red wine vinegar
- 2 garlic cloves, minced
- 1 teaspoon mustard
- ¼ cup olive oil
- 1 tablespoon lemon juice
- Sea salt and black pepper to the taste
- ½ cup kalamata olives, pitted and chopped
- 1 tablespoon parsley, chopped
- 10 cups mixed radicchio and lettuce leaves, torn
- 2 endives, roughly chopped
- 3 medium navel oranges, peeled and cut into medium segments
- 2 bulbs fennel, roughly chopped

Directions:

In a bowl, combine vinegar with lemon juice, garlic, salt, pepper, mustard, parsley and oil and whisk well. In a salad bowl, mix radicchio and lettuce with endive, fennel and oranges. Drizzle salad dressing, toss to coat and serve right away for breakfast! Enjoy!

Nutrition: calories 100, fat 1, fiber 2, carbs 3, protein 2

Breakfast Egg Delight

Preparation time: 10 minutes
Cooking time: 5 minutes
Servings: 2

Ingredients:

- 2 tomatoes, sliced
- 2 eggs, hard-boiled, peeled and sliced
- ¼ cup goat cheese, crumbled
- 1 breakfast whole wheat muffin, halved and toasted
- 1 tablespoon olive oil
- A pinch of chipotle chili powder

Directions:

Drizzle the oil over each muffin half, divide tomato slices and egg pieces. Sprinkle cheese and chili powder all over and broil them over medium heat for 5 minutes. Divide between 2 plates and serve. Enjoy!

Nutrition: calories 145, fat 2, fiber 2, carbs 5, protein 2

Delicious Banana Bowl

Preparation time: 5 minutes
Cooking time: 0 minutes
Servings: 2

Ingredients:

- 2 bananas, peeled and roughly chopped
- 2 cups raspberries
- ½ cup Greek yogurt
- ½ cup low fat milk
- Coconut flakes, toasted for serving

Directions:

In your blender, mix banana with raspberries, milk and yogurt, pulse well and divide into 2 bowls. Top with coconut flakes and serve right away. Enjoy!

Nutrition: calories 100, fat 1, fiber 8, carbs 5, protein 4

Unbelievable Breakfast Farro And Spinach

Preparation time: 10 minutes
Cooking time: 4 minutes
Servings: 2

Ingredients:

- 1 tablespoon olive oil
- A pinch of salt and black pepper
- 1 bunch spinach, chopped
- 1 avocado, pitted, peeled and chopped
- 1 garlic clove, minced
- 2 cups farro, already cooked
- 1 tomato, chopped

Directions:

Heat up a pan with the oil over medium heat, add garlic, stir and cook for 1 minute. Add spinach, salt and pepper, stir and cook for 2 minutes. Divide avocado and tomato into serving bowls, top each with spinach and farro, stir gently and serve right away. Enjoy!

Nutrition: calories 120, fat 1, fiber 3, carbs 3, protein 6

Tasty Almond Bars

Preparation time: 40 minutes
Cooking time: 4 minutes
Servings: 12

Ingredients:

- 12 dates, pitted and chopped
- 1 teaspoon vanilla extract
- ¼ cup honey
- ½ cup rolled oats
- ¾ cup cranberries, dried
- ¼ cup almond butter
- 1 cup almonds, toasted and chopped
- ¼ cup pumpkin seeds

Directions:

Put the almond butter in a small pot, heat it up over medium heat, add vanilla and honey, stir, cook for 1 minutes and transfer to a bowl. Add oats, cranberries, almonds and pumpkin seeds, stir and press everything on a lined baking sheet. Keep in the freezer for 30 minutes, divide into 12 pieces and serve for breakfast when you are on the run. Enjoy!

Nutrition: calories 140, fat 1, fiber 3, carbs 2, protein 3

Easy Eggs Sandwich

Preparation time: 10 minutes
Cooking time: 2 minutes
Servings: 2

Ingredients:

- 2 whole wheat muffins, toasted and halved
- 1 tablespoon chives, chopped
- 1 tablespoon dill, chopped
- A pinch of salt and black pepper
- 2 cheddar cheese slices
- 1 tomato, sliced
- 2 eggs

Directions:

In a bowl, mix eggs with salt, pepper, dill and chives, whisk well, divide this into 2 ramekins, introduce in the oven at 400 degrees F and cook for 6 minutes. Divide 2 muffin halves between plates, add an egg on each, add cheddar and tomato slices, top with the other muffin halves and serve right away. Enjoy!

Nutrition: calories 125, fat 1, fiber 1, carbs 4, protein 8

Easy Pancetta Breakfast

Preparation time: 10 minutes
Cooking time: 1 hour and 5 minutes
Servings: 4

Ingredients:

- 28 ounces small potatoes, cut into medium wedges
- 1 yellow onion, chopped
- 3 ounces pancetta, chopped
- 2 garlic cloves, minced
- 1 and ½ tablespoons olive oil
- 2 eggs, whisked
- 2 ounces goat cheese, crumbled
- A pinch of salt and black pepper
- A bunch of parsley, chopped

Directions:

Put potatoes in a pot, add water to cover, add a pinch of salt, bring to a boil over medium heat, simmer for 15 minutes, drain, put them in a bowl and leave aside to cool down. Heat up ½ tablespoons olive oil in a pot over low heat, add onion and garlic, stir, cook for 15 minutes and add over potatoes. Heat up the same pan over medium heat , add pancetta, stir, cook for 3-4 minutes and add to the same bowl with the potatoes and onion and garlic. Add cheese and eggs, salt, pepper and parsley and stir everything well. Heat up a pan with the rest of the oil over medium heat, add potato mix , cook for 15 minutes, flip and cook for 15 more minutes. Divide between plates and serve for breakfast. Enjoy!

Nutrition: calories 250, fat 4, fiber 4, carbs 7, protein 10

Special Omelet

Preparation time: 5 minutes
Cooking time: 5 minutes
Servings: 1

Ingredients:

- 1 egg, whisked
- ½ teaspoon olive oil
- 1 teaspoon cinnamon powder
- 1 tablespoon almond milk
- 3 ounces cottage cheese
- 4 ounces mixed raspberries and blueberries

Directions:

In a bowl, mix the egg with milk and cinnamon and whisk. Heat up a pan over a medium high heat, pour the egg mix, spread into the pan, cook for 2 minutes and transfer to a plate. Spread cheese and berries all over, roll and serve. Enjoy!

Nutrition: calories 140, fat 1, fiber 4, carbs 6, protein 10

Simple And Easy Breakfast

Preparation time: 10 minutes
Cooking time: 5 minutes
Servings: 2

Ingredients:

- A handful cherry tomatoes, halved
- 1 cucumber, sliced
- 1 avocado, pitted, peeled and chopped
- 2 tablespoons parsley, chopped
- 1 red bell pepper, chopped
- 1 tablespoon basil, chopped
- 1 tablespoon olive oil+ a drizzle more
- ¼ cup pine nuts, toasted
- Sea salt to the taste
- 2 eggs

Directions:

In a large bowl mix tomatoes, cucumber, bell pepper, avocado, basil, parsley, pine nuts and oil and toss to coat. Heat up a pan with a drizzle of oil over medium heat, crack eggs and fry them. Divide mixed salad into 2 bowls, top each with an egg and serve. Enjoy!

Nutrition: calories 140, fat 3, fiber 4, carbs 6, protein 5

Light And Healthy Salad

Preparation time: 5 minutes
Cooking time: 0 minutes
Servings: 2

Ingredients:

- 1 white grapefruit, peeled and cut into small segments
- 1 pink grapefruit, peeled and cut into small segments
- 1 teaspoon pistachios, chopped
- 1 tablespoon agave nectar

Directions:

In a bowl, mix white and pink grapefruits with agave nectar and pistachios, toss well, divide into 2 smaller bowls and serve. Enjoy!

Nutrition: calories 100, fat 1, fiber 2, carbs 2. protein 1

Breakfast Broccoli Frittata

Preparation time: 5 minutes
Cooking time: 25 minutes
Servings: 4

Ingredients:

- 17 ounces potatoes, roughly chopped
- 1 tablespoon olive oil
- 2 salmon fillets, skinless and boneless
- 1 small broccoli, florets separated
- 8 eggs, whisked
- 1 teaspoon mint, chopped

Directions:

Put potatoes in a pot, add water to cover, bring to a boil over medium heat and cook for 8 minutes. Add broccoli, cook everything for 4 minutes more, drain everything and put in a bowl. Place salmon fillets in an oven-proof dish, introduce in the microwave, cook for 3 minutes at a high temperature and flake into a bowl. Heat up a pan with the oil over medium heat, add potatoes, broccoli, salmon, salt, pepper, mint and eggs, stir and cook for 10 minutes. Divide between plates and serve. Enjoy!

Nutrition: calories 140, fat 2, fiber 3, carbs 6, protein 3

Breakfast Mushroom Salad

Preparation time: 10 minutes
Cooking time: 7 minutes
Servings: 6

Ingredients:

- ½ pounds mushrooms, sliced
- 1 tablespoon extra virgin olive oil
- 3 garlic cloves, minced
- 1 teaspoon basil, dried
- Salt and black pepper to the taste
- 1 tomato, diced
- 3 tablespoons lemon juice
- ½ cup water
- 1 tablespoons coriander, chopped

Directions:

Heat up a pan with the oil over medium heat, add mushrooms, stir and cook for 3 minutes. Add basil, garlic, salt, pepper, water, tomato and lemon juice, stir and cook for 4 minutes more. Divide into bowls, leave aside to cool down, sprinkle coriander on top and serve for breakfast. Enjoy!

Nutrition: calories 140, fat 4, fiber 4, carbs 7, protein 4

Healthy Breakfast Lentils

Preparation time: 10 minutes
Cooking time: 10 minutes
Servings: 4

Ingredients:

- ½ cup almonds, toasted chopped
- 1 apple, cored, peeled and chopped
- 3 tablespoons maple syrup
- 4 cups low fat milk
- ½ cup red lentils
- ½ teaspoon cinnamon powder
- ½ cup cream of wheat
- ½ cup cranberries, dried
- 1 teaspoon vanilla extract

Directions:

In a bowl, mix apple with 1 tablespoon maple syrup and almonds, stir and leave aside. Put milk in a pot, heat up over medium heat, add cream of wheat, the rest of the maple syrup, cinnamon, cranberries and lentils, stir, bring to a simmer and cook for 10 minutes Add vanilla, stir, divide into a bowl, top each with apple mixture and serve. Enjoy!

Nutrition: calories 150, fat 2, fiber 1, carbs 3, protein 5

Special Frittata

Preparation time: 10 minutes
Cooking time: 15 minutes
Servings: 3

Ingredients:

- 1 yellow onion, chopped
- 2 tablespoons butter
- 1 cup potatoes, boiled and chopped
- ¼ cup parsley, chopped
- ¾ cup ham, finely chopped
- 4 eggs
- ¾ cup lentils, cooked
- 2 tablespoons half and half
- Salt and black pepper to the taste
- ½ cup cherry tomatoes, halved
- ¾ cup cheddar cheese, shredded

Directions:

Heat up a pan with the butter over medium heat, add onions, stir and cook for 2 minutes. Add ham and potatoes, stir and cook for 4 more minutes. In a bowl, mix egg with parsley, salt, pepper, lentils and half and half and whisk well. Pour this into the pan, spread, stir gently and cook for 3 minutes. Arrange halved tomatoes and shredded cheese on top, introduce in preheated broiler and broil for 5 minutes. Divide between plates and serve for breakfast. Enjoy!

Nutrition: calories 156, fat 3, fiber 2, carbs 5, protein 7

Easy Lentils Mix

Preparation time: 10 minutes
Cooking time: 1 hour
Servings: 4

Ingredients:

- ½ cup red lentils, soaked for 12 hours and drained
- ¼ cup pumpkin seeds
- 3 tablespoons hemp seeds
- 2 teaspoons olive oil
- ¼ cup rolled oats
- ¼ cup coconut, shredded and toasted
- 1 tablespoon honey+ 1 teaspoon
- 1/3 cup cranberries, dried
- 1 tablespoon orange zest, grated
- 1 cup Greek yogurt
- 1 cup blackberries

Directions:

Spread lentils on a lined baking sheet, introduce in the oven at 370 degrees F and roast them for 30 minutes, flipping them from time to time. Heat up a pan over medium high heat, add pumpkin seeds, toast them for 2-3 minutes, transfer to a bowl Mix pumpkin seeds with hemp seeds, oats, coconut and roasted lentils, and stir. Add orange zest, 1-tablespoon honey and oil and toss everything to coat. Spread this on a lined baking tray, introduce in the oven at 370 degrees F, bake for 20 minutes, transfer everything to a bowl and mix with cranberries. Put half of the yogurt in a bowl, add half of the lentils granola and half of the berries. Add the rest of the yogurt and the rest of the lentils mix, drizzle 1 teaspoon honey on top and serve. Enjoy!

Healthy And Special Breakfast

Preparation time: 10 minutes
Cooking time: 3 minutes
Servings: 2

Ingredients:
- 1 whole wheat muffin, halved
- 6 ounces canned tuna, drained and flaked
- 2 tablespoons tomato sauce
- A pinch of sea salt and black pepper
- 2 mozzarella slices
- 1 teaspoon oregano, dried

Directions:
Spread tomato sauce on each muffin half, add tuna, salt and pepper to the taste and sprinkle oregano at the end. Top with mozzarella slices, arrange them all a tray, introduce in the oven at 325 degrees F, bake for 3 minutes and serve hot. Enjoy!

Nutrition: calories 110, fat 1, fiber 2, carbs 3, protein 4

Simple Tuna Frittata

Preparation time: 5 minutes
Cooking time: 15 minutes
Servings: 4

Ingredients:
- 10 ounces canned tuna, drained and flaked
- 5 eggs, whisked
- ½ cup feta cheese, shredded
- Salt and black pepper to the taste
- 3 teaspoons olive oil

Directions:
In a bowl, mix tuna with eggs, salt and pepper to the taste and whisk. Pour this into a dish which you've greased with the olive oil, introduce in the oven at 370 degrees F and bake for 14 minutes. Sprinkle shredded cheese on top, introduce in the oven for 3 more minutes, divide between plates and serve. Enjoy!

Nutrition: calories 143, fat 2, fiber 4, carbs 5, protein 7

Spinach And Tuna Sandwich

Preparation time: 5 minutes
Cooking time: 0 minutes
Servings: 2

Ingredients:
- 6 ounces canned tuna, drained and flaked
- 1 tablespoon mayonnaise
- 4 slices whole wheat bread
- A pinch of sea salt and black pepper
- A handful baby spinach
- 1 tablespoon feta cheese, crumbled
- A splash of white wine vinegar

Directions:
In a bowl, mix tuna with mayo, vinegar, salt and pepper and whisk well. Divide tuna and mayo mix on 2 bread slices, add baby spinach and cheese, top with the other 2 bread slices and serve. Enjoy!

Nutrition: calories 112, fat 2, fiber 1, carbs 2, protein 3

Easy Feta Omelet

Preparation time: 10 minutes
Cooking time: 6 minutes
Servings: 2

Ingredients:
- 4 sun dried tomatoes, chopped
- 2 eggs whisked
- 1 teaspoon olive oil
- A small handful of mixed salad leaves
- ½ tablespoon feta cheese, crumbled

Directions:
Heat up a pan with the olive oil over medium heat, add eggs and scramble them for 4-5 minutes. Add tomatoes and feta cheese, stir, cook for 1 minute, divide between 2 plates and serve with salad leaves on the side. Enjoy!

Nutrition: calories 140, fat 2, fiber 1, carbs 5, protein 3

Amazing Breakfast Salad

Preparation time: 10 minutes
Cooking time: 0 minutes
Servings: 4

Ingredients:
- 5 lettuce leaves, roughly chopped
- 1 peach, stone removed and chopped
- 1 cup baby spinach, chopped
- ½ mango, peeled and chopped
- 10 strawberries, halved
- 1 tablespoon hemp seeds
- 1 cucumber, sliced
- For the dressing:
- 1 tablespoon lime juice
- 1 tablespoon tahini
- 1 tablespoon date syrup
- 1 tablespoon coconut water
- ½ teaspoon spirulina powder

Directions:
In a salad bowl, mix lettuce with spinach, mango, peach, cucumber, strawberries and hemp seeds. In another bowl, mix lime juice with date syrup, tahini, coconut water and spirulina powder and whisk well. Add dressing to salad, toss to coat and serve right away for breakfast. Enjoy!

Nutrition: calories 130, fat 2, fiber 3, carbs 5, protein 3

Breakfast Quinoa Muffins

Preparation time: 10 minutes
Cooking time: 35 minutes
Servings: 6

Ingredients:
- 1 cup quinoa
- 2 cups water
- 1 cup spinach, torn
- 1 small yellow onion, chopped
- 2 eggs
- ¼ cup cheddar cheese, grated
- ½ teaspoon garlic powder
- Sea salt and black pepper to the taste
- ½ teaspoon oregano, dried
- A drizzle of olive oil

Directions:
Put water in a pan, heat up over medium heat, add quinoa, stir, simmer for 10 minutes, take off heat and leave aside for now. Heat up a pan with some oil over medium heat, add onion, stir and cook for 2-3 minutes. Add spinach, cook for 2 more minutes, take off heat and also leave aside. In a bowl, mix quinoa with spinach and onion, eggs, cheese, salt, pepper, garlic powder and oregano and stir well. Divide this mix into a greased muffin pan, introduce in the oven at 350 degrees F and bake for 20 minutes. Leave muffins to cool down before serving them for breakfast. Enjoy!

Nutrition: calories 87, fat 3, fiber 1, carbs 5, protein 4

The Most Amazing Breakfast Potatoes

Preparation time: 10 minutes
Cooking time: 45 minutes
Servings: 6

Ingredients:

- 2 pounds potatoes, peeled and sliced
- ½ white onion, sliced
- 1 teaspoon garlic powder
- 1 red bell pepper, chopped
- 2 tablespoons olive oil
- Sea salt and black pepper to the taste

Directions:

In a bowl, mix potatoes with onion, bell pepper, oil, salt, pepper and garlic powder and toss well. Spread these on a lined baking sheet, introduce in the oven at 425 degrees F and bake for 45 minutes, stirring often. Divide between plates and serve warm for breakfast! Enjoy!

Nutrition: calories 160, fat 3, fiber 3, carbs 7, protein 3

Greek Tapioca Porridge

Preparation time: 30 minutes
Cooking time: 15 minutes
Servings: 3

Ingredients:

- ¼ cup pearl tapioca
- ¼ cup sugar
- 2 cups water
- ½ cup coconut flakes
- 1 and ½ teaspoon lemon juice

Directions:

Put tapioca in a pan, add the water, stir, cover and leave aside for 30 minutes. Add milk and palm sugar to tapioca mix, heat everything up over medium heat and simmer for 15 minutes stirring often. Add lemon juice, stir, divide into breakfast bowls, top with coconut flakes and serve. Enjoy!

Nutrition: calories 120, fat 1, fiber 3, carbs 5, protein 2

Superb Breakfast Burrito

Preparation time: 10 minutes
Cooking time: 25 minutes
Servings: 4

Ingredients:

- 1 yellow onion, chopped
- 2 garlic cloves, minced
- 1 tablespoon olive oil
- 1 small green bell pepper, sliced
- 3 cups canned pinto beans, drained
- 2 hot chili peppers, chopped
- 4 tablespoon cilantro, chopped
- 1 teaspoon cumin, ground
- A pinch of salt
- 8 whole wheat Greek tortillas
- Salsa for serving
- 1 cup cheddar cheese, shredded
- Lettuce leaves shredded for serving
- Black olives, pitted and chopped for serving

Directions:

Heat up a pan with the oil over medium heat, add onion and cook for 3 minutes stirring from time to time. Add garlic, stir and cook for 1 minute. Add green pepper and stir for 3 minutes. Add pinto beans, chili peppers, salt, cumin and cilantro, stir and cook for 10 minutes. Mash everything using a potato masher, stir and cook for 5 minutes more. Divide this beans mix on each Greek tortilla, also divide cheese, salsa, lettuce and olives, fold, divide them between plates and serve. Enjoy!

Nutrition: calories 132, fat 2, fiber 4, carbs 5, protein 3

Breakfast Cauliflower And Potatoes

Preparation time: 10 minutes
Cooking time: 1 hour
Servings: 4

Ingredients:

- 2 cups cauliflower florets
- 8 medium potatoes
- 2 cups white mushrooms, roughly chopped
- 6 tomatoes, cubed
- 1 yellow onion, chopped
- 1 small garlic clove, minced
- ¼ teaspoon onion powder
- 3 tablespoons basil, chopped
- 3 tablespoons parsley, chopped

Directions:

Place potatoes in the oven at 350 degrees F, bake for 45 minutes, leave them aside to cool down, peel, chop them roughly and arrange on a lined baking sheet. Add tomatoes, cauliflower, mushrooms, garlic, onion and onion powder, toss, introduce in the oven at 350 degrees F and bake for 15 minutes. Sprinkle basil and parsley on top, divide between plates and serve for breakfast. .Enjoy!

Nutrition: calories 143, fat 1, fiber 1, carbs 3, protein 4

Delicious Eggs And Tomatoes

Preparation time: 10 minutes
Cooking time: 30 minutes
Servings: 2

Ingredients:
- 2 eggs
- 2 tomatoes, tops cut off and insides scooped out
-
- 1 teaspoon parsley, chopped
- Salt and black pepper to the taste

Directions:

Season tomato cups with salt and pepper and arrange them on a lined baking sheet. Crack an egg into each tomato cup, introduce in the oven at 350 degrees F and bake for 30 minutes. Sprinkle parsley on top, leave them to cool down for a few minutes, divide between plates and serve. Enjoy!

Nutrition: calories 162, fat 1, fiber 2, carbs 4, protein 4

Breakfast Tomato Sandwich

Preparation time: 5 minutes
Cooking time: 5 minutes
Servings: 1

Ingredients:
- 1 whole wheat muffin, halved and toasted
- 1 tablespoon homemade mayonnaise
- 3 bacon slices, halved
- Salt and black pepper to the taste
- 2 tomato slices

Directions:

Heat up a pan over medium heat, add bacon, cook for 5 minutes, transfer to paper towels, drain excess grease and leave aside for now. Spread mayo on muffin halves, add tomato slices on one-half, season with salt and pepper, add bacon, top with the other muffin half and serve. Enjoy!

Nutrition: calories 110, fat 1, fiber 2, carbs 2, protein 1

Greek Breakfast Salad

Preparation time: 15 minutes
Cooking time: 20 minutes
Servings: 6

Ingredients:

- 2 pounds new potatoes, halved
- 2 tomatoes, cut in medium segments
- 2 bell peppers, chopped
- 1 cucumber, chopped
- 1 small red onion, sliced
- ½ cup kalamata olives, pitted and sliced
- 4 ounces feta cheese, crumbled
- ¼ cup lemon juice
- ½ cup olive oil
- 1 tablespoon oregano, chopped
- 1 tablespoon mustard
- Salt and black pepper to the taste
- 1 teaspoon sugar
- 2 garlic cloves, minced

Directions:

Put potatoes in a pot, add water to cover, add salt, bring to a boil over medium high heat, cook for 20 minutes, drain, leave aside to cool down, chop and put in a salad bowl. Add tomatoes, bell peppers, cucumber, onion and olives. In a bowl, mix oil with lemon juice, oregano, mustard, garlic, salt, pepper and sugar and stir well. Pour this over salad, add feta on top, toss to coat and keep in the fridge until you serve it. Enjoy!

Nutrition: calories 132, fat 1, fiber 2, carbs 5, protein 5

Bulgur Salad

Preparation time: 40 minutes
Cooking time: 10 minutes
Servings: 4

Ingredients:

- 1 pound salmon fillet, skinless and boneless
- 1 tablespoon olive oil+ 1 teaspoon
- 1 cup bulgur
- 1 cup parsley, chopped
- 2 medium cucumbers, sliced
- ¼ cup mint, chopped
- 3 tablespoons lemon juice
- 1 small red onion, sliced
- Salt and black pepper to the taste
- 2 cup hot water

Directions:

Heat up a pan with 1 teaspoon oil over medium heat, add salmon, season with salt and pepper, cook for 5 minutes on each side, take off heat, transfer to a plate and keep in the fridge for about 15 minutes. In a bowl, mix bulgur with hot water, stir, cover, leave aside for 25 minutes, drain and transfer to another bowl. Add parsley, cucumbers, onion, mint, lemon juice, salt, pepper, salmon and the rest of the olive oil, toss to coat, divide between plates and serve. Enjoy!

Nutrition: calories 142, fat 2, fiber 1, carbs 4, protein 7

Quinoa And Bacon Salad

Preparation time: 10 minutes
Cooking time: 10 minutes
Servings: 4

Ingredients:

- ½ cup peas
- 2 and ½ cups asparagus, roughly chopped
- 3 bacon slices, chopped
- 1 tablespoon butter
- 3 tablespoons white vinegar
- 1 and ¾ cups quinoa
- 2 teaspoons mustard
- Salt and black pepper to the taste
- 5 ounces baby spinach
- ½ cup parsley, chopped
- 1 tablespoon thyme, chopped
- 1 tablespoon tarragon, chopped
- 3 tablespoons almonds, chopped

Directions:

Put water in a pot, bring to a boil over medium high heat, add peas and asparagus, boil for 2 minutes, drain, rinse under cold water, put in a bowl and leave aside for now. Heat up a pan over medium high heat, add bacon, cook for 4 minutes stirring from time to time, take off heat, transfer to a bowl and leave aside. Heat up the pan again over medium high heat, add butter, mustard and vinegar, stir well, add quinoa, salt and pepper and cook for 1 minute. Transfer quinoa to a bowl, add asparagus mix, thyme, tarragon, parsley and spinach and stir gently. Divide between plates and serve with bacon and almonds on top. Enjoy!

Nutrition: calories 187, fat 4, fiber 2, carbs 4, protein 6

Breakfast Strawberry Salad

Preparation time: 10 minutes
Cooking time: 0 minutes
Servings: 6

Ingredients:

- 3 tablespoons mayonnaise
- 3 tablespoons sugar
- 2 tablespoons low fat milk
- 1 tablespoon poppy seeds
- 10 ounces romaine lettuce leaves, torn
- 1 tablespoon white wine vinegar
- 1 cup strawberries sliced
- 2 tablespoons almonds, toasted and chopped

Directions:

In a bowl, mix sugar with mayo, milk, poppy seeds and vinegar and whisk. In a salad bowl, mix lettuce with strawberries and almonds. Add salad dressing, toss to coat and serve right away for breakfast. Enjoy!

Nutrition: calories 78, fat 2, fiber 1, carbs 2, protein 4

Breakfast Asparagus Salad

Preparation time: 10 minutes
Cooking time: 22 minutes
Servings: 6

Ingredients:
- 1 tablespoon parmesan, grated
- A pinch of sea salt and black pepper
- 1 tablespoon lemon juice
- 2 cups fava beans
- 1 shallot, chopped
- 2 bunches asparagus, trimmed
- 1 cup peas
- ½ cup olive oil+ 3 tablespoons
- 4 bacon slices, cooked and crumbled

Directions:

In a bowl, mix parmesan with lemon juice, 3 tablespoons olive oil, salt and pepper and whisk well. Put some water in a pot, add a pinch of salt, bring to a boil over medium heat, add fava beans, cook for 4 minutes, drain, transfer to a bowl and leave aside. Heat up the same pot with the water over medium heat, add asparagus and peas, stir, cook for 3 minutes, drain and add to fava beans. Heat up a small pan with ½ cup olive oil over medium high heat, add shallot, stir, cook for 10 minutes and add to asparagus mix. Season salad with salt and pepper, and dressing you've made earlier and top with bacon. Enjoy!

Nutrition: calories 164, fat 3, fiber 1, carbs 3, protein 2

Breakfast Corn Salad

Preparation time: 10 minutes
Cooking time: 20 minutes
Servings: 6

Ingredients:
- 8 ears of corn, husks removed
- 3 tablespoons mayonnaise
- 2/3 cup feta cheese, crumbled
- ¼ cup lime juice
- 1 lime cut into 4 wedges
- 1/3 cup chives, chopped
- Salt and black pepper to the taste

Directions:

Preheat your grill to 450 degrees F. Brush corn with mayo, season with salt and pepper, place on preheated grill over medium heat and cook for 12 minutes, turning it occasionally. Cut kernels from cobs, put corn into a bowl and mix with cheese, lime juice and chives. Toss to coat and serve this salad right away with lime wedges. Enjoy!

Nutrition: calories 132, fat 2, fiber 3, carbs 5, protein 4

Fresh Corn Breakfast

Preparation time: 10 minutes
Cooking time: 20 minutes
Servings: 8

Ingredients:

- ½ cup sweet onion, chopped
- ½ cup green bell pepper, chopped
- ¼ pound spicy smoked sausage, sliced
- 3 cups corn
- 2 garlic cloves, minced
- 1 cup tomato, chopped
- 1 cup okra, sliced
- Salt and black pepper to the taste

Directions:

Heat up a pan over medium high heat, add sausage, stir and cook for 3 minutes. Add onion, bell pepper and garlic, stir and cook 5 more minutes. Add okra, tomato and corn, and cook for 10 minutes. Add with salt and black pepper to the taste, transfer to a bowl and serve right away! Enjoy!

Nutrition: calories 143, fat 2, fiber 1, carbs 2, protein 3

Eggplant And Tomato Breakfast Hash

Preparation time: 20 minutes
Cooking time: 25 minutes
Servings: 4

Ingredients:

- 1 eggplant, chopped
- ½ cup extra-virgin olive oil
- ½ pound cherry tomatoes, halved
- A pinch of sea salt and black pepper
- 4 eggs, poached
- 1 teaspoon hot sauce
- ¼ cup basil, chopped
- ¼ cup mint, chopped

Directions:

In a bowl, mix eggplant with salt, stir, leave aside for 20 minutes, drain excess liquid and transfer to another bowl. Heat up a pan with half of the olive oil over medium high heat, add eggplant pieces, cook for 3 minutes on each side and return them to the bowl. Heat up the same pan with the rest of the oil over medium heat, add tomatoes, stir and cook for 8 minutes. Return eggplant to the pan, add hot sauce, stir and cook for 2 minutes. Add basil, mint, salt and pepper, stir, cook for 1 minute. Divide between plates, top with poached eggs and serve for breakfast. Enjoy!

Nutrition: calories 132, fat 1, fiber 2, carbs 2, protein 2

Breakfast Eggplant Crostini

Preparation time: 10 minutes
Cooking time: 15 minutes
Servings: 8

Ingredients:

- ¼ cup extra-virgin olive oil+ a drizzle
- 1 eggplant, sliced
- Salt and black pepper to the taste
- 2 and ½ tablespoons lemon juice
- ¼ cup Greek yogurt
- 1 cup arugula
- 1 cup mixed green, yellow, red and orange cherry tomatoes, halved
- 1 garlic clove, minced
- 1 ounce parmesan, grated
- 2 tablespoon mint, torn

Directions:

Brush eggplant slices with the olive oil, place them on preheated grill over medium heat, cook them for 6 minutes on each side and transfer them to a plate. Transfer eggplant to your blender, add salt, pepper, 1 tablespoon lemon juice, yogurt and garlic and blend well. Meanwhile, in a bowl, mix tomatoes with mint, arugula, the rest of the lemon juice and a drizzle of oil, salt and pepper to the taste and toss to coat. Spread eggplant paste on whole wheat bread slices, add tomatoes salad on top and sprinkle parmesan at the end. Serve for breakfast. Enjoy!

Nutrition: calories 185, fat 1, fiber 2, carbs 3, protein 3

Amazing Eggplant Sandwich

Preparation time: 10 minutes
Cooking time: 25 minutes
Servings: 2

Ingredients:

- 2 tablespoons olive oil
- 1 eggplant, sliced
- 4 slices cheddar cheese
- Salt and black pepper to the taste
- 4 tablespoons kale pesto
- 1 avocado, pitted, peeled and chopped
- 2 ciabatta rolls, halved

Directions:

Mix eggplant with the oil, season with salt and pepper to the taste, toss, arrange on a baking sheet, introduce them in the oven at 356 degrees F and bake for 10 minutes on each side. Meanwhile, arrange ciabatta rolls on another baking sheet., introduce them in the oven next to the eggplant slices and brown them for a few minutes. Take rolls out of the oven, spread kale pesto and arrange cheese slices on 2 ciabatta halves. Arrange baked eggplant slices and avocado over cheese, top with the other 2 ciabatta halves, divide between 2 plates and serve. Enjoy

Nutrition: calories 120, fat 1, fiber 2, carbs 3, protein 4

Mediterranean Diet Side Dish Recipes

Spicy Escarole
Preparation time: 10 minutes
Cooking time: 20 minutes
Servings: 4

Ingredients:
- 4 escarole heads, leaves separated and roughly chopped
- 14 ounces canned tomatoes, chopped
- Salt and black pepper to the taste
- 2 garlic cloves, minced
- ¼ pound soppressata, chopped
- ½ teaspoon red pepper, crushed
- 3 tablespoons olive oil
- ¼ cup panko
- 1 tablespoon oregano, chopped
- 2 tablespoons parmesan, grated

Directions:
Heat up a pan with 2 tablespoons oil over medium heat, add garlic, red pepper and soppressata, stir and cook for 2 minutes. Add escarole, salt, pepper, tomatoes and oregano, stir, bring to a boil, reduce heat to low and cook for 15 minutes. Take mixture off heat and transfer to a bowl. Heat up another pan with the rest of the oil over medium heat, add panko, stir and cook for 1 minute. Take off heat, add parmesan, stir well and sprinkle over escarole. Serve as a side dish right away. Enjoy!

Nutrition: calories 60, fat 3.5, fiber 4, carbs 5, protein 3

Eggplant Side Dish
Preparation time: 10 minutes
Cooking time: 10 minutes
Servings: 4

Ingredients:
- 1 eggplant, diced
- 5 tablespoons olive oil
- 3 shallots, chopped
- 3 garlic cloves, minced
- Salt and black pepper to the taste
- A handful dill, chopped
- ½ cup Greek yogurt

Directions:
Heat up a pan with the oil over medium high heat, add shallots and garlic, stir and cook for 3 minutes. Add eggplant, stir and cook for 10 minutes. Add salt, pepper, dill and yogurt, stir well again, cook for 1 minute more, divide between plates and serve as a side dish. Enjoy!

Nutrition: calories 254, fat 21, fiber 4, carbs 14, protein 5

Artichokes Side Dish

Preparation time: 10 minutes
Cooking time: 12 minutes
Servings: 4

Ingredients:

- 1 small yellow onion, chopped
- 2 garlic cloves, minced
- Salt and black pepper to the taste
- ½ cup white wine
- 2 tomatoes, chopped
- 9 ounces artichoke hearts, frozen
- 1 tablespoon extra-virgin olive oil
- 1 strip lemon zest
- A handful basil, chopped
- 3 tablespoons water
- A few black olives, pitted and chopped

Directions:

Heat up a pan with the oil over medium high heat, add onion, garlic and some salt, stir and cook for 5 minutes. Add wine, stir and cook for 3 minutes more. Add tomatoes, artichokes, water, lemon zest, salt and pepper, stir and cook for 6 minutes. Add olives and basil, stir again, cook for 1 minute, take off heat, divide between plates and serve. Enjoy!

Nutrition: calories 145, fat 7.6, fiber 8, carbs 18, protein 5

Flavored Broccoli Side Dish

Preparation time: 10 minutes
Cooking time: 10 minutes
Servings: 4

Ingredients:

- 2 bunches broccoli rabe
- 2 garlic cloves, minced
- 1 tablespoon olive oil
- ¼ cup jarred cherry peppers, chopped
- 2 tablespoons liquid from the peppers
- Salt and black pepper to the taste
- Some parmesan, grated for serving

Directions:

Put broccoli in a pot, add water to cover, bring to a boil over medium heat, cook for 7 minutes, drain and put in a bowl. Heat up a pan with the oil over medium high heat, add garlic and peppers, stir and cook for 2 minutes. Add liquid from the jar, stir and cook for 2 minutes more. Pour this over broccoli, add salt, pepper and parmesan, toss to coat, divide between plates and serve as a side dish. Enjoy!

Nutrition: calories 177, fat 8, fiber 3, carbs 16, protein 13

Cauliflower Couscous

Preparation time: 10 minutes
Cooking time: 10 minutes
Servings: 4

Ingredients:

- 1 and ½ cups couscous, already cooked
- 3 tablespoons olive oil
- 3 cups cauliflower florets
- 1 shallot, chopped
- Salt and pepper to the taste
- A pinch of cinnamon, ground
- ¼ cup dates, chopped
- A splash of red wine vinegar
- A handful parsley, chopped

Directions:

Put already cooked couscous in a bowl, add 1 tablespoon oil, toss to coat and leave aside for now. Heat up a pan with the rest of the oil over medium high heat, add shallot, stir and cook for 2 minutes. Add cauliflower florets, stir and cook for 4 minutes. Add dates, cinnamon, salt and pepper, stir and cook for 2 minutes more. Add couscous, vinegar, parsley, more salt and pepper if needed, cook for 1 minute, divide between plates and serve. Enjoy!

Nutrition: calories 345, fat 11, fiber 5, carbs 55, protein 9

Tasty Lentils And Ruby Chard

Preparation time: 10 minutes
Cooking time: 1 hour
Servings: 4

Ingredients:

- ½ cup celery, chopped
- ½ cup carrot, chopped
- ½ cup onion, chopped
- ½ cup red bell pepper, chopped
- ½ teaspoon coriander, chopped
- 1 tablespoon olive oil
- ½ cup dry white wine
- ½ teaspoon marjoram, dried
- 1 cup lentils, rinsed
- 2 teaspoons kalamata olives, pitted and chopped
- 8 ounces ruby chard, leaves torn
- 2 tablespoons sun-dried tomatoes, chopped
- Salt and black pepper to the taste
- 2 and ½ cups water
- 1 teaspoon balsamic vinegar

Directions:

Heat up a pot with the oil over medium high heat, add celery, carrot, onion, coriander, bell pepper, marjoram, salt and pepper, stir and cook for 4 minutes. Add wine, stir and cook for 3 minutes. Add lentils and water, stir, bring to a boil, reduce heat and simmer for 40 minutes. Add tomatoes, olives and chard, stir and cook for 5 minutes. Add more salt and pepper to the taste and the vinegar, stir and cook for 2 minutes. Transfer to plates and serve as a side dish. Enjoy!

Nutrition: calories 180, fat 3.5, fiber 9, carbs 24, protein 10

Spicy Cauliflower

Preparation time: 10 minutes
Cooking time: 30 minutes
Servings: 4

Ingredients:

- ½ cauliflower head, florets separated
- 12 small carrots
- 1 tablespoon olive oil
- 1 tablespoon harissa paste
- Salt and black pepper to the taste
- A handful mint, chopped
- 2 tablespoons almonds, toasted and chopped

Directions:

In a bowl, mix cauliflower florets with carrots, harissa, salt, pepper and oil and toss to coat. Spread this on a lined baking sheet, introduce in the oven at 400 degrees F and bake for 30 minutes. Take out of the oven, divide between plates, sprinkle mint and almonds on top and serve. Enjoy!

Nutrition: calories 70, fat 4, fiber 2, carbs, 6, protein 2

Roasted Carrots

Preparation time: 10 minutes
Cooking time: 45 minutes
Servings: 4

Ingredients:

- 3 tablespoons olive oil
- 16 slender carrots, peeled
- Salt and black pepper to the taste
- ½ teaspoon lemon zest, grated
- 1/3 cup yogurt
- 1 garlic clove, minced
- A pinch of cumin, ground
- 2 tablespoons homemade dukkah
- 2 teaspoons honey

Directions:

In a bowl, mix carrots with salt and pepper. Spread this on a lined baking sheet, cover, introduce in the oven at 425 degrees F and bake for 20 minutes. In a bowl, mix yogurt with garlic, salt, pepper, cumin and lemon zest and stir well. Take carrots out of the oven, drizzle honey over them, introduce in the oven again and roast for 25 minutes more. Transfer carrots to a platter, drizzle yogurt mix, sprinkle dukkah and serve them as a side dish. Enjoy!

Nutrition: calories 200, fat 12, fiber 5, carbs 20, protein 3

Delicious Roasted Potatoes

Preparation time: 10 minutes
Cooking time: 50 minutes
Servings: 4

Ingredients:

- 6 red potatoes, cut into medium wedges
- Salt and black pepper to the taste
- 2 tablespoons extra virgin olive oil
- 1 teaspoon lemon zest, grated
- 1 teaspoon oregano, dried

Directions:

In a bowl, mix potatoes with salt, pepper and oil, toss to coat and spread on a lined baking sheet. Cover and introduce in the oven at 425 degrees F and bake for 20 minutes. Take potatoes out of the oven, toss them a bit, introduce in the oven again and roast for 20 minutes more. Take them out of the oven again, add lemon zest and oregano, introduce in the oven and cook for 10 minutes more. Divide them among plates and serve. Enjoy!

Nutrition: calories 190, fat 7, fiber 3, carbs 30, protein 3

Squash With Chorizo And Chickpeas

Preparation time: 10 minutes
Cooking time: 10 minutes
Servings: 4

Ingredients:

- 3 ounces chorizo, cut in half lengthwise and thinly sliced
- 2 and ½ tablespoon extra-virgin olive oil
- ½ teaspoon smoked paprika
- 10 ounces baby squash, sliced
- 1 tablespoon sherry vinegar
- 15 ounces canned chickpeas, drained
- Salt and black pepper to the taste

Directions:

Heat up a pan with 1 and ½ tablespoons oil over high heat, add chorizo, cook for 1 minute and transfer to a bowl. Heat up the pan again, add paprika and squash, stir and cook for 3 minutes. Add chickpeas, vinegar, salt, pepper and chorizo, stir and cook for 2 minutes. Transfer to a platter, add the rest of the oil, toss to coat and serve as a side dish. Enjoy!

Nutrition: calories 240, fat 12, fiber 6, carbs 21, protein 10

Bulgur With Mushrooms

Preparation time: 10 minutes
Cooking time: 20 minutes
Servings: 4

Ingredients:

- 1 cup bulgur
- 2 cups chicken stock
- 1 tablespoon butter
- 1 tablespoon extra-virgin olive oil
- 6 ounces mushrooms, chopped
- 1 teaspoon garlic, minced
- Salt and black pepper to the taste
- ½ cup parmesan, grated
- 2 tablespoons parsley, finely chopped
- ½ cup cashews, toasted and chopped

Directions:

Put the stock in a pot, bring to a boil over medium high heat, add bulgur, reduce temperature to medium-low, cover and simmer for 12 minutes. Heat up a pan with the oil and butter over medium heat, add mushrooms, stir and cook for 4 minutes. Add salt and pepper, stir and cook for 5 minutes more. Add garlic, stir and cook for 1 minute. Take bulgur off heat, uncover the pot, fluff a bit, add sautéed mushrooms, cashews, parmesan and parsley, stir, divide between plates and serve as a side dish. Enjoy!

Nutrition: calories 330, fat 15, fiber 4, carbs 35, protein 11

Delicious Mediterranean Jasmine Rice

Preparation time: 10 minutes
Cooking time: 5 minutes
Servings: 4

Ingredients:

- 3 tablespoons butter
- 1 cup jasmine rice
- 2 tablespoons chives, chopped
- Salt and black pepper to the taste
- ¼ cup pine nuts
- 2 teaspoons lemon juice

Directions:

Cook rice according to package instructions, fluff with a fork and leave aside for now. Heat up a pan with the butter over medium high heat, add pine nuts, stir and brown for 3 minutes. Add chives, lemon juice, rice, salt and pepper, stir, cook for 2 minutes more, divide among plates and serve. Enjoy!

Nutrition: calories 280, fat 14, fiber 1, carbs 34, protein 5

Tasty Green Beans

Preparation time: 10 minutes
Cooking time: 6 minutes
Servings: 4

Ingredients:

- 2 tablespoons olive oil
- 1 and ½ pounds green beans
- Salt and black pepper to the taste
- 2 tablespoons tahini
- 1 teaspoon lemon zest, grated
- 1 tablespoon lemon juice
- 2 tablespoons water
- 2 tablespoons mint leaves, chopped
- A pinch of red pepper flakes, crushed

Directions:

Put green beans in a steamer basket, place in a pot filled with 1 inch water, bring to a boil over high heat, add salt and pepper to beans, cover pot and cook for 5 minutes. In a bowl, mix oil with lemon zest, lemon juice, tahini, salt, pepper and water and whisk well. Transfer green beans to a bowl, add lemon and tahini mix over them, also add mint and pepper flakes, toss to coat, divide between plates and serve. Enjoy!

Nutrition: calories 179, fat 11, fiber 5, carbs 14, protein 5

Perfect Snap Peas Side Dish

Preparation time: 10 minutes
Cooking time: 5 minutes
Servings: 4

Ingredients:

- ½ cup almonds, blanched
- 2 teaspoons lemon juice
- ¼ cup extra virgin olive oil
- ½ cup water
- 1 and ½ teaspoons garlic, minced
- 1 pound sugar snap peas
- Salt and black pepper to the taste

Directions:

In your blender, mix almonds with lemon juice, olive oil, water and garlic, blend for 3 minutes, add salt and pepper to the taste, blend again and transfer to a bowl. Heat up a pot with water over medium high heat, add salt and peas, cook for 1 minute, drain them and transfer to a bowl filled with ice water. Drain peas again and divide them on serving plates. Drizzle almonds sauce over them and serve as a side dish. Enjoy!

Nutrition: calories 240, fat 23, fiber 4, carbs 12, protein 7

Flavored Corn On The Cob With Olive Tapenade

Preparation time: 10 minutes
Cooking time: 4 minutes
Servings: 4

Ingredients:

- 4 ears of corn
- 4 ounces green olives, pitted
- ½ teaspoon anchovy paste
- 1 teaspoon thyme, chopped
- Salt and black pepper to the taste
- 2 tablespoons extra virgin olive oil

Directions:

In your blender, mix thyme with olives, anchovy paste, oil, salt and some black pepper and pulse well. Shuck corn, place in a pot filled with boiling water, cover, take the pot off the heat and leave aside for 5 minutes. Drain corn, arrange on plates, drizzle 2 tablespoons of olives tapenade over each piece and serve. Enjoy!

Nutrition: calories 160, fat 10, fiber 4, carbs 20, protein 3

Delicious Quinoa Pilaf

Preparation time: 10 minutes
Cooking time: 35 minutes
Servings: 6

Ingredients:

- 4 cups chicken stock
- 2 cups red quinoa, rinsed and drained
- 1 yellow onion, chopped
- 2 tablespoons vegetable oil
- 1 tablespoon garlic, minced
- 1 teaspoon lemon zest, grated
- 2 tablespoons lemon juice
- ½ cup sun-dried tomatoes, chopped
- Salt and black pepper to the taste
- 2 tablespoons olive oil
- ½ cup basil, chopped

Directions:

Heat up a pan over medium high heat, add quinoa, fry for 8 minutes stirring often and transfer to a plate. Put the stock in a pot, bring to a boil over medium heat, add quinoa, stir, cover and cook for 15 minutes. Heat up a pan with the vegetable oil over medium heat, add onion, stir and cook for 8 minutes. Add garlic, stir, cook for 1 minute more and take off heat. In a bowl, mix lemon zest with lemon juice, salt, pepper and olive oil and whisk well. Add quinoa, tomatoes, onions mix, more salt and pepper if needed and basil, toss to coat and divide among plates. Enjoy!

Nutrition: calories 260, fat 11, fiber 4, carbs 41, protein 10

Couscous With Corn And Cheese

Preparation time: 10 minutes
Cooking time: 4 minutes
Servings: 4

Ingredients:

- 2 cup hot water
- 2 tablespoons butter
- 1 teaspoon thyme, chopped
- 1 cup scallions, sliced
- 2 cups corn kernels
- Salt and black pepper to the taste
- A pinch of cayenne pepper
- 1 cup couscous
- 2 tablespoons blue cheese, crumbled

Directions:

Heat up a pot with the butter over medium heat, add thyme and cook for 10 seconds. Add scallions, salt, pepper and corn, stir and cook for 1 minute. Add couscous, hot water and cayenne, stir, take off heat, cover and leave aside for 5 minutes. Uncover pot, fluff with a fork, add more salt and pepper to the taste and crumbled cheese, stir, divide between plates and serve as a side dish. Enjoy!

Nutrition: calories 200, fat 8, fiber 5, carbs 32, protein 9

Simple Sautéed Carrots

Preparation time: 10 minutes
Cooking time: 45 minutes
Servings: 4

Ingredients:

- 1 tablespoon mint, chopped
- 1 tablespoon parsley, chopped
- 1 tablespoon green olives, pitted and chopped
- 4 and ½ tablespoons olive oil
- 2 teaspoons capers, drained and chopped
- ½ teaspoon lemon zest, grated
- 1 and ½ teaspoons sherry vinegar
- ¼ teaspoon cumin, ground
- ¼ teaspoon sugar
- Salt and black pepper to the taste
- 1 and ¼ pounds carrots, chopped
- 5 shallots, cut into wedges
- 2 turnips, trimmed and roughly chopped
- 2 ounces kale leaves, thinly sliced

Directions:

In a bowl, mix 1 and ½ tablespoons olive oil with olives, parsley, mint, capers, lemon zest, vinegar, cumin, sugar and some black pepper, whisk well and leave aside. Heat up a pan with the rest of the oil over medium high heat, add turnips, carrots, salt and pepper, stir and cook for 10 minutes. Add shallots, reduce heat to medium-low and cook for 20 minutes stirring every 2 minutes. Add kale, parsley and mint sauce, more salt and pepper, stir take off heat and serve as a side dish. Enjoy!

Nutrition: calories 104, fat 7, fiber 2.6, carbs 10, protein 2

Tasty Braised Fennel

Preparation time: 10 minutes
Cooking time: 2 hours
Servings: 4

Ingredients:

- 3 lemon slices, cut in quarters
- Salt and black pepper to the taste
- 3 tablespoons extra virgin olive oil
- 1 tablespoon water
- 2 fennel bulb, cut in halves and sliced into medium wedges

Directions:

Place fennel wedges in a baking dish, sprinkle with salt and pepper, drizzle the oil, add lemon pieces and the water, toss to coat, cover with tin foil, introduce in the oven at 375 degrees F and bake for 1 hour and 40 minutes. Take the dish out of the oven, uncover, introduce in the oven again and bake for 20 minutes more. Serve as a side dish at room temperature. Enjoy!

Nutrition: calories 190, fat 11, fiber 9, carbs 22, protein 4

Braised Leeks And Thyme

Preparation time: 10 minutes
Cooking time: 1 hour
Servings: 4

Ingredients:

- 2 pounds leeks, white and green parts separated and halved
- 1 tablespoon dry white wine
- 12 thyme sprigs
- 1 tablespoon water
- Salt and black pepper to the taste
- ¼ cup olive oil

Directions:

Arrange leeks in a baking dish and add thyme sprigs on top. In a bowl, mix oil with wine, water, salt and pepper and whisk well. Pour this over leeks and thyme, toss to coat, cover the dish with tin foil, introduce in the oven at 375 degrees F and bake for 45 minutes. Uncover the dish, bake leeks for 15 minutes more, discard thyme, divide between plates and serve as a side dish. Enjoy!

Nutrition: calories 180, fat 13, fiber 2, carbs 14, protein 1

Grilled Asparagus

Preparation time: 30 minutes
Cooking time: 15 minutes
Servings: 4

Ingredients:
- 5 tablespoons olive oil
- 1 garlic head
- 2 tablespoons shallot, chopped
- Salt
- Black pepper to the taste
- 1 and ½ teaspoons white wine vinegar
- 1 and ½ pound asparagus
- ½ teaspoon red wine vinegar

Directions:
Season garlic with salt, pepper and 1 tablespoon olive oil, arrange on a baking tray and bake at 350 degrees F for 40 minutes. Squeeze garlic into a bowl, add salt, pepper and 2 tablespoons of oil and leave aside. In a bowl, mix shallot with the white and red vinegar, stir well and leave aside for 30 minutes. Add remaining oil, salt and pepper and the asparagus. Preheat your kitchen grill over medium high heat, add asparagus in and cook for 10 minutes. Meanwhile, spread roasted garlic mix over bread and grill it for a few minutes. Divide asparagus on plates, drizzle vinegar mix and garlic all over and serve as a side dish. Enjoy!

Nutrition: calories 132, fat 1, fiber 2, carbs 4, protein 4, carbs 3

Cucumber Side Dish

Preparation time: 1 hour
Cooking time: 0 minutes
Servings: 12

Ingredients:
- 2 cucumbers, chopped
- 2 tomatoes, chopped
- ½ cup green bell pepper, chopped
- 1 yellow onion, chopped
- 1 jalapeno pepper, chopped
- 1 garlic clove, minced
- 1 teaspoon parsley, chopped
- 2 tablespoons lime juice
- 2 teaspoons cilantro, chopped
- ½ teaspoon dill, dried
- Salt to the taste

Directions:
In a large salad bowl, mix cucumbers with tomatoes and jalapeno pepper. Add green pepper, onion, garlic and salt and stir. Add dill, parsley, cilantro and lime juice and toss to coat. Introduce in the fridge about 1 hour before serving. Serve as a side dish. Enjoy!

Nutrition: calories 132, fat 3, fiber 1, carbs 2, protein 4

Cucumber And Peanut Salad

Preparation time: 10 minutes
Cooking time: 5 minutes
Servings: 2

Ingredients:

- 1 big cucumber, chopped
- 1 tablespoon butter
- Salt to the taste
- 1 red chili pepper, dried
- ½ teaspoon cumin, ground
- 1 tablespoon lemon juice
- 3 tablespoons peanuts, chopped
- 1 teaspoon sugar
- 1 teaspoon cilantro, chopped

Directions:

In a bowl, mix cucumber with salt, leave aside for 10 minutes, pat dry and transfer to a bowl. Heat up a small pan with the butter over medium heat, add chili pepper and cumin and stir well. Add peanuts and sugar, stir, take off heat and add to cucumber. Add lemon juice, sprinkle cilantro on top and serve right away as a side dish. Enjoy!

Nutrition: calories 132, fat 2, fiber 1, carbs 2, protein 2

Easy Beet Salad

Preparation time: 10 minutes
Cooking time: 1 hour
Servings: 4

Ingredients:

- 4 fresh beets
- Salt and black pepper to the taste
- ½ cup olive oil + a drizzle
- ¼ cup lemon juice
- 8 slices goat cheese, crumbled
- 1/3 cup walnuts, chopped
- 8 lettuce leaves

Directions:

Arrange beets on a lined, baking sheet, add a drizzle of oil, season with some salt and pepper, introduce in the oven at 400 degrees F and bake for 1 hour. Peel beets, cut them and transfer to a bowl. In a small bowl mix lemon juice with ½ cup olive oil, salt and black pepper to the taste and whisk. Add this to beets, also add lettuce and cheese, toss to coat, divide between plates and serve. Enjoy!

Nutrition: calories 121, fat 1, fiber 2, carbs 3, protein 3

Grilled Beets

Preparation time: 10 minutes
Cooking time: 30 minutes
Servings: 6

Ingredients:

- 3 medium beets, sliced
- 1/3 cup balsamic vinegar
- 1 teaspoon rosemary, chopped
- 1 garlic clove, minced
- ½ teaspoon Italian seasoning
- A drizzle of olive oil

Directions:

In a bowl, mix rosemary with vinegar, garlic and Italian seasoning and whisk. Add beets, toss and leave aside for 10 minutes. Place beets and the marinade on tin foil pieces, add a drizzle of oil, seal edges, place on preheated grill over medium heat and cook for 25 minutes. Unwrap beets, peeled and cube them. Arrange beets and the marinade on serving plates and serve right away as a side dish. Enjoy!

Nutrition: calories 100, fat 2, fiber 2, carbs 2, protein 4

Grilled Squash

Preparation time: 10 minutes
Cooking time: 10 minutes
Servings: 6

Ingredients:

- 5 medium assorted squash cut in medium slices
- ¼ teaspoon kosher salt
- 3 tablespoons olive oil
- 1 cup pepitas, shelled, unsalted and toasted
- ¼ cup goat cheese
- For the salsa:
- 7 tomatillos
- Salt to the taste
- ½ onion chopped
- 2 tablespoons cilantro chopped
- 2 tablespoons lime juice

Directions:

Heat up a pan over medium heat, add tomatillos, onion and salt to the taste, stir, cook for 3 minutes, transfer to your blender and pulse. Add lime juice and cilantro to tomatillo mix, blend well, pour into a small bowl and leave aside. Preheated your grill over medium heat, add squash, drizzle olive oil, cook for 5 minutes on each side and divide o plates. Sprinkle pepitas and goat cheese, top with the salsa and serve as a side dish. Enjoy!

Nutrition: calories 100, fat 1, fiber 1, carbs 2, protein 2

Delicious Eggplant Side Dish

Preparation time: 10 minutes
Cooking time: 5 minutes
Servings: 6

Ingredients:
- 1/3 cup homemade mayonnaise
- 2 tablespoons balsamic vinegar
- A pinch of salt and black pepper
- 1 tablespoon lime juice
- 2 big eggplants, sliced
- ¼ cup cilantro, chopped
- ¼ cup olive oil

Directions:
In a small bowl, mix mayonnaise with vinegar, lime juice and black pepper, stir well and leave aside. Brush each eggplant slice with some olive oil, season them with salt and pepper, place on preheated grill over medium high heat, cook for 5 minutes on each side and divide between plates. Drizzle the mayo mix all over, sprinkle cilantro and serve as a side dish. Enjoy!

Nutrition: calories 100, fat 1, fiber 2, carbs 2, protein 2

Barley Risotto

Preparation time: 10 minutes
Cooking time: 1 hour
Servings: 4

Ingredients:
- 1 tablespoon butter
- 1 yellow onion, chopped
- 4 parsnips, roughly chopped
- 10 sage leaves, chopped
- 1 garlic clove, minced
- 14 ounces barley
- ½ tablespoon parmesan, grated
- 6 cups hot veggie stock
- Salt and black pepper

Directions:
Heat up a pan with the butter over medium high heat, add onion, some salt and pepper, stir and cook for 5 minutes. Add parsnips and cook for 10 more minutes. Add sage, garlic, barley and stock, stir well, bring to a simmer and cook for 40 minutes. Add parmesan, stir, divide between plates and serve with sage on top. Enjoy!

Nutrition: calories 132, fat 1, fiber 1, carbs 2, protein 2

Lentils Side Salad

Preparation time: 15 minutes
Cooking time: 30 minutes
Servings: 4

Ingredients:

- 7 ounces lentils
- 3 tablespoons capers, chopped
- Juice of 1 lemon
- Zest and juice from 1 lemon
- 1 red onion, chopped
- 3 tablespoons olive oil
- 14 ounces canned chickpeas, drained
- 8 ounces already cooked beetroot, chopped
- 1 small hand parsley, chopped
- Salt and pepper to the taste

Directions:

Put lentils in a pot, add water to cover, bring to a simmer over medium heat, boil for 20 minutes, drain and leave aside. Put lemon juice from 1 lemon in a bowl, add onion, salt and pepper, whisk and leave aside. Put the juice and zest from the second lemon in a bowl, add oil, salt, pepper and the capers, whisk well and leave aside. Add chickpeas to lentils, also add beets, parsley and pickled onions you've prepared and toss to coat. Add capers mix as well, toss well and serve. Enjoy!

Nutrition: calories 132, fat 1, fiber 2, carbs 2, protein 3

Sweet Potatoes Side Dish

Preparation time: 10 minutes
Cooking time: 1 hour
Servings: 4

Ingredients:

- 4 tablespoons olive oil
- 1 garlic clove, minced
- 4 medium sweet potatoes
- 1 shallot, chopped

For the tahini yogurt:

- 1 and ½ tablespoons Greek yogurt
- ½ tablespoon pine nuts
- 2 tablespoons tahini paste
- 14 ounces canned chickpeas, drained
- 3 ounces baby spinach
- Zest and juice from 1 lemon
- A small bunch dill, chopped

- 4 ounces pomegranate seeds
- Salt and pepper to the taste

Directions:

Wrap potatoes in tin foil, arrange them on a lined baking sheet, introduce in the oven at 350 degrees F and cook them for 1 hour. Meanwhile, heat up a pan with 1 tablespoon olive oil over medium high heat, add shallot and garlic, stir and cook for 3 minutes. Add chickpeas, stir and cook for 1 more minute. Add spinach and dill, stir, take off heat and leave aside. In a bowl, mix the rest of the oil with lemon zest and juice and whisk Add to chickpeas mix and mash everything with a potato masher. In another bowl, mix yogurt with tahini, salt and pepper and stir well. Take potatoes out of the oven, unwrap, split them lengthwise, divide between plates, stuff with chickpeas mix, drizzle tahini mix all over them serve with pine nuts and pomegranate seeds on top as a side dish. Enjoy!

Nutrition: calories 120, fat 1, fiber 1, carbs 2, protein 2

Special Side Dish

Preparation time: 10 minutes
Cooking time: 10 minutes
Servings: 2

Ingredients:
- 1 yellow onion, sliced
- 2 tablespoons olive oil
- 10 shitake mushrooms

For the sauce:
- 2 tablespoons soy sauce
- 1 tablespoon Worcestershire sauce

- ¼ head cabbage, roughly chopped
- 4 spring onions, chopped
- Salt and black pepper to the taste

- A pinch of stevia

Directions:
Heat up a pan with the oil over medium heat, add onion and cabbage, stir and cook for 5 minutes. Add mushrooms and spring onions and cook for 1 more minute. Add salt, and pepper, stir and cook for 1-2 more minutes. In a bowl, mix Worcestershire sauce with stevia and soy sauce, stir and add to mushrooms. Toss to coat, take off heat and serve as a side dish. Enjoy!

Nutrition: calories 132, fat 2, fiber 1, carbs 2, protein 1

Mushroom Pilaf

Preparation time: 10 minutes
Cooking time: 30 minutes
Servings: 4

Ingredients:
- 2 cups chicken stock
- 1 yellow onion, chopped
- 10 ounces mixed mushrooms, sliced
- 2 garlic cloves, minced
- 8 ounces wild and basmati rice

- Juice and zest of 1 lemon
- A small bunch of chives, chopped
- 6 tablespoons light goat cheese with herbs, crumbled
- Salt and black pepper to the taste

Directions:
Heat up a pot with 2 tablespoons of stock over medium high heat, add onion, stir and cook for 5 minutes. Add stock, mushrooms and garlic and cook for 2 more minutes. Add rice, lemon juice, lemon zest, salt and pepper, stir, bring to a simmer, cover and cook for 25 minutes. Add half of the chives and half of the cheese and stir gently. Divide between plates and serve with the rest of the chives and the cheese sprinkled on top. Enjoy!

Nutrition: calories 142, fat 1, fiber 2, carbs 2, protein 2

Delicious Potatoes

Preparation time: 10 minutes
Cooking time: 1 hour and 10 minutes
Servings: 4

Ingredients:

- 4 potatoes, scrubbed and pricked with a fork
- 1 carrot, chopped
- 1 tablespoon olive oil
- 1 celery stalk, chopped
- 2 tomatoes, chopped
- A splash of water
- 1 teaspoon sweet paprika
- 14 ounces canned haricot beans, drained
- 1 teaspoon Worcestershire sauce
- Salt and black pepper to the taste
- 2 tablespoons chives, chopped

Directions:

Place potatoes on a lined baking sheet, introduce in the oven and bake at 350 degrees F for 1 hour. Heat up a pan with the oil over medium heat, add celery and carrot, stir for 10 minutes. Add beans, tomatoes, salt, pepper and sweet paprika, stir and cook for 5 more minutes. Add a splash of water, Worcestershire sauce, stir and cook for 5 minutes. Take potatoes out of the oven, split them, spoon beans mix in each, sprinkle chives on top, arrange on plates and serve as a side dish. Enjoy!

Nutrition: calories 123, fat 1, fiber 2, carbs 2, protein 1

Kale Salad

Preparation time: 10 minutes
Cooking time: 15 minutes
Servings: 6

Ingredients:

- 4 ounces bulgur wheat
- 4 ounces kale
- A bunch of mints, chopped
- A bunch of spring onions, chopped
- ½ cucumber, chopped
- A pinch of cinnamon powder
- A pinch of allspice
- 6 tablespoons olive oil
- Zest and juice from ½ lemon
- 4 ounces feta cheese, crumbled

Directions:

Put bulgur in a bowl, cover with hot water and aside for 10 minutes. Put kale in your food processor and blend a bit. Drain bulgur, transfer to another bowl and mix with kale, mint, spring onions, cucumber and tomatoes. Add cinnamon and allspice and stir. Add olive oil and lemon juice and toss to coat. Add feta cheese and lemon zest on top, toss and serve as a side dish. Arrange lettuce leaves on plates and scoop salad into each. Enjoy!

Nutrition: calories 100, fat 1, fiber 2, carbs 2, protein 4

Spicy Beans Side Dish

Preparation time: 10 minutes
Cooking time: 25 minutes
Servings: 4

Ingredients:

- 4 teaspoons olive oil
- 1 garlic clove, minced
- ½ teaspoon smoked paprika
- ¾ cup veggie stock
- 1 yellow onion, sliced
- 1 red bell pepper, chopped
- 15 ounces canned butter beans, drained
- 4 cups baby spinach
- ½ cup goat cheese, shredded
- 2 teaspoon sherry vinegar

Directions:

Heat up a pan with the oil over medium heat, add garlic, stir and cook for 30 seconds. Add onion, paprika and bell pepper and cook for 6 minutes. Add beans, spinach and stock and cook for 3 minutes more. Add cheese and vinegar, divide between plates and serve as a side dish. Enjoy!

Nutrition: calories 140, fat 1, fiber 2, carbs 2, protein 2

Amazing Rice

Preparation time: 10 minutes
Cooking time: 1 hour
Servings: 6

Ingredients:

- 1 tablespoon olive oil
- 1 yellow onion, chopped
- 2 celery stalks, chopped
- 2 garlic cloves, minced
- 2 cups brown rice
- 1 and ½ cup canned black beans, rinsed and drained
- 4 cups water
- 2 cups corn
- Salt and black pepper to the taste

Directions:

Heat up a pan with the olive oil over medium heat, add celery and onion, stir and cook for 8 minutes. Add corn, beans and garlic, stir and sauté them as well for about 5 minutes. Add rice, water, salt and pepper to the taste, stir, cover and cook for 45 minutes. Divide between plates and serve right away! Enjoy!

Nutrition: calories 132, fat 1, fiber 2, carbs 2, protein 1

Delicious Side Dish

Preparation time: 10 minutes
Cooking time: 20 minutes
Servings: 6

Ingredients:

- 4 tablespoons olive oil
- 1 cup millet
- 2 small bunches green onions, chopped
- 2 tomatoes, chopped
- ½ cup cilantro, chopped
- 5 drops hot sauce
- 6 cups cold water
- ½ cup lemon juice
- Salt and black pepper to the taste

Directions:

Heat up a pan with 2 tablespoons oil over medium high heat, add millet, stir and cook for 4 minutes. Add water, bring to a boil, cover and boil for 20 minutes. Transfer millet to a bowl, add tomatoes, onions, lemon juice, cilantro, hot sauce, the rest of the oil, salt and pepper, toss and serve as a side dish. Enjoy!

Nutrition: calories 163, fat 1, fiber 2, carbs 5, protein 3

Quinoa Side Salad

Preparation time: 10 minutes
Cooking time: 0 minutes
Servings: 4

Ingredients:

- 1 cup quinoa, cooked
- 1 avocado, chopped
- 1 medium bunch collard greens, chopped
- 1 handful strawberries, sliced
- 4 tablespoons walnuts, chopped
- 2 tablespoons white wine vinegar
- 4 tablespoons tahini
- 4 tablespoons cold water
- 1 tablespoon maple syrup

Directions:

In a bowl, mix tahini with maple syrup, water and vinegar and pulse well. In a salad bowl, mix collard green leaves with half of the salad dressing and toss to coat. Add avocado, walnuts, quinoa and strawberries and toss again. Add the rest of the dressing on top and serve as a side dish. Enjoy!

Nutrition: calories 175, fat 3, fiber 3, carbs 5, protein 3

Grain Side Salad

Preparation time: 10 minutes
Cooking time: 40 minutes
Servings: 4

Ingredients:
- 10 tablespoons pepitas, roasted
- 3 cups water
- 1 handful cilantro, chopped
- 4 tablespoons parsley, chopped
- 1 and ½ cups raw einkorn
- 1 cup radish sprouts
- 2 avocados, peeled, pitted and chopped
- 2 mangos, peeled and chopped
- 3 tablespoons olive oil
- 4 tablespoons Greek yogurt
- 1 teaspoons sherry vinegar
- 2 tablespoons lemon juice
- Salt and black pepper to the taste

Directions:

In your blender, mix olive oil with avocados, salt, pepper, lemon juice and vinegar and pulse. Add yogurt, pulse again, transfer to a bowl and leave aside for now. Heat up a large pot with the water over medium high heat, add einkorn, bring to a boil, simmer for about 30 minutes, drain and transfer to a bowl. Add pepitas, parsley, cilantro, radish sprouts, mango, salt and pepper to the taste. Add salad dressing, toss to coat and serve as a side dish. Enjoy!

Nutrition: calories 200, fat 1, fiber 2, carbs 2, protein 3

Beet And Cheese Side Salad

Preparation time: 15 minutes
Cooking time: 0 minutes
Servings: 6

Ingredients:
- 2 pounds beets, baked, peeled and cubed
- 2 tablespoons olive oil
- 1 tablespoon lemon juice
- 2 tablespoons red wine vinegar
- 1 cup blue cheese, crumbled
- 3 small garlic cloves, minced
- 4 green onions, chopped
- 5 tablespoons dill, chopped
- Salt and black pepper to the taste

Directions:

In a bowl, mix vinegar with oil, lemon juice, garlic, salt and pepper, whisk well and leave aside. Add green onions, cheese, beets and dill and toss to coat. Leave it in the fridge for 15 minutes and then serve as a side dish. Enjoy!

Nutrition : calories 180, fat 2, fiber 3, carbs 2, protein 3

Broccoli Side Dish

Preparation time: 10 minutes
Cooking time: 30 minutes
Servings: 5

Ingredients:
- 2 and ½ cups quinoa
- 4 and ½ cups veggie stock
- ½ teaspoon salt
- 2 tablespoons pesto sauce
- 2 tablespoons arrowroot powder
- 12 ounces mozzarella cheese
- 2 cups spinach
- 12 ounces broccoli
- 1/3 cup parmesan
- 3 green onions, chopped

Directions:
Put quinoa and green onions in a baking dish. Put broccoli in a heatproof bowl, introduce in the microwave, cook on high for 5 minutes and leave a side. In a bowl, mix veggie stock with arrowroot powder, pesto sauce and some salt, stir well, transfer to a pot and bring to a boil over medium heat. Pour this over quinoa, add broccoli, spinach, parmesan and mozzarella cheese. Introduce in the oven at 400 degrees F and bake for 30 minutes. Divide between plates and serve as a side dish.
Enjoy!

Nutrition: calories 210, fat 2, fiber 2, carbs 3, protein 3

Peas Side Dish

Preparation time: 10 minutes
Cooking time: 0 minutes
Servings: 8

Ingredients:
- 60 ounces peas
- 1 yellow bell pepper, chopped
- 2 ounces Cheddar cheese, grated
- ½ cup mayonnaise
- 3 tablespoon basil, dried
- 2 tablespoons red onion, chopped
- 2 teaspoons chili pepper, chopped
- 1 teaspoon apple cider vinegar
- 1 teaspoon sugar
- Salt and black pepper to the taste
- 1 teaspoon garlic powder
- A drizzle of hot sauce

Directions:
In a salad bowl, mix bell pepper with cheese, onion, basil, chili pepper, salt and pepper and stir. Add mayo, sugar, vinegar, hot sauce and garlic powder and stir. Add peas, toss well, introduce in the fridge and serve cold as a side dish. Enjoy!

Nutritional value: calories 120, fat 2, fiber 1, carbs 2, protein 3

Mashed Potatoes

Preparation time: 10 minutes
Cooking time: 40 minutes
Servings: 10

Ingredients:

- 2 pounds gold potatoes, cut into small pieces
- 1 and ½ cup fresh ricotta cheese
- Sea salt and black pepper to the taste
- ½ cup low fat milk
- 3 tablespoons butter

Directions:

Put potatoes in a pot, add water to cover, add a pinch of salt, bring to a simmer over medium heat, cook for 20 minutes, drain and mash them well. Add salt, pepper, milk, butter and ricotta and stir well. Spoon mashed potatoes into 10 ramekins, place them in a baking pan and broil them for a few minutes. Serve hot! Enjoy!

Nutrition: calories 180, fat 3, fiber 1, carbs 2, protein 3

Veggie Mix

Preparation time: 5 minutes
Cooking time: 20 minutes
Servings: 4

Ingredients:

- 1 and ½ cups yellow onion, chopped
- 1 and ½ cups red bell pepper, chopped
- 5 teaspoons olive oil
- 1 cup celery, chopped
- 1 tablespoon garlic, minced
- ¾ cup veggie stock
- ½ cup brown rice
- ½ cup water
- Salt and black pepper to the taste
- ½ teaspoon thyme, chopped
- ¾ teaspoon sweet paprika
- ¼ teaspoon red pepper, ground
- 1/3 cup tomato, chopped
- 4 teaspoons green onions, chopped
- 45 ounces canned black peas, drained

Directions:

Heat up a pan with the oil over medium high heat, add onion, celery and bell pepper, stir and cook for 7 minutes. Add garlic, cook 1 more minute. Add rice, stock, water, salt, pepper, paprika, thyme, red pepper, stir, bring to a boil, cover and simmer for 10 minutes. Add peas, stir and cook 2 more minutes. Add tomato, green onions, stir gently, divide between plates and serve as a side dish. Enjoy!

Nutrition: calories 187, fat 2, fiber 2, carbs 2, protein 3

Creamy Barley Side Salad

Preparation time: 15 minutes
Cooking time: 30 minutes
Servings: 4

Ingredients:

- ½ cup barley
- 1 and ½ cup water
- ½ cup Greek yogurt
- Salt and black pepper to the taste
- 2 tablespoons olive oil
- 1 teaspoon mustard
- 1 tablespoon lemon juice
- 2 celery stalks, sliced
- ¼ cup mint, chopped
- 1 apple, cored and chopped

Directions:

Put barley in a pan, add the water and some salt, bring to a boil, cover, simmer for 25 minutes, drain, spread on a baking sheet and leave aside. In a bowl, mix yogurt with lemon juice, oil, salt, pepper and mustard and stir well. Add mint, apple, celery and barley, toss to coat and serve as a side dish. Enjoy!

Nutrition: calories 132, fat 2, fiber 3, carbs 3, protein 1

Easy Couscous

Preparation time: 10 minutes
Cooking time: 10 minutes
Servings: 4

Ingredients:

- 10 ounces couscous
- 1 and ½ cup hot water
- ½ cup pine nuts
- 2 garlic cloves, minced
- 3 tablespoons olive oil
- 15 ounces canned chickpeas, rinsed
- ½ cup raisins
- 2 bunches Swiss chard
- Salt and black pepper to the taste

Directions:

Put couscous in a bowl, add water, stir, cover and leave aside for 10 minutes. Meanwhile, heat up a pan over medium high heat, add pine nuts, toast them for 4 minutes, transfer to a plate and leave aside. Return the pan to medium heat, add oil, heat up, add garlic, stir and cook for 1 minute. Add raisins, chickpeas, chard, salt, pepper, stir and cook for 5 minutes. Fluff couscous, divide between plates, add chard and chickpeas mix, top with pine nuts and serve as a side dish. Enjoy!

Nutrition: calories 153, fat 2, fiber 3, carbs 6, protein 4

Amazing Cabbage

Preparation time: 10 minutes
Cooking time: 20 minutes
Servings: 4

Ingredients:

- 3 tablespoons olive oil
- 1 tablespoon black lentils
- 2 dried red chilies, chopped
- 1 spring curry leaves, chopped
- 1 teaspoon mustard seeds
- 1 pinch asafetida powder
- 1 cabbage head, shredded
- 4 green chili peppers, chopped
- ¼ cup peas
- ¼ coconut grated
- Salt and black pepper to the taste

Directions:

Heat up a pan with the oil over medium heat, add red chili peppers, mustard seeds and black lentils, stir and fry for 3-4 minutes. Add curry leaves, asafetida powder, green chili peppers, stir and cook for 1 more minute. Add peas, cabbage, salt and black pepper, stir and fry for 10 minutes. Add coconut, cook for 2 more minutes, divide between plates and serve right away! Enjoy!

Nutrition: calories 153, fat 3, fiber 2, carbs 2, protein 5

Chickpeas Delight

Preparation time: 10 minutes
Cooking time: 25 minutes
Servings: 4

Ingredients:

- 1 yellow onion, chopped
- 2 tablespoons olive oil
- 2 garlic cloves, minced
- 2 teaspoons spice mix
- 28 ounces canned chickpeas, drained
- 14 ounces canned tomatoes, chopped
- 2 cups veggie stock
- 2 zucchinis, chopped
- 6 ounces green beans, halved
- 2 cups couscous, cooked
- 2 tablespoons coriander, chopped
- ½ cup figs, dried and chopped
- Salt and pepper to the taste

Directions:

Heat up a pan with the oil over medium high heat, add onion, stir and cook for 3-4 minutes. Add garlic, spice mix, salt and pepper, stir and cook for 5 minutes. Add tomato, stock and chickpeas, bring to a boil, cover and simmer for 10 minutes. Add beans, figs and zucchinis, stir and cook for 8 more minutes. Divide couscous on serving plates, add veggie mix, top with coriander and serve. Enjoy!

Nutrition: calories 200, fat 1, fiber 2, carbs 3, protein 4

Greek Tomato Side Salad

Preparation time: 10 minutes
Cooking time: 0 minutes
Servings: 4

Ingredients:

- 4 pounds heirloom tomatoes, sliced
- 1 yellow bell pepper, chopped
- 1 green bell pepper, chopped
- 1 red onion, chopped
- Sea salt and black pepper to the taste
- 4 ounces feta cheese, crumbled
- ½ teaspoon oregano, dried
- 2 tablespoons mint, chopped
- A drizzle of olive oil

Directions:

In a salad bowl, mix tomatoes with yellow and green bell peppers, onion, salt and pepper, toss to coat and leave aside for 10 minutes. Add cheese, oregano, mint and olive oil and toss to coat. Serve right away as a side dish. Enjoy!

Nutrition: calories 142, fat 1, fiber 1, carbs 1, protein 2

Tomato And Bocconcini Side Salad

Preparation time: 6 minutes
Cooking time: 6 minutes
Servings: 4

Ingredients:

- 20 ounces tomatoes, cut in wedges
- 2 tablespoons olive oil
- 1 and ½ tablespoons balsamic vinegar
- 1 teaspoon sugar
- 1 garlic clove, minced
- 8 ounces baby bocconcini, drain and torn
- 1 cup basil, chopped
- Salt and black pepper to the taste

Directions:

In a bowl, mix sugar with vinegar, garlic, oil, salt and pepper and whisk very well. In a salad bowl, mix bocconcini with tomato and basil. Add dressing, toss to coat and serve right away. Enjoy!

Nutrition: calories 121, fat 1, fiber 1, carbs 2, protein 2

cious Side Salad

Preparation time: 10 minutes
Cooking time: 5 minutes
Servings: 6

Ingredients:

- 1 tablespoon olive oil
- 1 cucumber, chopped
- 2 pints colored cherry tomatoes, halved
- Salt and black pepper to the taste
- 1 red onion, chopped

- 3 tablespoons red wine vinegar
- 1 garlic clove, minced
- 1 bunch basil, chopped
- 1 teaspoon honey

Directions:

In a bowl, mix vinegar with salt, pepper, honey and the oil and whisk very well. In a salad bowl mix cucumber with tomatoes, onion and garlic. Add vinegar dressing, toss to coat, sprinkle basil, toss to coat and serve as a side dish. Enjoy!

Nutrition: calories 153, fat 2, fiber 1, carbs 2, protein 2

Avocado Side Salad

Preparation time: 10 minutes
Cooking time: 0 minutes
Servings: 4

Ingredients:

- 1 cucumber, chopped
- 1 pound tomatoes, chopped
- 2 avocados, pitted, peeled and chopped
- 1 small red onion, sliced

- 2 tablespoons olive oil
- 2 tablespoons lemon juice
- ¼ cup cilantro, chopped
- Sea salt and black pepper to the taste

Directions:

In a salad bowl, mix tomatoes with onion, avocado, cucumber and cilantro. In a small bowl, mix oil with lemon juice, salt and pepper to the taste and whisk well. Pour this over salad, toss to coat and serve right away. Enjoy!

Nutrition: calories 173, fat 1, fiber 1, carbs 2, protein 2

Eggplant Side Salad

Preparation time: 10 minutes
Cooking time: 1 hour
Servings: 5

Ingredients:
- 1 red bell pepper
- 1 green bell pepper
- 7 tomatoes
- 1 eggplant, cut into thin strips
- 2 tablespoons tomato paste
- Salt and black pepper to the taste
- A pinch of cayenne pepper
- 4 garlic cloves, crushed
- ¼ cup extra-virgin olive oil

Directions:

Place bell peppers on stove burners, roast them until they turn black, transfer to a bowl, cover, leave them to cool down, peeled, cut into thin strips, put in a bowl and leave aside. Put some water in a pot, bring to a boil over medium high heat, add tomatoes, steam them for 1 minute, transfer to a bowl filled with ice water, allow them to cool down. Heat up a pan with the oil over medium high heat, add eggplant strips, stir and cook them for 8 minutes. Add garlic, stir and cook for 2 more minutes. Add bell peppers strips, stir and cook for 1 minute more. Peel tomatoes, chop them and add them to eggplant mix. Add salt, pepper to the taste, cayenne and tomato paste, stir, bring to a boil, reduce heat and cook for 30 minutes. Transfer salad to bowls and serve hot as a side dish. Enjoy!

Nutrition: calories 200, fat 1, fiber 2, carbs 2, protein 4

Tomato Risotto

Preparation time: 10 minutes
Cooking time: 25 minutes
Servings: 4

Ingredients:
- 5 cups chicken stock
- 1 garlic clove, minced
- 1 yellow onion, chopped
- 10 ounces sun dried tomatoes in olive oil, chopped
- 1 and ½ cup Arborio rice
- Salt and black pepper to the taste
- 1 and ½ cup pecorino, grated
- 1 cup white wine
- 2 tablespoons butter
- ¼ cup basil leaves, chopped

Directions:

Heat up a pot over medium high heat, add dried tomatoes, onions, garlic, salt and pepper, stir and cook for 2 minutes. Add wine and rice, stir well and cook for another 2 minutes. Add 3 cups stock, stir and cook for 7 minutes. Add the rest of the stock, stir again, cover pot, introduce in the oven at 425 degrees F and bake for 15 minutes. Take risotto out of the oven, add cheese and butter and stir until they melt. Sprinkle basil, stir gently, transfer to plates and serve as a side dish. Enjoy!

Nutrition: calories 110, fat 1, fiber 1, carbs 2, protein 2

Simple Cucumber Side Salad

Preparation time: 1 hour and 10 minutes
Cooking time: 0 minutes
Servings: 8

Ingredients:

- 4 cucumbers, sliced
- 1 cup white wine vinegar
- 1 white onion, sliced
- 1 tablespoon dill, dried
- ¾ cup sugar
- ½ cup water

Directions:

In a bowl, mix onion with cucumbers. Heat up a pot with the water over medium high heat, vinegar and sugar, stir well, bring to a boil and take off heat. Pour over cucumber, add dill, stir gently and keep in the fridge for 1 hour before serving as a side dish for a beef based meal. Enjoy!

Nutrition: calories 112, fat 1, fiber 1, carbs 2, protein 2

Special And Tasty Side Salad

Preparation time: 10 minutes
Cooking time: 0 minutes
Servings: 4

Ingredients:

- 1 big English cucumber, chopped
- 1 avocado, pitted, peeled and chopped
- 2 tomatoes, chopped
- 1 tablespoon lime juice
- 3 tablespoons olive oil
- 2 teaspoons balsamic vinegar
- 1 teaspoon Greek herb salad dressing mix

Directions:

In a bowl, mix tomato with avocado and cucumber. In another bowl, mix oil with vinegar, lime juice and dressing mix and stir very well. Pour salad dressing over salad, toss to coat and serve as a side dish. Enjoy!

Nutrition: calories 100, fat 1, fiber 1, carbs 2, protein 2

Quick Mediterranean Side Salad

Preparation time: 6 minutes
Cooking time: 0 minutes
Servings: 6

Ingredients:

- 2 big cucumbers, sliced
- ½ cup balsamic vinegar
- 2 tablespoons olive oil
- Sesame seeds, toasted for serving
- Salt and black pepper to the taste

Directions:

In a small bowl, mix vinegar with salt, pepper and oil and whisk very well. Put cucumbers in a bowl and mix with sesame seeds. Add salad dressing, toss to coat and serve as a side dish. Enjoy!

Nutrition: calories 100, fat 1, fiber 1, carbs 1, protein 1

Wonderful Dates Salad

Preparation time: 10 minutes
Cooking time: 0 minutes
Servings: 4

Ingredients:

- 2 cucumbers, chopped
- 8 dates, pitted and sliced
- ¾ cup fennel, sliced
- 2 tablespoons chives, chopped
- ½ cup walnuts, chopped
- 2 tablespoons lemon juice
- 4 tablespoons fruity olive oil
- Salt and black pepper to the taste

Directions:

Put the cucumber in a salad bowl and mash a bit using a fork. Add dates, fennel, chives and walnuts and stir gently. Add salt, pepper to the taste, lemon juice and the oil, toss to coat and serve right away as a side dish. Enjoy!

Nutrition: calories 90, fat 1, fiber 1, carbs 2, protein 2

Cucumber And Beans Side Salad

Preparation time: 10 minutes
Cooking time: 0 minutes
Servings: 4

Ingredients:

- 1 big cucumber, cut into chunks
- 15 ounces canned black beans, drained
- 1 cup corn
- 1 cup cherry tomatoes, halved
- 1 small red onion, chopped
- 3 tablespoons olive oil
- 4 and ½ teaspoons orange marmalade
- 1 teaspoon honey
- Salt and black pepper to the taste
- ½ teaspoon cumin, ground
- 1 tablespoon lemon juice

Directions:

In a bowl, mix beans with cucumber, corn, onion and tomatoes. In another bowl, mix marmalade with oil, honey, lemon juice, salt, pepper to the taste and cumin and whisk very well. Pour this over salad, toss to coat and serve right away as a side dish. Enjoy!

Nutrition: calories 193, fat 1, fiber 1, carbs 2, protein 2

Beet And Cucumber Side Salad

Preparation time: 10 minutes
Cooking time: 2 minutes
Servings: 8

Ingredients:

- 4 small beets, peeled and sliced
- 3 cucumbers, sliced
- 6 scallions, chopped
- 3 chili peppers, sliced
- Zest from 1 lemon, sliced
- 5 ounces dry ricotta, crumbled
- 2 cups mixed basil with mint, parsley and cilantro, chopped
- ¼ cup white wine vinegar
- 2 teaspoons poppy seeds
- ½ teaspoon sugar
- A drizzle of olive oil
- Salt and black pepper to the taste

Directions:

In a salad bowl mix cucumbers with beets, scallions, chili peppers, mixed herbs, lemon zest and ricotta. In another bowl, mix vinegar with sugar, poppy seeds, salt, pepper and a drizzle of olive oil and whisk very well. Pour this over salad, toss to coat, divide between plates and serve. Enjoy!

Nutrition: calories 112, fat 1, fiber 2, carbs 2, protein 2

Mediterranean Diet Snack And Appetizer Recipes

Mediterranean Sandwiches

Preparation time: 10 minutes
Cooking time: 0 minutes
Servings: 12

Ingredients:

- 1 cucumber, peeled and sliced
- 8 slices whole wheat bread
- 2 tablespoons soft butter
- 1 tablespoon chives, chopped
- ¼ cup homemade mayonnaise
- 1 teaspoon mustard
- Salt and black pepper to the taste

Directions:

Spread butter on one side of each bread slice. Divide cucumbers on 4 bread slices. In a bowl, mix chives with mayo, mustard, salt and pepper to the taste and whisk well. Spread this over cucumbers slices, top with the other 4 buttered bread slices, cut each sandwich in 3 pieces, arrange on a platter and serve right away as an appetizer. Enjoy!

Nutrition: calories 110, fat 1, fiber 2, carbs 2, protein 2

Delicious Rolls

Preparation time: 10 minutes
Cooking time: 0 minutes
Servings: 6

Ingredients:

- 1 big cucumber, sliced lengthwise
- 1 tablespoon cilantro, chopped
- 1 tablespoon cranberries, dried
- 4 ounces canned sardines, drained and flaked
- 3 ounces canned tuna pate
- Salt and black pepper to the taste
- 1 teaspoon lemon juice

Directions:

Arrange cucumber slices on a working surface. In a bowl, mix sardines with tuna paste, salt and pepper to the taste and lemon juice and mash everything well. Spoon this mix on each cucumber slice, add cilantro and cranberries on top, roll, arrange on a platter and serve. Enjoy!

Nutrition: calories 80, fat 1, fiber 2, carbs 2, protein 1

Easy Stuffed Tomatoes

Preparation time: 10 minutes
Cooking time: 2minutes
Servings: 24

Ingredients:

- 24 cherry tomatoes, top cut off and insides scooped out
- 2 tablespoons olive oil
- A pinch of salt
- ¼ teaspoon red pepper flakes
- ½ cup feta cheese, cut into 24 pieces
- 1 tablespoon black olive paste
- 1 tablespoon water
- ¼ cup mint, torn

Directions:

Season each tomato with pepper flakes and drizzle half of the oil. Insert a feta cheese cube in each tomato, introduce them in preheated broiler over medium heat and broil them for 2 minutes. In a bowl, mix the olive paste with the water and spread it on a platter. Arrange tomatoes on top, drizzle the rest of the oil, sprinkle mint and serve. Enjoy!

Nutrition: calories 110, fat 1, fiber 2, carbs 2, protein 2

Mediterranean Surprise

Preparation time: 10 minutes
Cooking time: 5 minutes
Servings: 6

Ingredients:

- 1 garlic clove, minced
- 4 tablespoons olive oil
- 5 tomatoes, chopped
- 1 tablespoon balsamic vinegar
- ¼ cup basil, chopped
- A pinch of red pepper flakes
- 14 slices whole wheat baguette
- Salt and black pepper to the taste

Directions:

In a bowl, mix tomatoes with 3 tablespoons oil, garlic, basil, pepper flakes, balsamic vinegar, salt and pepper to the taste, stir well and leave aside. Arrange bread slices on a lined baking sheet, introduce them in the oven at 350 degrees F, toast for 5 minutes, arrange them on a platter and divide tomato mix on them. Drizzle the rest of the oil and serve right away. Enjoy!

Nutrition: calories 84, fat 1, fiber 1, carbs 1, protein 1

Easy Mediterranean Salsa

Preparation time: 2 hours and 5 minutes
Cooking time: 0 minutes
Servings: 16

Ingredients:
- 3 yellow tomatoes, seedless and chopped
- 1 red tomato, seedless and chopped
- Salt and black pepper to the taste
- 1 cup watermelon, seedless and chopped
- 1/3 cup red onion, chopped
- 1 mango, peeled, seedless and chopped
- 2 jalapeno peppers, chopped
- ¼ cup cilantro, chopped
- 3 tablespoons lime juice
- 2 teaspoons honey

Directions:

In a bowl, mix yellow and red tomatoes with mango, watermelon, onion and jalapeno. Add cilantro, lime juice, salt, pepper to the taste and honey and stir well. Cover bowl, keep in the fridge for 2 hours and then serve. Enjoy!

Nutrition: calories 83, fat 2, fiber 1, carbs 2, protein 1

Spinach Dip

Preparation time: 15 minutes
Cooking time: 0 minutes
Servings: 4

Ingredients:
- 1 bunch spinach, roughly chopped
- 1 scallion, sliced
- 2 tablespoons mint, chopped
- ¾ cup sour cream
- Salt and black pepper to the taste

Directions:

Put some water in a pot, bring to a boil over medium heat, add spinach, cook for 20 seconds, rinse and drain well, chop and put in a bowl. Add sour cream, scallion, salt, pepper to the taste and of course, the mint, stir well, leave aside for 15 minutes and then serve. Enjoy!

Nutrition: calories 110, fat 1, fiber 1, carbs 1, protein 5

Artichoke Dip

Preparation time: 10 minutes
Cooking time: 30 minutes
Servings: 10

Ingredients:
- 8 ounces artichoke hearts
- ¾ cup basil, chopped
- ¾ cup green olive paste
- 1 cup parmesan cheese, grated
- 5 ounces garlic and herb cheese

Directions:
In your food processor, mix artichokes with basil and pulse. Spread this into a baking dish, add olive paste, parmesan cheese, herbed cheese and stir. Introduce in the oven at 375 degrees F and bake for 30 minutes. Serve warm. Enjoy!

Nutrition: calories 152, fat 2, fiber 3, carbs 3, protein 1

Delicious Mediterranean Dip

Preparation time: 10 minutes
Cooking time: 0 minutes
Servings: 8

Ingredients:
- ½ cup sour cream
- 1 chili pepper, chopped
- Salt and pepper to the taste
- 4 avocados, pitted, peeled and chopped
- 1 cup cilantro, chopped
- ¼ cup lemon juice
- Carrot sticks for serving

Directions:
Put avocados in your blender and pulse a few times. Add sour cream and pulse again. Add chili pepper, lemon juice, cilantro, salt and pepper to the taste and pulse well again. Transfer to a bowl and serve as a snack. Enjoy!

Nutrition: calories 112, fat 1, fiber 2, carbs 2, protein 4

Chives Dip

Preparation time: 10 minutes
Cooking time: 10 minutes
Servings: 4

Ingredients:
- 2 ounces goat cheese, soft
- ¾ cup sour cream
- 1 shallot, minced
- 1 tablespoon chives, chopped
- 1 tablespoon lemon juice
- Salt and black pepper to the taste
- ½ pound potatoes, sliced
- ½ pound purple potatoes, sliced
- 2 tablespoons extra virgin olive oil

Directions:
In a bowl, mix chives with sour cream, goat cheese, shallot, lemon juice, salt and pepper to the taste and stir very well. In another bowl, mix potato slices with salt and olive oil and toss to coat. Heat up your kitchen grill over medium high heat, add potato slices, grill for 5 minutes on each side and transfer them to a bowl. Serve your potato chips with the chives dip on the side. Enjoy!

Nutrition: calories 110, fat 2, fiber 2, carbs 2, protein 5

Chickpeas Appetizer

Preparation time: 10 minutes
Cooking time: 0 minutes
Servings: 6

Ingredients:
- 4 scallions, sliced
- 1 cup arugula, chopped
- 15 ounces canned chickpeas, chopped
- Salt and black pepper to the taste
- 2 jarred red peppers, roasted and chopped
- 2 tablespoons olive oil
- 2 tablespoons lemon juice

Directions:

In a bowl, mix chickpeas with arugula, scallions, red peppers, salt, pepper, lemon juice and olive oil and stir very well. Transfer to a bowl and serve. Enjoy!

Nutrition: calories 74, fat 2, fiber 2, carbs 6, protein 2

Cilantro Dip

Preparation time: 10 minutes
Cooking time: 0 minutes
Servings: 6

Ingredients:
- ½ cup ginger, sliced
- 2 bunches cilantro, chopped
- 3 tablespoons balsamic vinegar
- ½ cup olive oil
- 2 teaspoons sesame oil
- 2 tablespoons soy sauce

Directions:

In your blender mix cilantro with olive oil, ginger, vinegar, soy sauce and sesame oil and pulse very well. Transfer to a bowl and serve. Enjoy!

Greek Yogurt Dip

Preparation time: 10 minutes
Cooking time: 0 minutes
Servings: 8

Ingredients:
- 1 garlic clove, minced
- 2 cups Greek yogurt
- ¼ cup dill, chopped
- ¼ cup walnuts, chopped
- Salt and black pepper to the taste

Directions:

In a bowl, mix yogurt with garlic, salt and pepper and whisk. Add dill and walnuts, stir again and serve. Enjoy!

Nutrition: calories 73, fat 2, fiber 1, carbs 2, protein 3

Mediterranean Goat Cheese Dip

Preparation time: 10 minutes
Cooking time: 0 minutes
Servings: 4

Ingredients:

- ¼ cup mixed parsley and chives, chopped
- 8 ounces goat cheese, soft
- Black pepper to the taste

Directions:

In your food processor mix cheese with black pepper, parsley and chives and pulse well. Transfer to a bowl and serve with graham crackers on the side as a snack. Enjoy!

Nutrition: calories 152, fat 2, fiber 2, carbs 2, protein 1

Mediterranean Party Dip

Preparation time: 10 minutes
Cooking time: 0 minutes
Servings: 8

Ingredients:

- 19 ounces canned cannellini beans, drained
- 3 scallions, chopped
- 1 garlic clove, minced
- 3 tablespoons olive oil
- Salt and black pepper to the taste
- 1 tablespoon lemon juice
- 2 ounces prosciutto, chopped

Directions:

In a bowl, mix beans with scallions, garlic, salt, pepper, oil and lemon juice and stir well. Add prosciutto, stir well again and serve as a Mediterranean snack. Enjoy!

Nutrition: calories 62, fat 4, fiber 1, carbs 1, protein 3

Simple Tomato Delight

Preparation time: 10 minutes
Cooking time: 0 minutes
Servings: 6

Ingredients:

- 12 ounces Greek cream cheese
- 1 big tomato, cut in quarters
- ¼ cup homemade mayonnaise
- 2 garlic clove, minced
- 2 tablespoons yellow onion, chopped
- 1 celery stalk, chopped
- 1 teaspoon sugar
- 2 tablespoons lemon juice
- Salt and black pepper to the taste
- 4 drops hot sauce

Directions:

In your blender, mix cream cheese with tomato, onion, garlic and celery and pulse a few times. Add mayo, lemon juice, sugar, salt, pepper and hot sauce, blend again very well, transfer to a bowl and serve as a snack. Enjoy!

Nutrition: calories 74, fat 3, fiber 1, carbs 3, protein 4

Green Dip

Preparation time: 10 minutes
Cooking time: 0 minutes
Servings: 6

Ingredients:
- 1 cup homemade mayonnaise
- 7 ounces Greek basil pesto sauce
- Salt and black pepper to the taste
- 1 cup sour cream

Directions:

In a bowl, mix pesto with mayo and sour cream and whisk very well. Add salt and pepper, stir well again and keep in the fridge until your serve it. Enjoy!

Nutrition: calories 87, fat 2, fiber 0, carbs 1, protein 2

Tasty Beet Chips

Preparation time: 1 hour and 10 minutes
Cooking time: 30 minutes
Servings: 4

Ingredients:
- 2 beets, sliced

For the vinaigrette:
- 1/3 cup champagne vinegar
- A pinch of black pepper
- A pinch of sea salt
- 1 cup olive oil
- 1 teaspoon green tea powder

Directions:

Put the vinegar in a small pot and heat up over medium heat. Add green tea powder, stir well, bring to a simmer, take off heat and leave aside to cool down completely. Add the oil and a pinch of black pepper, whisk really well and keep in the fridge for 1 hour. Add beets slices and a pinch of salt, toss to coat well and spread them on a lined baking sheet. Introduce beets chips in the oven at 350 degrees F and bake for 30 minutes. Leave them to cool down completely before serving them for your next party as a snack. Enjoy!

Nutrition: calories 100, fat 2, fiber 2, carbs 3, protein 2

Mediterranean Appetizer Salad

Preparation time: 10 minutes
Cooking time: 0 minutes
Servings: 4

Ingredients:

- ½ cup black olives, pitted and sliced
- 3 zucchinis, cut with a spiralizer
- 1 cup cherry tomatoes, halved
- Salt and black pepper to the taste

For the mint tea vinaigrette:

- 1 tablespoon shallot, chopped
- ½ cup sunflower oil
- ½ cup olive oil

- 1 small red onion, chopped
- ½ cup canned chickpeas, drained
- ½ cup feta cheese, crumbled

- ¼ cup apple cider vinegar
- 2 teaspoons mint tea powder
- 1 teaspoon mustard

Directions:

In a bowl, mix shallot with sunflower oil, olive oil, vinegar, mustard and mint tea powder and whisk really well. In a salad bowl, mix zucchini noodles with olives, tomatoes, onion, chickpeas, salt and pepper and stir gently. Add the vinaigrette, toss to coat well and serve with the cheese on top as an appetizer. Enjoy!

Nutrition: calories 200, fat 3, fiber 2, carbs 4, protein 2

Elegant Veggie Appetizer

Preparation time: 10 minutes
Cooking time: 0 minutes
Servings: 4

Ingredients:

- 2 carrots, peeled and grated
- 1 avocado, pitted, peeled and chopped
- ½ green cabbage head, shredded
- 10 strawberries, halved
- Salt and black pepper to the taste
- ¼ teaspoon lemon matcha powder

- 1 teaspoon maple syrup
- 2 tablespoons white wine vinegar
- 1 tablespoon Dijon mustard
- ¼ cup lemon juice
- ¾ cup olive oil

Directions:

In a bowl, mix lemon juice with oil, vinegar, matcha tea powder, maple syrup, mustard, salt and pepper and whisk well. In a salad bowl, mix avocado with cabbage, strawberries and carrots. Add salad dressing, toss to coat, divide on appetizer plates and serve. Enjoy!

Nutrition: calories 100, fat 1, fiber 2, carbs 2, protein 4

Delicious Glazed Squash

Preparation time: 10 minutes
Cooking time: 25 minutes
Servings: 6

Ingredients:

- 6 tablespoons grape seed oil
- 2 tablespoons white miso paste
- 3 acorn squash, halved and sliced
- 2 tablespoons maple syrup

Directions:

In a bowl, mix miso, maple syrup and oil and whisk well. Brush a baking sheet with some of the oil and arrange squash pieces on it. Drizzle half of the glaze over them, introduce in the oven at 400 degrees F and roast for 5 minutes. Brush acorn squash pieces with the rest of the glaze, flip them and roast for 20 minutes. Serve as a snack. Enjoy!

Nutrition: calories 143, fat 4, fiber 3, carbs 20, protein 4

Great Mediterranean Delight

Preparation time: 10 minutes
Cooking time: 0 minutes
Servings: 8

Ingredients:

- 1 big cucumber, thinly sliced
- 12 small shrimp, already cooked
- 2 tablespoons sour cream
- Salt and black pepper to the taste
- 12 whole grain crackers

Directions:

Arrange crackers on a platter. Add cucumber slices on each. Spoon some sour cream over cucumber slices, top each with shrimps, sprinkle salt and pepper all over them and serve right away. Enjoy!

Nutrition: calories 84, fat 2, fiber 1, carbs 2, protein 3

Unbelievable Appetizer Cups

Preparation time: 10 minutes
Cooking time: 0 minutes
Servings: 20

Ingredients:

- 2 big cucumbers, cut into ½ inch thick slices and seeds scooped out
- 2 cups canned chickpeas, drained
- 7 ounces canned red peppers, roasted, drained and chopped
- ¼ cup lemon juice
- 1/3 cup tahini paste
- 1 garlic clove, minced
- Salt and black pepper to the taste
- ¼ teaspoon cumin, ground
- 3 tablespoons olive oil
- 1 tablespoon hot water

Directions:

In your food processor, mix red peppers with chickpeas, olive oil, tahini, lemon juice, salt, pepper, garlic, cumin and hot water and blend very well. Arrange cucumber cups on a platter, fill each with chickpeas mix and serve right away as an appetizer. Enjoy!

Nutrition: calories 182, fat 1, fiber 3, carbs 4, protein 2

Salmon Appetizer

Preparation time: 7 minutes
Cooking time: 0 minutes
Servings: 44

Ingredients:

- 1 big long cucumber, sliced into 44 pieces
- 2 teaspoons lemon juice
- 4 ounces sour cream
- 1 teaspoon lemon zest, finely grated
- Salt and black pepper to the taste
- 2 teaspoons dill, chopped
- 4 ounces smoked salmon, cut into 44 strips

Directions:

In a bowl, mix lemon juice with lemon zest, salt, pepper to the taste and sour cream and stir well. Arrange cucumber slices on a platter, add salmon strips and ½ teaspoon cream mix on each and sprinkle dill at the end. Enjoy!

Nutrition: calories 142, fat 3, fiber 1, carbs 3, protein 3

Eggplant Balls

Preparation time: 15 minutes
Cooking time: 1 hour
Servings: 6

Ingredients:

- 4 cups eggplants, cubed
- 3 tablespoons olive oil
- 3 garlic cloves, minced
- 1 tablespoon water
- 2 eggs, whisked
- Salt and black pepper to the taste
- 1 cup parsley, chopped
- ½ cup parmesan cheese, finely grated
- ¾ cups breadcrumbs

Directions:

Heat up a pan with the oil over medium high heat, add garlic, stir and brown it for a few minutes. Add eggplant cubes and water, stir, reduce heat to low, cover pan, cook for 20 minutes and transfer them to a bowl. Add eggs, cheese, parsley, breadcrumbs, salt and pepper, stir well, keep in the fridge for 15 minutes, shape medium balls and spread them on a lined baking sheet. Introduce them in the oven at 350 degrees F and bake for 30 minutes. Sprinkle parmesan over them, arrange on a platter and serve as an appetizer. Enjoy!

Nutrition: calories 142, fat 1, fiber 3, carbs 2, protein 3

Grilled Appetizer

Preparation time: 10 minutes
Cooking time: 15 minutes
Servings: 8

Ingredients:
- 2 eggplants, cut into 20 slices

For the tapenade:
- 2 tablespoons olive oil
- ½ cup bottled roasted peppers, chopped
- ½ cup kalamata and black olives, pitted and chopped
- 1 tablespoon lemon juice

For serving:
- 2 tablespoons pine nuts, toasted
- 4 tablespoons feta cheese, crumbled

- A drizzle of olive oil

- 1 teaspoon red pepper flakes, crushed
- Salt and black pepper to the taste
- 2 tablespoons mixed mint, parsley, oregano and basil, chopped

- A drizzle of olive oil

Directions:

In a bowl, mix roasted peppers with olives, 2 tablespoons olive oil, lemon juice, mixed herbs, red pepper flakes, salt and pepper to the taste, stir well and keep in the fridge. Brush eggplant slices with a drizzle of olive oil on both sides, place them on preheated grill over medium high heat, cook for 7 minutes on each side and transfer them to a platter. Top each eggplant slice with some tapenade mix, sprinkle pine nuts, feta cheese and drizzle olive oil on top of each and serve. Enjoy!

Nutrition: calories 132, fat 2, fiber 3, carbs 4, protein 4

Eggplant Chips

Preparation time: 10 minutes
Cooking time: 1 hour
Servings: 2

Ingredients:
- A drizzle of oilve oil
- 2 eggplants, sliced
- ½ tablespoon garlic powder
- ½ tablespoon smoked paprika
- 1 teaspoon oregano, dried
- Salt and black pepper to the taste

- ½ teaspoon turmeric, ground
- ½ teaspoon thyme, dried
- ½ teaspoon onion powder
- A pinch of cayenne pepper
- ¼ teaspoon sage, dried and ground

Directions:

Arrange eggplant slices on a lined baking sheet, season with salt and pepper, drizzle some olive oil and rub well. Sprinkle half of garlic powder, onion powder, paprika, oregano, turmeric, thyme, sage and a pinch of cayenne. Flip them and sprinkle the rest of the seasoning mix. Introduce them in the oven at 250 degrees F and bake them for 1 hour. Transfer them to bowls and serve as a snack. Enjoy!

Nutrition: calories 110, fat 1, fiber 2, carbs 2, protein 4

Simple Appetizer Salad

Preparation time: 10 minutes
Cooking time: 20 minutes
Servings: 4

Ingredients:
- 1 tomato, diced
- 1 eggplant, pricked
- Salt and black pepper to the taste
- 1 and ½ teaspoons red wine vinegar
- ½ teaspoon oregano, chopped
- 3 tablespoons olive oil
- 2 garlic cloves, minced
- 3 tablespoons parsley, chopped
- Capers, chopped for serving

Directions:

Heat up your grill over medium high heat, add eggplant, cook for 15 minutes, turning from time to time, cool down, scoop flesh, chop and put in a bowl. Add salt, pepper to the taste, tomatoes, garlic, vinegar and oregano and stir gently. Add parsley and oil and stir again. Top with capers and serve as an appetizer. Enjoy!

Nutrition: calories 132, fat 1, fiber 2, carbs 2, protein 4

Easy And Delicious Appetizer Salad

Preparation time: 10 minutes
Cooking time: 10 minutes
Servings: 4

Ingredients:
- 1 eggplant, sliced
- 1 red onion, sliced
- A drizzle of olive oil
- 1 avocado, pitted and chopped
- 1 teaspoon mustard
- 1 tablespoon red wine vinegar
- 1 tablespoon oregano, chopped
- 1 teaspoon honey
- Salt and black pepper to the taste
- Zest from 1 lemon
- Some parsley sprigs, chopped for serving

Directions:

Brush red onion slices and eggplant ones with a drizzle of olive oil, place them on preheated kitchen grill, cook for a few minutes on each side, cool down, chop and put in a bowl. Add avocado and stir gently. In a bowl, mix vinegar with mustard, oregano, honey, olive oil, salt and pepper to the taste and whisk well. Add this to eggplant mix, toss to coat, add lemon zest and parsley on top and serve as an appetizer. Enjoy!

Nutrition: calories 142, fat 2, fiber 1, carbs 5, protein 2

Gorgeous Appetizer

Preparation time: 2 hours and 10 minutes
Cooking time: 1 hour and 30 minutes
Servings: 12

Ingredients:

- 1 garlic clove, minced
- 6 eggplants, pricked with a fork
- 1 teaspoon parsley, dried
- 1 teaspoon oregano, dried
- ¼ teaspoon basil, dried
- 3 tablespoons olive oil
- 2 tablespoons sugar
- 1 tablespoon balsamic vinegar
- Salt and black pepper to the taste

Directions:

Arrange eggplants on a lined baking sheet, introduce in the oven at 350 degrees F, bake for 1 hour and 30 minutes, leave them to cool down, peel, chop and transfer to a salad bowl. Add garlic, oil, parsley, sugar, oregano, basil, salt and pepper to the taste, toss to coat, keep in the fridge for 2 hours and then serve as an appetizer. Enjoy!

Nutrition: calories 200, fat 3, fiber 1, carbs 3, protein 3

Chickpeas Appetizer

Preparation time: 30 minutes
Cooking time: 10 minutes
Servings: 4

Ingredients:

- 1 eggplant, cut in half lengthwise and sliced
- 1 small red onion, chopped
- Juice of 1 lemon
- Zest from 1 lemon
- A drizzle of olive oil
- 28 ounces canned chickpeas, drained
- 1 bunch parsley, chopped
- 2 tomatoes, chopped
- A pinch of cayenne pepper
- 2 teaspoons garlic infused olive oil
- Some silver almonds for serving
- Salt to the taste

Directions:

Put the onion in a bowl, add water to cover and leave aside for 30 minutes. Spread eggplant slices on a lined baking sheet, brush with a drizzle of olive oil, introduce in a preheated broiler for 5 minutes, brush them again with some olive oil and with half of the lemon juice, broil again until they are soft, transfer to a salad bowl and leave aside. Spread chickpeas on the same baking sheet, broil for a few minutes and add them to the bowl with the eggplant pieces Add tomatoes, parsley, drained onion, cayenne pepper, the rest of the lemon juice, salt to the taste, garlic oil, lemon zest and almonds, toss to coat and serve as an appetizer. Enjoy!

Nutrition: calories 154, fat 3, fiber 2, carbs 2, protein 4

Special Egg Salad

Preparation time: 10 minutes
Cooking time: 35 minutes
Servings: 4

Ingredients:

- 1 big purple eggplant, cubed
- ¼ cup olive oil
- 12 eggs, hard-boiled, peeled and chopped
- Juice of 1 lemon
- 14 ounces feta cheese, crumbled
- Salt and black pepper to the taste
- 1/3 cup pine nuts
- ¼ cup mustard
- ¾ cup sun dried tomatoes, marinade and chopped
- 1 cup walnuts, halved

Directions:

Spread eggplant cubes on a lined baking sheet. In a bowl, mix half of the lemon juice with the oil, salt and pepper to the taste, stir well, add to eggplant, toss to coat, introduce in the oven at 400 degrees F and bake for 30 minutes. In your food processor, mix cheese with the rest of the lemon juice, mustard, salt and pepper and blend. Add walnuts, sun dried tomatoes and pine nuts and blend again. Put chopped eggs in a bowl, crush them with a fork, add eggplant cubes and cheese mix, toss to coat well and serve as a side dish. Enjoy!

Nutrition: calories 153, fat 3, fiber 3, carbs 2, protein 2

Stuffed Eggplant

Preparation time: 10 minutes
Cooking time: 45 minutes
Servings: 6

Ingredients:

- 6 baby eggplants, sliced in halves
- 2 garlic cloves, minced
- 12 oregano sprigs
- 1 lemon, sliced
- Juice from 2 lemons
- Salt and black pepper to the taste
- ¾ cup olive oil
- 8 ounces feta cheese, sliced

Directions:

Arrange eggplant pieces in a baking pan, insert lemon slices, garlic and oregano into each and season them with salt and pepper. Drizzle olive oil and lemon juice, cover with tin foil, introduce in the oven at 450 degrees F and bake for 40 minutes. Uncover pan, bake for 5 more minutes, leave aside to cool down for 3-4 minutes, transfer to plates, top with feta cheese slices and pan juices and serve. Enjoy!

Nutrition: calories 200, fat 1, fiber 1, carbs 4, protein 3

Simple Eggplant Appetizer

Preparation time: 6 hours and 30 minutes
Cooking time: 10 minutes
Servings: 4

Ingredients:

- 1 and ½ pounds eggplants, sliced
- ½ jalapeno pepper, chopped
- ¾ cup olive oil
- 1 red bell pepper, roasted and chopped
- 1 and ½ teaspoons capers, drained and chopped
- 1 big garlic clove, minced
- 1 bunch parsley, chopped
- Salt and black pepper to the taste

Directions:

Sprinkle eggplant slices with salt on both sides, leave them aside for 30 minutes, pat dry and brush them with ¼ cup olive oil. Heat up a pan over medium high heat, add eggplant slices, cook for 5 minutes on each side and arrange in a baking dish. In a bowl, mix chili pepper with roasted pepper, parsley, capers, garlic, the rest of the oil, salt and pepper to the taste and stir very well. Pour this over eggplants, cover and leave in the fridge for 6 hours. Divide on plates and serve as an appetizer. Enjoy!

Flavored Appetizer

Preparation time: 8 hours
Cooking time: 30 minutes
Servings: 6

Ingredients:

- 2 big eggplants, peeled and sliced
- 3 tablespoons lemon juice
- Salt to the taste
- 3 garlic cloves
- 1/8 teaspoon cumin
- 6 tablespoons cold water
- ½ cup tahini paste
- Some olive oil for frying
- ½ cup pomegranate seeds
- 3 tablespoons carob molasses
- ¼ cup pistachios, halved

Directions:

Arrange eggplant slices on a lined baking sheet, season with salt on both sides and introduce them in the fridge for 8 hours. In your kitchen blender, mix lemon juice with salt to the taste and garlic and blend well. Strain this into a bowl and mix with cumin, tahini and the cold water and stir well. Heat up a pan with some olive oil over medium high heat, pat dry eggplant slices, add them to pan and cook for 5 minutes on each side. Drain excess grease and arrange eggplant pieces on a platter. Drizzle ¼ cup of tahini sauce you've just made, add molasses, sprinkle pomegranate seeds and pistachios on top and serve hot as an appetizer. Enjoy!

Nutrition: calories 142, fat 3, fiber 3, carbs 5, protein 3

Lentils Dip

Preparation time: 1 hour and 10 minutes
Cooking time: 10 minutes
Servings: 6

Ingredients:

- 1 cup red lentils, soaked overnight
- Salt and black pepper to the taste
- 1 bay leaf
- 2 tablespoons lemon juice
- 1 garlic clove, finely chopped
- 1 tablespoon tomato paste
- 2 tablespoon cilantro, finely chopped
- 2 teaspoons cumin
- 2 teaspoons harissa
- 2 tablespoons extra virgin olive oil

Directions:

Put lentils in a pot, add salt, bay leaf and water to cover, bring to a boil over medium high heat, reduce temperature to medium and cook for 10 minutes. Drain lentils, leave aside for 10 minutes to cool down, transfer to your blender, add tomato paste, lemon juice, cilantro, garlic, cumin, olive oil, harissa, salt and pepper to the taste and pulse until you obtain a smooth spread. Transfer to a bowl and leave aside for 1 hour before serving. Enjoy!

Nutrition: calories 132, fat 1, fiber 2, carbs 3, protein 3

Stuffed Baby Potatoes

Preparation time: 10 minutes
Cooking time: 40 minutes
Servings: 36

Ingredients:

- 18 red baby potatoes
- ½ cup goat cheese, crumbled
- ¾ cup red lentils, cooked and drained
- 2 tablespoons butter, melted
- 1 garlic clove, minced
- 1 tablespoon chives, chopped
- ½ teaspoon Sriracha sauce
- Salt and black pepper to the taste

Directions:

Put potatoes in a pot, add water to cover, bring to a boil over medium low heat, simmer for 15 minutes, drain, rinse and leave them aside to cool down. Cut potatoes in halves, remove pulp leaving a bit on the bottom and transfer potato flesh to your kitchen blender. Add lentils, goat cheese, butter, chives, garlic, salt, pepper and Sriracha sauce and blend everything well. Arrange potatoes on a lined baking sheet, stuff with the lentils and potato mix you've made, introduce them in the oven at 375 degrees F and bake for 15 minutes. Divide between plates and serve right away as an appetizer. Enjoy!

Nutrition: calories 210, fat 2, fiber 3, carbs 3, protein 1

Lentils Balls

Preparation time: 10 minutes
Cooking time: 45 minutes
Servings: 4

Ingredients:

- 1 cup red lentils
- 3 cups water
- 2 cups bulgur
- Some sea salt
- 3 teaspoons cumin, ground
- 1 tablespoon tomato paste
- 1 teaspoon red pepper flakes
- 1 and ½ tablespoons olive oil
- 3 scallions, chopped
- 1 yellow onion, chopped
- ½ bunch parsley, chopped
- Lemon slices for serving
- Lettuce leaves for serving

Directions:

Put lentils in a pot, add 3 cups water and some salt, stir, heat up over medium high heat, cook for 20 minutes and take off heat. Add bulgur, stir, cover pot and leave aside for 15 minutes. Transfer mix to a large bowl and leave aside. Heat up a pan with the oil over medium high heat, add onion, stir and cook for 3-4 minutes. Add tomato paste, red pepper flakes and cumin, stir and cook for 4 minutes. Transfer this to lentils and bulgur mix, add some more salt and knead well for 10 minutes. Add parsley and scallions and stir. Shape balls out of this mix, arrange them all on a platter and serve with lemon slices on the side. Enjoy!

Nutrition: calories 167, fat 3, fiber 4, carbs 3, protein 2

Divine Okra Salad

Preparation time: 40 minutes
Cooking time: 0 minutes
Servings: 4

Ingredients:

- 1 pound okra, cut into medium pieces
- A pinch of sea salt
- Black pepper to the taste
- 15 ounces canned black beans, drained
- 1 cup corn
- 1 pound cherry tomatoes, halved
- 1 white onion, chopped
- 3 tablespoons olive oil
- 1 avocado, pitted, peeled and chopped

Directions:

Put okra in a salad bowl, add beans, corn, onion, tomatoes and avocado and stir. Add a pinch of salt, black pepper and olive oil ,toss to coat and keep in the fridge for 30 minutes before you serve it. Enjoy!

Nutrition: calories 120, fat 1, fiber 1, carbs 0, protein 7

Tuna Spread

Preparation time: 10 minutes
Cooking time: 0 minutes
Servings: 12

Ingredients:

- 6 ounces canned tuna, drained and flaked
- 3 teaspoons lemon juice
- 1 teaspoon onion salt
- 8 ounces cream cheese
- 4 drops hot pepper sauce
- ¼ cup parsley, chopped

Directions:

In a bowl, mix tuna with cream cheese, lemon juice, hot pepper sauce and onion salt and stir well. Shape a big ball, roll in chopped parsley and keep in the fridge until you serve. Enjoy!

Nutrition: calories 132, fat 2, fiber 3, carbs 2, protein 4

Mediterranean Spinach Cakes

Preparation time: 10 minutes
Cooking time: 30 minutes
Servings: 4

Ingredients:

- 12 ounces spinach
- ½ cup ricotta cheese
- 2 eggs, whisked
- ½ cup parmesan, grated
- Salt and black pepper to the taste
- 1 garlic clove, minced
- Olive oil spray

Directions:

Put spinach in your food processor, pulse well and transfer to a bowl. Add ricotta, parmesan, eggs, salt and pepper to the taste and garlic and stir very well. Spray a muffin pan with some olive oil, divide spinach into all cups, introduce in the oven at 400 degrees F and bake for 20 minutes. Take spinach cakes out of the oven, transfer them to a platter and serve as an appetizer. Enjoy!

Nutrition: calories 141, fat 4, fiber 2, carbs 6, protein 13

Mediterranean Diet Meat Recipes

Mediterranean Pork And Rice Salad

Preparation time: 3 hours and 10 minutes
Cooking time: 0 minutes
Servings: 10

Ingredients:

- 1 green cabbage head, shredded
- 1 and ½ cups rice, already cooked
- 2 cups pork roast, already cooked
- ounces peas
- ounces water chestnuts, drained and sliced
- ½ cup sour cream
- ½ cup mayonnaise
- A pinch of salt
- 1 teaspoon celery seed

Directions:

In a bowl, mix cabbage with rice, peas, pork and chestnuts and toss. In another bowl, mix sour cream with mayo, salt and celery seed and whisk. Pour this over salad, toss to coat and keep in the fridge for 3 hours before you serve it. Enjoy!

Nutrition: calories 285, fat 4, fiber 2, carbs 7, protein 15

Amazing Pork Stew

Preparation time: 10 minutes
Cooking time: 40 minutes
Servings: 6

Ingredients:

- 2 pounds pork meat, boneless and cubed
- 2 yellow onions, chopped
- 1 tablespoon canola oil
- 1 garlic clove, minced
- 3 cups chicken stock
- 2 tablespoons paprika
- 1 teaspoon caraway seeds
- Salt and black pepper to the taste
- ¼ cup water
- 2 tablespoons white flour
- 1 and ½ cups sour cream
- 2 tablespoons dill, chopped
- Boiled potatoes for serving

Directions:

Heat up a pot with the oil over medium heat, add pork and brown it for a few minutes. Add onions, stir and cook for 3 minutes. Add garlic, stir and cook 1 minute more. Add stock, caraway seeds, paprika, salt and pepper, bring to a boil, reduce temperature, cover and cook for 30 minutes. Add flour mixed with water, stir and boil 2 minutes more. Take off heat, add dill and cream, stir and return to heat. Cook stew for 2 minutes, take off heat and serve with boiled potatoes on the side. Enjoy!

Nutrition: calories 300, fat 4, fiber 4, carbs 6, protein 12

Mediterranean Grilled Pork Chops

Preparation time: 1 day
Cooking time: 20 minutes
Servings: 6

Ingredients:
- 2 pork chops
- ¼ cup olive oil
- 2 yellow onions, sliced
- 2 garlic cloves, minced
- 2 teaspoons mustard
- 1 teaspoon sweet paprika
- Salt and black pepper to the taste
- ½ teaspoon oregano, dried
- ½ teaspoon thyme, dried
- A pinch of cayenne pepper

Directions:

In a small bowl, mix oil with garlic, mustard, paprika, black pepper, oregano, thyme and cayenne and whisk well. In a bowl, combine onions with meat and mustard mix, toss to coat, cover and keep in the fridge for 1 day. Place meat on preheated grill over medium high heat, season with salt and cook for 10 minutes on each side. Meanwhile, heat up a pan over medium heat, add marinated onions, stir and sauté for 4 minutes. Divide pork chops on plates, add sautéed onions on top and serve. Enjoy!

Nutrition: calories 284, fat 4, fiber 4, carbs 7, protein 12

Simple Pork Stir Fry

Preparation time: 10 minutes
Cooking time: 15 minutes
Servings: 4

Ingredients:
- 4 ounces bacon, chopped
- 4 ounces snow peas
- 2 tablespoons butter
- 1 pound pork loin, cut into thin strips
- 2 cups mushrooms, sliced
- ¾ cup white wine
- ½ cup yellow onion, chopped
- 3 tablespoons sour cream
- Salt and white pepper to the taste

Directions:

Put snow peas in a pot, add water to cover, also add a pinch of salt, bring to a boil over medium heat, cook until they are soft, drain and leave aside. Heat up a pan over medium high heat, add bacon, cook for a few minutes, drain grease, transfer to a bowl and also leave aside. Heat up a pan with 1 tablespoon butter over medium heat, add pork strips, salt and pepper to the taste, brown for a few minutes and transfer to a plate as well. Return pan to medium heat, add the rest of the butter and melt it. Add onions and mushrooms, stir and cook for 4 minutes. Add wine, and simmer until it's reduced. Add cream, peas, pork, salt and pepper to the taste, stir, heat up, divide between plates, top with bacon and serve. Enjoy!

Nutrition: calories 310, fat 4, fiber 6, carbs 9, protein 10

The Best Mediterranean Pork Soup

Preparation time: 10 minutes
Cooking time: 1 hour
Servings: 6

Ingredients:
- 1 small yellow onion, chopped
- 1 tablespoon olive oil
- 1 and ½ teaspoons basil, chopped
- 1 and ½ teaspoons ginger, grated
- 3 garlic cloves, chopped
- Salt and black pepper to the taste
- ½ teaspoon cumin, ground
- 1 carrot, chopped
- 1 pound pork chops, bone-in
- 3 ounces brown lentils, rinsed
- 3 cups chicken stock
- 2 tablespoons tomato paste
- 2 tablespoons lime juice
- 1 teaspoon red chili flakes, crushed

Directions:

Heat up a pot with the oil over medium heat, add garlic, onion, basil, ginger, salt, pepper and cumin, stir well and cook for 6 minutes. Add carrots, stir and cook 5 more minutes. Add pork and brown for a few minutes. Add lentils, tomato paste and stock, stir, bring to a boil, cover pot and simmer for 50 minutes. Transfer pork to a plate, discard bones, shred it and return to pot. Add chili flakes and lime juice, stir, ladle into bowls and serve. Enjoy!

Nutrition: calories 263, fat 4, fiber 6, carbs 8, protein 10

Simple Braised Pork

Preparation time: 40 minutes
Cooking time: 1 hour
Servings: 4

Ingredients:
- 2 pounds pork loin roast, boneless and cubed
- 5 tablespoons butter
- Salt and black pepper to the taste
- 2 cups chicken stock
- ½ cup dry white wine
- 2 garlic cloves, minced
- 1 teaspoon thyme, chopped
- 1 thyme spring
- 1 bay leaf
- ½ yellow onion, chopped
- 2 tablespoons white flour
- ¾ pound pearl onions
- ½ pound red grapes

Directions:

Heat up a pan with 2 tablespoons butter over high heat, add pork loin, some salt and pepper, stir, brown for 10 minutes and transfer to a plate. Add wine to the pan, bring to a boil over high heat and cook for 3 minutes. Add stock, garlic, thyme spring, bay leaf, yellow onion and return meat to the pan, bring to a boil, cover, reduce heat to low, cook for 1 hour, strain liquid into another pot and transfer pork to a plate. Put pearl onions in a small pot, add water to cover, bring to a boil over medium high heat, boil them for 5 minutes, drain, peel them and leave aside for now. In a bowl, mix 2 tablespoons butter with flour and stir very well. Add ½ cup of strained cooking liquid and whisk well. Pour this into cooking liquid, bring to a simmer over medium heat and cook for 5 minutes. Add salt and pepper, chopped thyme, pork and pearl onions, cover and simmer for a few minutes. Meanwhile, heat up a pan with 1 tablespoon butter, add grapes, stir and cook them for 1-2 minutes. Divide pork meat on plates, drizzle the sauce all over and serve with onions and grapes on the side. Enjoy!

Nutrition: calories 320, fat 4, fiber 5, carbs 9, protein 18

Delicious Pork Stew

Preparation time: 20 minutes
Cooking time: 8 hours
Servings: 4

Ingredients:

- 2 tablespoons white flour
- ½ cup chicken stock
- 1 tablespoon ginger, grated
- 1 teaspoon coriander, ground
- 2 teaspoons cumin, ground
- Salt and black pepper to the taste
- 2 and ½ pounds pork butt, cubed
- 28 ounces canned tomatoes, drained and chopped
- 4 ounces carrots, chopped
- 1 red onion cut in wedges
- 4 garlic cloves, minced
- ½ cup apricots, cut in quarters
- 1 cup couscous, cooked
- 15 ounces canned chickpeas, drained
- Cilantro, chopped for serving

Directions:

Put stock in your slow cooker. Add flour, cumin, ginger, coriander, salt and pepper and stir. Add tomatoes, pork, carrots, garlic, onion and apricots, cover pot and cook on Low for 7 hours and 50 minutes. Add chickpeas and couscous, cover and cook for 10 more minutes. Divide on plates, sprinkle cilantro and serve right away. Enjoy!

Nutrition: calories 216, fat 6, fiber 8, carbs 10, protein 20

Wonderful Pork Salad

Preparation time: 10 minutes
Cooking time: 10 minutes
Servings: 4

Ingredients:

- 1 red chili, chopped
- 2 tablespoons rice vinegar
- 1/3 cup soy sauce
- 1 tablespoon lime juice
- 1 teaspoon olive oil
- 4 ounces mixed salad greens
- 1 tablespoon pickled ginger
- 4 ounces snow peas, blanched
- 1 red bell pepper, sliced
- 4 ounces pork, cooked and cut into thin strips

Directions:

In a salad bowl, mix greens with peas, bell pepper, pork and ginger. In a small bowl, mix vinegar with soy sauce, chili, oil and lime juice and whisk. Add this to your salad, toss to coat and serve. Enjoy!

Nutrition: calories 235, fat 4, fiber 4, carbs 8, protein 10

Special Ground Pork Dish

Preparation time: 10 minutes
Cooking time: 7 minutes
Servings: 4

Ingredients:

- 12 ounces pasta, already cooked
- Salt and black pepper to the taste
- 1 and ½ tablespoon olive oil
- 5 scallions, chopped
- 2 tablespoons ginger, grated
- 2 garlic cloves, minced
- 1 pound pork, ground
- 3 tablespoons soy sauce
- 1 tablespoon chili paste
- 2 tablespoons balsamic vinegar
- 1 tablespoon sugar
- 2/3 cup chicken stock
- ½ cup peanut butter
- 1 lime, cut into wedges
- ¼ cup cilantro, chopped

Directions:

Heat up a pan with the oil over medium high heat, add scallions, stir and cook for 1-2 minutes. Add garlic and ginger, stir and cook for 1 more minute. Add pork, stir and cook for 5 minutes. Add chili paste, vinegar, soy sauce and sugar, stir and cook for 1-2 minutes. Add peanut butter, stock, salt and pepper, stir, bring to a simmer and cook for 2 minutes. Add pasta, toss to coat, divide between plates, sprinkle cilantro on top and serve with lime wedges on the side. Enjoy!

Nutrition: calories 220, fat 3, fiber 4, carbs 7, protein 12

Slow Cooked Mediterranean Pork

Preparation time: 20 hours and 10 minutes
Cooking time: 8 hours
Servings: 6

Ingredients:

- 3 pounds pork shoulder boneless
- ¼ cup olive oil
- 2 teaspoons oregano, dried
- ¼ cup lemon juice
- 2 teaspoons mustard
- 2 teaspoons mint, chopped
- 3 garlic cloves, minced
- 2 teaspoons pesto sauce
- Salt and black pepper to the taste

Directions:

In a bowl, mix olive oil with lemon juice, oregano, mint, mustard, garlic, pesto, salt and pepper and whisk very well. Rub pork with the marinade, cover and keep in a cold place for 10 hours. Flip pork shoulder and leave aside for 10 more hours. Transfer to your slow cooker along with the marinade juices, cover and cook on low for 8 hours. Uncover, slice, divide between plates and serve! Enjoy!

Nutrition: calories 300, fat 4, fiber 6, carbs 7, protein 12

Orange Scented Roast

Preparation time: 10 minutes
Cooking time: 4 hours
Servings: 8

Ingredients:

- 1 pound small potatoes, chopped
- 2 medium carrots, chopped
- 15 ounces stewed tomatoes, drained
- 1 yellow onion, chopped
- Zest and juice from 1 orange
- 4 garlic cloves, minced
- 3 and ½ pounds pork roast, trimmed
- 3 bay leaves
- Salt and black pepper to the taste
- ½ cup kalamata olives, pitted

Directions:

Put potatoes in your slow cooker. Add carrots, tomatoes, onions, orange juice and zest. Also add bay leaves, garlic and pork. Season with salt and pepper, cover and cook on High for 4 hours. Transfer meat to a cutting board, slice it and divide among plates. Discard bay leaves, add veggies to a bowl, crush them a bit with a fork and mix with olives. Divide this next to pork and serve. Enjoy!

Nutrition: calories 240, fat 4, fiber 7, carbs 9, protein 12

Incredible Pork Stew

Preparation time: 20 minutes
Cooking time: 4 hours
Servings: 4

Ingredients:

- 2 pounds pork neck
- 1 tablespoon white flour
- 1 and ½ tablespoons olive oil
- 2 eggplants, chopped
- 1 brown onion, chopped
- 1 red bell pepper, chopped
- 3 garlic cloves, minced
- 1 tablespoon thyme, dried
- 2 teaspoons sage, dried
- 4 ounces canned white beans, drained
- 1 cup chicken stock
- 12 ounces zucchinis, chopped
- 2 tablespoons tomato paste

Directions:

In a bowl, mix flour with salt, pepper and pork neck and toss. Heat up a pan with 2 teaspoons oil over medium high heat, add pork and cook for 3 minutes on each side. Transfer pork to a slow cooker and leave aside. Heat up the rest of the oil in the same pan over medium heat, add eggplant, onion, bell pepper, thyme, sage and garlic, stir and cook for 5 minutes. Add reserved flour, stir and cook for 1 more minute. Add to pork, also add beans, stock, tomato paste and zucchinis. Cover and cook on High for 4 hours. Uncover, transfer to plates and serve. Enjoy!

Nutrition: calories 310, fat 3, fiber 5, carbs 8, protein 12

Pork With Couscous

Preparation time: 10 minutes
Cooking time: 7 hours
Servings: 6

Ingredients:
- 2 and ½ pounds pork loin boneless and trimmed
- ¾ cup chicken stock
- 2 tablespoons olive oil
- ½ tablespoon sweet paprika
- 2 and ¼ teaspoon sage, dried
- ½ tablespoon garlic powder
- ¼ teaspoon rosemary, dried
- ¼ teaspoon marjoram, dried
- 1 teaspoon basil, dried
- 1 teaspoon oregano, dried
- Salt and black pepper to the taste
- 2 cups couscous, cooked

Directions:

In a bowl, mix oil with stock, paprika, garlic powder, sage, rosemary, thyme, marjoram, oregano, salt and pepper to the taste and whisk well. Put pork loin in your crock pot, add stock and spice mix, stir, cover and cook on Low for 7 hours. Slice pork, return to pot and toss with cooking juices. Divide between plates and serve with couscous on the side. Enjoy!

Nutrition: calories 310, fat 4, fiber 6, carbs 7, protein 14

Easy Roasted Pork Shoulder

Preparation time: 30 minutes
Cooking time: 4 hours
Servings: 6

Ingredients:
- 3 tablespoons garlic, minced
- 3 tablespoons olive oil
- 4 pounds pork shoulder
- Salt and black pepper to the taste

Directions:

In a bowl, mix olive oil with salt, pepper and oil and whisk well. Brush pork shoulder with this mix, arrange in a baking dish and introduce in the oven at 425 degrees for 20 minutes. Reduce heat to 325 degrees F and bake for 4 hours. Take pork shoulder out of the oven, slice and arrange on a platter. Serve with your favorite Mediterranean side salad. Enjoy!

Nutrition: calories 221, fat 4, fiber 4, carbs 7, protein 10

Crazy Pork Roast

Preparation time: 20 minutes
Cooking time: 2 hours
Servings: 10

Ingredients:

- 5 and ½ pounds pork loin roast, trimmed, chine bone removed
- Salt and black pepper to the taste
- 3 garlic cloves, minced
- 2 tablespoons rosemary, chopped
- 1 teaspoon fennel, ground
- 1 tablespoon fennel seeds
- 2 teaspoons red pepper, crushed
- ¼ cup olive oil

Directions:

In your food processor mix garlic with fennel seeds, fennel, rosemary, red pepper, some black pepper and the olive oil and blend until you obtain a paste. Place pork roast in a roasting pan, spread 2 tablespoons garlic paste all over and rub well. Season with salt and pepper, introduce in the oven at 400 degrees F and bake for 1 hour. Reduce heat to 325 degrees F and bake for another 35 minutes. Carve roast into chops, divide between plates and serve right away! Enjoy!

Nutrition: calories 300, fat 4, fiber 2, carbs 6, protein 15

Braised Beef Brisket

Preparation time: 10 minutes
Cooking time: 7 hours and 15 minutes
Servings: 6

Ingredients:

- 1 pound sweet onion, chopped
- 4 pounds beef brisket
- 1 pound carrot, chopped
- 8 earl gray tea bags

For the sauce:

- 16 ounces canned tomatoes, chopped
- ½ pound celery, chopped
- 1 ounce garlic, minced
- 4 ounces vegetable oil
- ½ pound celery, chopped
- Salt and black pepper to the taste
- 4 cups water

- 1 pound sweet onion, chopped
- 1 cup brown sugar
- 8 earl gray tea bags
- 1 cup white vinegar

Directions:

Put the water in a pot, add 1 pound onion, 1 pound carrot, ½ pound celery, salt and pepper, stir and bring to a simmer over medium high heat. Add beef brisket and 8 tea bags, stir, cover, reduce heat to medium low and cook for 7 hours. Meanwhile, heat up a pan with the vegetable oil over medium high heat, add 1 pound onion, stir and sauté for 10 minutes. Add garlic, ½ pound celery, tomatoes, sugar, vinegar, salt, pepper and 8 tea bags, stir, bring to a simmer and cook until veggies are tender enough. Transfer beef brisket to a cutting board, leave aside to cool down, slice and divide between plates. Discard tea bags from the sauce, drizzle it over meat and serve. Enjoy!

Nutrition: calories 400, fat 12, fiber 4, carbs 8, protein 14

Mediterranean Beef Dish

Preparation time: 10 minutes
Cooking time: 15 minutes
Servings: 6

Ingredients:

- 1 pound beef meat, ground
- 2 cups zucchinis, chopped
- ½ cup yellow onion, chopped
- Salt and black pepper to the taste
- 15 ounces canned roasted tomatoes and garlic
- 1 cup water
- ¾ cup cheddar cheese, shredded
- 1 and ½ cups white rice

Directions:

Heat up a pan over medium high heat, add beef, onion, salt, pepper and zucchini, stir and cook for 7 minutes. Add water, tomatoes and garlic, stir and bring to a boil. Add rice, more salt and pepper, stir, cover, take off heat and leave aside for 7 minutes. Divide between plates and serve with cheddar cheese on top. Enjoy!

Elegant Beef Tartar

Preparation time: 10 minutes
Cooking time: 0 minutes
Servings: 1

Ingredients:

- 1 shallot, chopped
- 4 ounces beef fillet, minced
- 5 small cucumbers, chopped
- 1 egg yolk
- A pinch of salt and black pepper
- 2 teaspoons mustard
- 1 tablespoon parsley, chopped
- 1 parsley spring, roughly chopped for serving

Directions:

In a bowl, mix meat with shallot, egg yolk, salt, pepper, mustard, cucumbers and parsley. Stir very well and arrange on a platter. Garnish with the chopped parsley spring and serve. Enjoy!

Nutrition: calories 210, fat 3, fiber 1, carbs 5, protein 8

Beef And Special Mediterranean Sauce

Preparation time: 15 minutes
Cooking time: 1 hour and 15 minutes
Servings: 4

Ingredients:

- 2 pounds round roast
- 2 carrots, chopped
- 1 leek, chopped
- 1 bay leaf
- 1 turnip, chopped
- 1 celery stalk, chopped
- 1 teaspoon black peppercorns
- 2 yellow onions, cut in quarters
- ounces mixed chives, parsley, cress and chervil, chopped
- 2 cups yogurt
- 3 tablespoons mayonnaise
- 1 cup sour cream
- 1 teaspoon mustard
- Salt and black pepper to the taste
- 2 eggs, hard boiled, peeled and chopped

Directions:

Put beef in a pot, add bay leaf, peppercorns, leek, carrots, celery, turnip, onions and water to cover them, bring to a boil over medium heat and cook for 1 hour. In a bowl, mix yogurt with sour cream, mayo, mustard, salt, pepper and chopped herbs and whisk well. Add this to the pot with the beef mix and stir. Also add eggs, stir, cook 1 minute, take off heat and leave aside for 15 minutes before serving the roast sliced and with veggies and sauce on top. Enjoy!

Nutrition: calories 263, fat 4, fiber 2, carbs 5, protein 9

Mediterranean Beef Surprise

Preparation time: 10 minutes
Cooking time: 20 minutes
Servings: 4

Ingredients:

- 12 ounces spaghetti
- Zest and juice from 1 lemon
- 2 garlic cloves, minced
- 2 tablespoons olive oil
- 1 pound beef meat, ground
- Salt and black pepper to the taste
- 1-pint cherry tomatoes, chopped
- 1 small red onion, chopped
- ½ cup white wine
- 2 tablespoons tomato paste
- Some basil leaves, chopped for serving
- Some parmesan, grated for serving

Directions:

Put water in a pot, add a pinch of salt, bring to a boil over medium high heat, add spaghetti, cook according to instructions, drain and return pasta to pot. Add lemon zest and juice and 1 tablespoon oil to pasta, toss to coat, heat up over medium heat for a couple of seconds, divide between plates and keep warm. Meanwhile, heat up a pan with the rest of the oil over medium heat, add garlic, stir and cook for 1 minute. Add beef, salt and pepper and brown it for 4 minutes. Add tomato paste and wine, stir and cook for 3 minutes. Divide beef on plates, add tomatoes, red onion, basil and parmesan and serve. Enjoy!

Nutrition: calories 284, fat 2, fiber 1, carbs 5, protein 15

Delightful Beef Salad

Preparation time: 10 minutes
Cooking time: 15 minutes
Servings: 4

Ingredients:

- 1 pound beef sirloin
- 1 red onion, sliced
- 1 big cucumber, sliced
- 1 red chili, sliced
- A handful coriander leaves, chopped

For the salad dressing:

- Juice from 3 lemons
- 1 tablespoon brown sugar

- A handful mint leaves, chopped
- 2 ounces peanuts, chopped
- A drizzle of olive oil
- Salt and black pepper to the taste

- 1 tablespoon fish sauce
- 1 garlic clove, minced

Directions:

Rub beef with some olive oil, season with salt and pepper to the taste, place on preheated grill over medium high heat and cook for 3 minutes on each side. Slice beef, put in a salad bowl and mix with cucumber, chili, onion, mint and coriander. In a small bowl, mix lemon juice with fish sauce, sugar and garlic and whisk very well. Pour this over beef salad, toss to coat, sprinkle peanuts on top and serve right away. Enjoy!

Nutrition: calories 231, fat 3, fiber 4, carbs 6, protein 9

Mediterranean Ground Beef Soup

Preparation time: 10 minutes
Cooking time: 30 minutes
Servings: 8

Ingredients:

- 1 yellow onion, chopped
- 1 tablespoon olive oil
- 1 garlic clove, minced
- 1 pound beef, ground
- 1 pound eggplant, chopped
- ¾ cup celery, chopped
- ¾ cup carrots, chopped
- Salt and black pepper to the taste

- 29 ounces canned tomatoes, drained and chopped
- 28 ounces beef stock
- ½ teaspoon nutmeg, ground
- 1 teaspoon sugar
- ½ cup macaroni
- 2 teaspoons parsley, chopped
- ½ cup parmesan cheese, grated

Directions:

Heat up a pot with the oil over medium heat, add onion, garlic and meat, stir and brown for a few minutes. Add celery, carrots, eggplant and tomatoes and stir. Add stock, salt, pepper to the taste, sugar and nutmeg, stir and cook for 20 minutes. Add macaroni, stir and cook for 12 more minutes. Ladle into soup bowls, top with grated cheese and serve. Enjoy!

Nutrition: calories 241, fat 3, fiber 5, carbs 7, protein 10

Beef And Lentils Soup

Preparation time: 10 minutes
Cooking time: 1 hour and 40 minutes
Servings: 8

Ingredients:
- 1 pound beef chuck, cubed
- 2 tablespoons olive oil
- 2 celery stalks, chopped
- 2 carrots, chopped
- 1 yellow onion, chopped
- Salt and black pepper to the taste
- 3 garlic cloves, chopped
- 2 cups lentils
- 32 ounces canned chicken stock
- 1 and ½ teaspoons cilantro, dried
- 1 teaspoon oregano, dried
- 28 ounces canned tomatoes, chopped
- ¼ cup parsley, chopped
- ½ cup parmesan, grated

Directions:

Heat up a pot with the oil over medium high heat, add beef, salt and pepper to the taste, stir, brown for 8 minutes, transfer to a plate and keep warm. Return pot to medium heat, add carrots, celery, garlic, onion, oregano and cilantro, stir and cook for 8 more minutes. Return beef to pot and also add stock and tomatoes, stir, bring to a boil, cover pot and cook for 1 hour. Add lentils, stir and simmer for 40 more minutes. Add salt, pepper to the taste and parsley, stir, ladle into bowls, sprinkle parmesan on top and serve. Enjoy!

Nutrition: calories 210, fat 4, fiber 6, carbs 8, protein 10

Special Beef Dish

Preparation time: 15 minutes
Cooking time: 2 hours and 45 minutes
Servings: 6

Ingredients:
- 4 tablespoons olive oil
- 3 pounds beef meat, cubed
- 6 ounces smoked bacon, chopped
- 1 pound carrots, cut into chunks
- 3 garlic cloves, chopped
- 2 yellow onions, chopped
- 3 cups beef stock
- 2 cups dry red wine
- 2 tablespoons tomato paste
- 4 tablespoons butter
- 1 teaspoon thyme, chopped
- 1 pound pearl onions
- 3 tablespoons white flour
- 3 bay leaves
- 1 pound button mushrooms, sliced
- Salt and black pepper to the taste
- Some chopped parsley for serving

Directions:

Heat up a Dutch oven with 2 tablespoons oil over medium heat, add bacon, stir, brown for 3 minutes and transfer to a plate. Return Dutch oven to medium heat, add beef, salt and pepper, stir, brown meat for 4 minutes, transfer to the same plate as the bacon and leave aside. Add 2 tablespoons oil to the pot, heat up over medium high heat, add garlic, onions, carrots, salt and pepper to the taste, stir and cook for 5 minutes. Return beef and bacon to pot, add wine, tomato paste and bay leaves, stir, bring to a boil, cover pot, introduce in the oven at 350 degrees and cook the stew for 2 hours. In a bowl, mix 2 tablespoons butter with the flour, stir well and leave aside. Heat up a pan with 2 tablespoons butter over medium heat, add mushrooms, stir and cook them for 3 minutes. Take stew out of the oven, add flour and butter mix, mushrooms and pearl onions, heat up over medium heat, reduce to a simmer, cover and cook for 30 minutes. Discard bay leaves, transfer to bowls and serve with chopped parsley on top. Enjoy!

Nutrition: calories 253, fat 4, fiber 2, carbs 6, protein 12

Unique Beef Salad

Preparation time: 10 minutes
Cooking time: 10 minutes
Servings: 4

Ingredients:

- 1 tablespoon soy sauce
- 1 pound beef steak
- 8 ounces noodles
- 1 cucumber, sliced
- ½ cup sweet chili sauce
- 1 cup carrot, chopped
- ½ cup water
- Some chopped cilantro for serving

Directions:

Mix steak with soy sauce, introduce in preheated broiler and broil for 15 minutes. Slice steak and transfer to a bowl. Cook noodles according to package instructions, drain, rinse with cold water and add to steak pieces. Add cucumber, carrots and cilantro and toss. In a bowl, mix chili with water and whisk very well. Add this to salad, toss again and serve. Enjoy!

Nutrition: calories 277, fat 4, fiber 3, carbs 8, protein 17

Tasty And Special Beef Stew

Preparation time: 20 minutes
Cooking time: 7 hours
Servings: 4

Ingredients:

- 2 pounds beef, cubed
- Salt and black pepper to the taste
- 2 cups beef stock
- 2 tablespoons olive oil
- 2 bay leaves
- ¼ cup white flour
- 1 yellow onion, chopped
- 2 tablespoons thyme, chopped
- 4 garlic cloves, minced
- 16 ounces mushrooms, chopped
- 3 carrots, chopped
- 3 celery stalks, chopped
- 28 ounces canned tomatoes, crushed
- ½ cup parsley, chopped
- ½ pound orzo

Directions:

In a bowl, mix beef with salt, pepper and flour. Heat up a pan with the oil over medium high heat, add meat, brown it for a few minutes and transfer to slow cooker. Heat up the same pan over medium high heat, add beef stock, bring to a simmer and pour over meat. Add thyme, garlic, bay leaves, carrots, onion, mushrooms, celery and tomatoes to your slow cooker as well. Add salt and pepper to the taste, cover and cook on Low for 7 hours. When the stew is almost done, put water in a pot, add salt, bring to a boil and add orzo. Cook according to instructions, take off heat and leave aside. Divide beef stew on plates, discard bay leaves, arrange orzo on the side and sprinkle parsley all over. Serve right away. Enjoy!

Nutrition: calories 240, fat 5, fiber 3, carbs 7, protein 11

Simple Beef Salad

Preparation time: 10 minutes
Cooking time: 5 minutes
Servings: 4

Ingredients:

- 2 apples, cored, peeled and sliced
- 3 red beetroot, peeled and sliced
- Juice of 1 lemon
- 2 sirloin steaks
- 1 tablespoon olive oil
- 1 small bunch dill, chopped
- 3 ounces low fat buttermilk
- 2 tablespoon olive oil
- Salt and pepper to the taste

Directions:

In a salad bowl, mix beetroot with apple pieces and some of the lemon juice, toss to coat and leave aside for now. Heat up your kitchen grill over medium high heat, season steaks with salt, pepper, rub them with some olive oil, place on grill and cook them for 2 minutes on each side. Slice steak and put in a bowl. Meanwhile, in another bowl, mix dill with buttermilk, lemon juice and the extra virgin olive oil and whisk. Mix beetroot and apple slices with beef, toss, divide between plates, drizzle the dill dressing you've just made and serve right away! Enjoy!

Nutrition: calories 210, fat 3, fiber 3, carbs 5, protein 8

New And Original Beef Steak

Preparation time: 10 minutes
Cooking time: 35 minutes
Servings: 4

Ingredients:

- 4 medium sirloin steaks
- Salt and black pepper to the taste
- 1 tablespoon olive oil
- 1 tablespoon butter
- 8 cherry tomatoes, halved
- A small handful tarragon, chopped

Directions:

Heat up a pan with the oil and the butter over medium high heat, add steaks, season with salt and pepper and cook them for 1 minute on each side. Transfer steaks to heated grill at 400 degrees F and cook them for 4 more minutes. Divide steaks on plates, sprinkle tarragon on them and serve right away cherry tomatoes on the side. Enjoy!

Nutrition: calories 213, fat 4, fiber 2, carbs 6, protein 9

Mediterranean Beef Meatballs

Preparation time: 10 minutes
Cooking time: 20 minutes
Servings: 4

Ingredients:
For the meatballs:

- 1 pound beef, ground
- 1/3 cup cilantro, chopped
- 1 cup red onion, chopped
- 4 garlic cloves, minced
- 1 tablespoon ginger, grated
- ½ tablespoon honey
- 1 and ½ tablespoon fish sauce
- 1 Thai chili, chopped
- 2 tablespoons olive oil

Directions:

Put meat in your food processor, add onion, garlic, cilantro, ginger, fish sauce, honey and chili and pulse a few times until everything is mixed. Heat up a pan with the oil over medium high heat, shape meatballs, add them to the pan, cover and cook for 5 minutes. Flip them, cover and cook for 5 more minutes, drain using paper towels and arrange them on a platter. Serve them with a side salad. Enjoy!

Nutrition: calories 200, fat 4, fiber 2, carbs 5, protein 9

Vibrant Beef Dish

Preparation time: 10 minutes
Cooking time: 20 minutes
Servings: 4

Ingredients:

- 2 tablespoons lime juice
- 2 tablespoons soy sauce
- 1 tablespoon fish sauce
- 1 and ½ tablespoons brown sugar
- 5 garlic cloves, minced
- 3 tablespoons olive oil
- Salt and black pepper to the taste
- 1 yellow onion, cut into wedges
- 1 and ½ pound beef tenderloin, cubed
- 3 tablespoons peanuts, toasted and chopped
- 2 scallions, chopped

Directions:

In a bowl, mix lime juice with soy sauce, sugar and fish sauce and stir very well. In another bowl, mix garlic with 1 and ½ teaspoon oil and some black pepper and also stir well. Heat up a pan with 3 teaspoons oil over medium high heat, add meat, cook for 3 minutes on each side and transfer to a bowl. Heat up the same pan with the rest of the oil over medium high heat, add onion, stir and cook for 3 minutes. Add the garlic mix, stir and cook for 1 more minute. Return beef and its juices to the pan, stir, add soy mix, stir again and cook for 3 minutes. Divide beef among plates and serve with peanuts and scallions on top. Enjoy!

Nutrition: calories 273, fat 4, fiber 5, carbs 7, protein 12

Garlic Beef

Preparation time: 40 minutes
Cooking time: 15 minutes
Servings: 4

Ingredients:

- 11 ounces steak fillets, sliced
- 4 garlic cloves, minced
- 2 tablespoons olive oil
- 1 red bell pepper, cut into strips
- Black pepper to the taste
- 1 tablespoon sugar
- 2 tablespoons fish sauce
- 2 teaspoons corn flour
- ½ cup beef stock
- 4 green onions, sliced

Directions:

In a bowl, mix beef with oil, garlic, black pepper and bell pepper, stir, cover and keep in the fridge for 30 minutes. Heat up a pan over medium high heat, add beef and its mixture, stir and cook for 1-2 minutes. In a bowl, mix sugar with fish sauce, stir well and pour over beef. Cook for 3 minutes, add stock mixed with corn flour and stir again. Add green onions, cook for 1-2 minutes, take off heat, transfer to plates and serve right away! Enjoy!

Nutrition: calories 243, fat 3, fiber 3, carbs 6, protein 9

Special Beef

Preparation time: 15 minutes
Cooking time: 15 minutes
Servings: 4

Ingredients:

- 1 cup green onion, chopped
- 1 cup soy sauce
- ½ cup water
- ¼ cup brown sugar
- ¼ cup sesame seeds
- 5 garlic cloves, minced
- 1 teaspoon black pepper
- 1 pound lean beef
- Brown rice, cooked for serving

Directions:

In a bowl, mix onion with soy sauce, water, sugar, garlic, sesame seeds and pepper and stir well. Place meat in a bowl, add marinade, toss, cover and leave aside for 10 minutes. Drain meat, place on preheated grill over medium heat and cook for 15 minutes flipping once. Slice, divide between plates and serve with brown rice on the side. Enjoy!

Nutritional value: calories 439, protein 30

Beef And Mushroom Soup

Preparation time: 20 minutes
Cooking time: 8 hours
Servings: 8

Ingredients:

- 2 tablespoons olive oil
- 2/3 cup barley soaked overnight, drained and rinsed
- 1 pound beef, cubed
- 2 yellow onions, chopped
- 4 ounces shitake mushrooms, quartered
- 5 ounces Portobello mushrooms, quartered
- 4 garlic cloves, minced
- 3 carrots, chopped
- 2 bay leaves
- 4 celery stalks, chopped
- 6 tablespoons dill, chopped
- 2 tablespoons tomato paste
- 90 ounces beef broth
- A pinch of salt and black pepper

Directions:

Heat up a pan with the oil over medium high heat, add beef and cook for 6 minutes. Transfer beef to slow cooker as well and leave aside. Heat up the same pan over medium heat, add onions, stir and cook for 10 minutes. Add mushrooms, stir and cook for 5 more minutes. Add garlic, cook for 5 minutes and transfer everything to the slow cooker. Add carrots, bay leaves, dill, celery, tomato paste, barley, salt, pepper and stock to your slow cooker, stir, cover and cook on Low for 8 hours. Discard bay leaves, ladle soup into bowls and serve. Enjoy!

Nutrition: calories 293, fat 4, fiber 2, carbs 7, protein 10

Mediterranean Beef And Cabbage Soup

Preparation time: 10 minutes
Cooking time: 9 hours
Servings: 12

Ingredients:

For the stock:

- 4 pounds beef shank, bone-in
- 3 carrots, cut into thirds
- 2 cups water
- 3 yellow onions
- 1 bay leaf
- 4 celery stalks
- 16 peppercorns

For the soup:

- 2 tablespoons olive oil
- 1 yellow onion, chopped
- 2 garlic cloves, minced
- 1 tablespoon sweet paprika
- 1 head cabbage, shredded
- 6 ounces canned diced tomatoes, juice reserved
- Juice of 1 lemon
- Salt and black pepper to the taste
- ¼ cup white sugar
- ¼ cup dill, chopped

Directions:

Put beef shanks and water in a pot and mix with carrot, onions, celery, bay leaf and peppercorns. Bring to a boil over medium heat, stir and simmer for 4 hours. Discard veggies, strain stock and leave aside to cool down. Heat up a pan with the oil over medium heat, add garlic and 1 chopped onion, stir and cook for a few minutes. Transfer this to your slow cooker, add cabbage, canned tomatoes and juice, paprika, salt and pepper. Add beef stock you've prepared, cover pot and cook on LOW for 5 hours. Uncover pot, add lemon juice, sugar and dill, stir well, ladle into bowls and serve. Enjoy!

Nutrition: calories 239, fat 6, fiber 8, carbs 9, protein 12

Special Lamb And Rice

Preparation time: 1 hour
Cooking time: 1 hour and 30 minutes
Servings: 6

Ingredients:

- 2 ounces raisins
- 4 ounces prunes, pitted
- 1 tablespoon lemon juice
- 1 yellow onion, chopped
- 1 pound lamb, boneless and cubed
- 1 ounce butter
- 3 ounces lamb meat, ground

- 2 garlic cloves, minced
- Salt and black pepper to the taste
- 2 and ½ cups veggie stock
- 2 cups white rice
- A handful parsley, chopped
- A pinch of saffron

Directions:

In a bowl, mix raisins with prunes and lemon juice, add water to cover, leave everything aside for 1 hour, drain and chop prunes. Heat up a pan with the butter over medium high heat, add onion, stir and cook for 5 minutes. Add cubed lamb, ground lamb, garlic, some salt and pepper, stir and cook for 5 minutes. Add half of the stock, bring to a boil, cover pan and cook for 1 hour. Add rice, the rest of the stock and the saffron, stir and cook for 15 minutes more. Add prunes, raisins, more salt and pepper, stir, divide between plates and serve with parsley sprinkled on top. Enjoy!

Nutrition: calories 210, fat 3, fiber 6, carbs 8, protein 10

Special Lamb

Preparation time: 10 minutes
Cooking time: 10 minutes
Servings: 3

Ingredients:

- 1 carrot, chopped
- 1 onion, sliced
- ½ tablespoon olive oil

For the marinade:

- 1 garlic clove, minced
- ½ apple, grated
- 1 small yellow onion, grated
- 1 tablespoon ginger, grated

- 3 ounces bean sprouts
- 8 ounces lamb loin, sliced

- 5 tablespoons soy sauce
- 1 tablespoons sugar
- 2 tablespoons orange juice
- A pinch of black pepper

Directions:

In a bowl, mix 1 grated onion with the apple, garlic, 1 tablespoon ginger, soy sauce, orange juice, sugar and black pepper and stir well. Add lamb pieces, toss to coat and leave aside for 15 minutes. Heat up a pan with the olive oil over medium high heat, add 1 sliced onion, carrot and bean sprouts, stir and cook for 3 minutes. Add lamb, cook for 5 minutes and pour the marinade over them. Cook for a few more minutes, ladle into bowls and serve. Enjoy!

Nutrition: calories 265, fat 3, fiber 7, carbs 8, protein 12

Delicious And Wonderful Lamb

Preparation time: 1 day
Cooking time: 2 hours and 15 minutes
Servings: 8

Ingredients:
- 5 pounds leg of lamb
- 2 cups low fat buttermilk
- 2 tablespoons mustard
- ½ cup butter
- 2 tablespoons basil and rosemary, chopped
- 2 tablespoons tomato paste
- 2 garlic cloves, minced
- Salt and black pepper to the taste
- 1 cup white wine
- 1 tablespoon cornstarch mixed with 1 tablespoon water
- ½ cup sour cream

Directions:

Put lamb roast in a big dish, add buttermilk, toss to coat, cover and keep in the fridge for 24 hours. Pat dry lamb and put in a baking dish. In a bowl, mix butter with tomato paste, mustard, basil, rosemary, salt, pepper and garlic and whisk well. Spread this over lamb, introduce in the oven at 160 degrees F and bake for 2 hours. Transfer cooking juices to a pan and heat up over medium heat. Add wine, cornstarch, salt, pepper and sour cream, whisk well and take off heat. Slice lamb, divide between plates, top with gravy and serve. Enjoy!

Nutrition: calories 287, fat 4, fiber 7, carbs 9, protein 12

Special Lamb Dish

Preparation time: 10 minutes
Cooking time: 1 hour and 30 minutes
Servings: 4

Ingredients:
- 1 red bell pepper, sliced
- 4 medium potatoes, chopped
- 1 green bell pepper, sliced
- 1 eggplant, chopped
- 2 tablespoons olive oil
- 1/3 cup mint jelly
- 1 garlic head, cut in half
- 1 and ½ tablespoon lemon juice
- 4 lamb chops
- 1 tablespoon thyme, chopped
- Salt flakes to the taste

Directions:

Put potatoes in a pan, add red, green bell pepper and eggplant and toss. Add 1 and ½ tablespoons olive oil and garlic, toss to coat, introduce in the oven at 400 degrees F and bake for 45 minutes. In a bowl, mix lemon juice with mint jelly and thyme and whisk well. Heat up a pan with the rest of the oil over medium high heat, add lamb chops, cook for 2 minutes on each side and brush them on both sides with half of the jelly mix. Take veggies out of the oven, put lamb chops on top, add salt to the taste, introduce in the oven again and cook for 15 minutes. Brush them with the rest of the jelly mix and bake for 10 minutes more. Transfer lamb and veggies to plates and serve. Enjoy!

Nutrition: calories 310, fat 4, fiber 6, carbs 7, protein 10

Lamb Soup

Preparation time: 20 minutes
Cooking time: 1 hour and 10 minutes
Servings: 8

Ingredients:

- 3 pounds lamb
- 2 tablespoons olive oil
- 1 teaspoon garlic, minced
- 1 yellow onion, chopped
- 1/3 cup brown rice
- ½ teaspoon thyme, dried
- 3 cups water
- ½ teaspoon oregano, dried
- 3 carrots, chopped
- ½ cabbage head, chopped
- 1 cup cauliflower florets
- 4 potatoes, chopped
- Salt and pepper to the taste

Directions:

Heat up a pot with the oil over medium high heat, add garlic, stir and sauté for 2 minutes. Add lamb and brown for a few minutes more. Add onion, rice and the water, stir, bring to a boil, reduce heat to medium and boil everything for 5 minutes. Add oregano and thyme, stir, cover pot and simmer for 40 minutes. Add carrots, cauliflower, cabbage and potatoes, cover pot and cook for 20 more minutes. Remove meat from pot, discard bones, chop it and return to pot again. Cook for 5 more minutes, ladle into soup bowls and serve right away! Enjoy!

Nutrition: calories 273, fat 3, fiber 6, carbs 9, protein 12

Delicious Hot Stew

Preparation time: 10 minutes
Cooking time: 8 hours
Servings: 6

Ingredients:

- 1 pound pork, cubed
- 1 pound lamb meat, cubed
- 1 tablespoon olive oil
- Salt to the taste
- 2 yellow onions, chopped
- 2 teaspoon peppercorns
- A pinch of whole allspice
- 3 cups water
- 2 bay leaves

Directions:

Heat up a pan over medium high heat, add pork and lamb and brown it on all sides. Meanwhile, put half of the onion slices in your slow cooker. Add half of the meat, add salt, pepper, half of the peppercorns, allspice and 1 bay leaf. Continue with the rest of the onion slices, the rest of the meat, more salt and pepper, the rest of the peppercorns, allspice and bay leaf. Add the water, cover slow cooker and cook on low for 8 hours. Divide plates and serve right away! Enjoy!

Nutrition: calories 300, fat 3, fiber 2, carbs 6, protein 10

Lamb Salad

Preparation time: 10 minutes
Cooking time: 10 minutes
Servings: 4

Ingredients:

- 1 garlic clove, minced
- 2 red chilies, chopped
- 1 tablespoon sugar
- 1 cucumber, sliced
- 2 tablespoons balsamic vinegar
- 1 carrot, sliced
- 1 radish, sliced
- 1 stick lemongrass, chopped
- ½ cup mint leaves, chopped
- ½ cup coriander leaves, chopped
- Salt and black pepper to the taste
- 2 tablespoons olive oil
- 3 ounces bean sprouts
- 2 lamb fillets
- 1 tablespoon fish sauce

Directions:

Put chilies in a pan, add sugar, garlic and vinegar, bring to a boil, stir well, take off heat, leave aside for a few minutes, add fish sauce and whisk well. In a bowl, mix cucumber with radish, carrot, lemongrass, coriander, mint and sprouts. Heat up your kitchen grill, brush lamb fillets with the oil, season them with salt and pepper and cook for 3 minutes on each side. Slice meat, add to the veggie mix, toss and divide among plates. Drizzle the dressing over salad, toss and serve! Enjoy!

Nutrition: calories 231, fat 3, fiber 5, carbs 7, protein 10

Tasty Lamb Ribs

Preparation time: 8 hours
Cooking time: 2 hours and 10 minutes
Servings: 4

Ingredients:
For the marinade:

- 2 garlic cloves, minced
- ¼ cup shallot, chopped
- 2 tablespoons fish sauce
- 2 tablespoons soy sauce
- 2 tablespoons brown sugar
- 2 tablespoons olive oil

For the sauce:

- 2 tablespoons balsamic vinegar
- 2 tablespoons fish sauce
- 1 tablespoon soy sauce
- 2 tablespoons lime juice
- 1 and ½ tablespoons lime juice
- 1 tablespoon coriander seeds, ground
- 1 tablespoon ginger, grated
- 1 teaspoon chili sauce
- Salt to the taste
- 2 pounds lamb riblets

- 2 tablespoons cilantro, chopped
- 1 garlic clove, minced
- 1 tablespoon sugar

Directions:

Put riblets in a bowl, add shallot, 2 garlic cloves, fish and soy sauce and toss. Also add the oil, brown sugar, lime juice, ginger, chili sauce, salt and coriander, toss again, cover and keep in the fridge for 8 hours. Transfer riblets roasting pan, introduce in the oven at 300 degrees F and cook for 2 hours. Turn oven to broiler, broil riblets for 4 minutes and divide them between plates. In a bowl, mix 2 tablespoons fish sauce with 2 tablespoons lime juice, vinegar, chopped cilantro, 1 tablespoons soy sauce, 1 tablespoon sugar and 1 garlic clove, whisk well and drizzle over riblets. Enjoy!

Nutrition: calories 232, fat 3, fiber 1, carbs 5, protein 8

n Slow Cooked Lamb

: 20 minutes
hours
Servings: 4

Ingredients:
- 4 and ½ pounds shoulder lamb steak, diced
- 2 tomatoes, chopped
- 1 garlic clove, minced
- 1 tablespoon cinnamon powder
- 2 teaspoons sugar
- Salt and white pepper to the taste
- ½ cup water
- ¾ cup raisins
- 1 bunch coriander, chopped

Directions:

Put lamb in your slow cooker. Add tomatoes, garlic, cinnamon, salt, pepper, sugar and water. Add coriander stems, cover and cook on Low for 6 hours. Add coriander leaves and raisins, stir, divide between plates and serve hot! Enjoy!

Nutrition: calories 283, fat 4, fiber 5, carbs 8, protein 10

Greek Style Lamb

Preparation time: 15 minutes
Cooking time: 6 hours
Servings: 4

Ingredients:
- 4 lamb shanks
- 1 yellow onion, chopped
- 1 tablespoon olive oil
- 4 teaspoons coriander seeds, crushed
- 2 tablespoons white flour
- 4 bay leaves
- 2 teaspoons honey
- 5 ounces dry sherry
- 2 and ½ cups chicken stock
- Salt and pepper to the taste

Directions:

Heat up a pan with the oil over medium high heat, add lamb shanks, brown them on all sides and transfer to slow cooker. Heat up the same pan over medium high heat, add onion, stir and cook for 5 minutes. Add coriander, stir and cook 1 more minute. Add flour, sherry, stock, honey and bay leaves, salt and pepper, stir and bring to a boil. Pour this over lamb, cover and cook on High for 6 hours turning meat once. Divide everything between plates and serve. Enjoy!

Nutrition: calories 283, fat 4, fiber 2, carbs 7, protein 10

Simple Lamb

Preparation time: 15 minutes
Cooking time: 6 hours
Servings: 6

Ingredients:

- 4 pounds lamb roast
- 1 spring rosemary
- 3 garlic cloves, minced
- 6 potatoes, halved
- ½ cup lamb stock
- 4 bay leaves
- Salt and black pepper to the taste

Directions:

Put potatoes in your slow cooker. Add lamb, garlic and rosemary spring. Season with salt and pepper. Add bay leaves and stock, cover and cook on High for 6 hours. Slice lamb, divide between plates and serve with cooking juices on top. Enjoy!

Nutrition: calories 273, fat 4, fiber 2, carbs 5, protein 12

Superb Lamb

Preparation time: 15 minutes
Cooking time: 8 hours and 10 minutes
Servings: 6

Ingredients:

- 4 pounds lamb leg
- 2 tablespoons olive oil
- 2 sprigs rosemary, chopped
- 2 tablespoons parsley, chopped
- 2 tablespoons oregano, chopped
- 1 tablespoon lemon rind, grated
- 3 garlic cloves, minced
- 2 tablespoons lemon juice
- 2 pounds baby potatoes
- 1 cup beef stock

Directions:

Make small cuts all over the lamb, insert rosemary, season with salt and pepper and leave aside. In a bowl, mix 1 tablespoon oil with oregano, parsley, garlic, lemon juice and rind and stir well. Rub lamb with this mix and leave aside again. Heat up a pan with the rest of the oil over medium high heat, add potatoes, stir, cook for 3 minutes and transfer to your slow cooker. Heat up the same pan over medium high heat, add lamb meat, cook for 3 minutes on each side and also transfer to your slow cooker. Add stock, cover and cook on High for 2 hours and on Low for 6 hours. Divide everything between plates and serve! Enjoy!

Nutrition: calories 264, fat 4, fiber 2, carbs 7, protein 12

Lamb And Feta Stew

Preparation time: 10 minutes
Cooking time: 8 hours
Servings: 8

Ingredients:

- 3 pounds lamb shoulder, boneless and trimmed
- 3 white onions, chopped
- 1 tablespoon olive oil
- 1 tablespoon oregano, dried
- 3 garlic cloves, minced
- 1 tablespoon lemon rind, grated
- Salt and black pepper to the taste
- A pinch of allspice
- 2 tablespoons white flour
- 1 and ½ cups beef stock
- 6 ounces artichoke hearts
- ¼ cup tomato paste
- ½ cup feta cheese
- 2 tablespoons parsley, chopped

Directions:

Heat up a pan with the olive oil over medium high heat, add lamb, brown for a few minutes and add to your slow cooker. Heat up the pan again over medium heat, add onion, rind, garlic, salt, pepper, oregano and allspice, stir and cook for 5 minutes. Add flour, stir and cook for 1 more minute. Add tomato paste and stock, bring to a boil, add over lamb, cover crock pot and cook on Low for 7 hours and 45 minutes. Add parsley, stir gently, cover and cook for 15 more minutes. Add feta, stir gently, transfer to plates and serve right away! Enjoy!

Nutrition: calories 310, fat 2, fiber 3, carbs 5, protein 9

Meatballs And Pomegranate Sauce

Preparation time: 30 minutes
Cooking time: 1 hour
Servings: 42 meatballs

Ingredients:

For the pomegranate sauce:
- 2 cups Greek yogurt
- 1 cup pomegranate juice

For the meatballs:
- 2 slices whole wheat bread
- 1 yellow onion, chopped
- 1/3 cup parsley, chopped
- 1 pound ground lamb meat
- ¾ teaspoon allspice
- 2 tablespoons pomegranate seeds

- ½ teaspoon red pepper flakes
- Salt to the taste
- 2 tablespoons olive oil
- ¼ teaspoon cinnamon powder
- 2 tablespoons canola oil

Directions:

Heat up a pan with the pomegranate juice, bring to a boil over medium heat, cook for 10 minutes, take off heat and keep warm. Meanwhile, put bread slices in a bowl, add water to cover, soak for a few minutes, squeeze them and leave aside for now. Put the onion in your food processor and pulse a few times. Add parsley and pulse again. Add bread, lamb, cinnamon, allspice, pepper flakes and salt and pulse again well. Shape your meatballs, place them on a plate and leave aside. Heat up a pan with the olive and canola oil over medium high heat, add meatballs and cook for 2 minutes on each side. Transfer them to a lined baking pan, introduce in the oven at 350 degrees F and bake for 15 minutes. Drain excess fat on paper towels and arrange on a platter. In a bowl, mix yogurt with warm pomegranate juice and with pomegranate seeds and whisk Serve meatballs with the dip on the side. Enjoy!

Nutrition: calories 265, fat 4, fiber 6, carbs 8, protein 12

Super Lamb Steaks

Preparation time: 10 minutes
Cooking time: 10 minutes
Servings: 4

Ingredients:

- 4 lamb leg steaks
- 1 teaspoon cumin, ground
- 2 teaspoons olive oil
- 1 tablespoon sugar
- 2 carrots, grated
- 3 tablespoons wine vinegar
- 2 spring onions, chopped
- 4 ounces white cabbage, shredded
- 5 sweet peppers
- 4 pita bread
- 3 tablespoons mayonnaise
- Salt and black pepper to the taste

Directions:

Rub lamb with olive oil, cumin, salt and pepper, place on preheated grill over medium high heat, cook for 4 minutes on each side, transfer to a plate and leave aside for now. In a bowl, mix sugar with vinegar and whisk well. Add carrots, cabbage, onion, salt and pepper and toss everything to coat. In your food processor, mix peppers and mayonnaise and blend well. Divide carrots and cabbage mix on each flatbread, add sliced lamb on top and drizzle mayonnaise mix at the end. Roll up flatbreads and serve right away! Enjoy!

Nutrition: calories 264, fat 4, fiber 2, carbs 5, protein 9

Stylish Lamb And Eggplant Delight

Preparation time: 15 minutes
Cooking time: 1 hour
Servings: 6

Ingredients:

- 4 eggplants, cut into halves lengthwise
- 4 ounces olive oil
- 2 yellow onions, chopped
- 4 ounces lamb meat, ground
- 2 green bell peppers, chopped
- 1 pound tomatoes, chopped
- 4 tomato slices
- 2 tablespoons tomato paste
- ½ cup parsley, chopped
- 4 garlic cloves, minced
- ½ cup hot water
- Greek yogurt for serving
- Salt and pepper to the taste

Directions:

Heat up a pan with the olive oil over medium high heat, add eggplant halves, cook for 5 minutes, flipping once and transfer to a plate. Heat up the same pan over medium high heat, add onion, stir and cook for 3 minutes. Add bell peppers and cook for 2 more minutes. Add lamb, tomato paste, salt, pepper and chopped tomatoes and stir again. Add parsley and cook for 5 more minutes. Place eggplant halves on a baking tray, open them up, divide garlic in each, spoon meat filling and top with a tomato slice. Pour the water over them, cover tray with foil and bake in the oven at 350 degrees F for 40 minutes. Take out of the oven, transfer to plates and serve with yogurt on top. Enjoy!

Nutrition: calories 253, fat 3, fiber 2, carbs 5, protein 10

Delicious Baked Chicken Thighs

Preparation time: 10 minutes
Cooking time: 25 minutes
Servings: 4

Ingredients:

- 1 and ½ pounds chicken thighs, boneless and skinless
- 2 tablespoons harissa paste
- ½ cup Greek yogurt
- Salt and black pepper to the taste
- 1 tablespoon lemon juice
- 1 tablespoon mint, finely chopped

Directions:

Put chicken thighs in a lined baking dish, add salt and pepper to the taste and leave aside for now. Meanwhile, in a bowl, mix lemon juice with yogurt, salt and pepper and stir. Add harissa, stir again and spread over chicken pieces. Introduce chicken thighs in the oven at 165 degrees F and bake for 20 minutes. Transfer dish to your preheated broiler and broil for 5 minutes. Divide chicken on plates, sprinkle mint on top and serve. Enjoy!

Nutrition: calories 250, fat 12, fiber 0, carbs 2, protein 31

Tasty Grilled Chicken And Amazing Vinaigrette

Preparation time: 10 minutes
Cooking time: 10 minutes
Servings: 4

Ingredients:

- 2 tablespoon vegetable oil
- 4 chicken breast halves, skinless and boneless
- Salt and black pepper to the taste
- 1 tablespoon shallot, chopped
- 1 tablespoon vinegar
- ½ teaspoon sugar
- ½ teaspoon mustard
- 6 tablespoons olive oil
- 2 tablespoons parsley chopped
- 2 tablespoons kalamata olives, pitted and chopped

Directions:

Place each chicken piece between 2 parchment paper pieces, brush meat with the vegetable oil, season with salt and pepper, place on preheated grill cook for 10 minutes turning once, transfer to a cutting board and leave aside for a few minutes. In a bowl, mix shallot with vinegar, mustard, sugar, salt, pepper, olive oil, parsley and olives and whisk well. Cut chicken in thin slices, arrange on a platter and serve with the vinaigrette on top. Enjoy!

Nutrition: calories 400, fat 32, fiber 0, carbs 2, protein 24

Braised Rabbit

Preparation time: 10 minutes
Cooking time: 1 hour and 30 minutes
Servings: 4

Ingredients:

- ½ rabbit lives
- 1 whole rabbit, cut into 12 pieces
- Salt and black pepper to the taste
- 3 garlic cloves, minced
- 3 tablespoons olive oil
- 1 yellow onion, chopped
- 3 tomatoes, seeded, peeled and grated
- ¼ cup dry white wine
- 3 carrots, chopped
- 1 thyme spring
- 1 cup chicken stock
- 12 almonds, toasted
- 1 tablespoon parsley, chopped
- Crusty bread

Directions:

Heat up a pan with the oil over medium high heat, add rabbit pieces, salt and pepper to the taste, brown them for 10 minutes, transfer to a platter and keep warm. Heat up the pan again over medium heat, add garlic, stir, cook for 1 minute, transfer to a bowl and leave aside as well. Add onion to the pan, stir and cook for 3 minutes. Add tomatoes, stir, reduce heat to low and cook for 15 minutes. Return rabbit pieces to the pan, add wine, stir and cook for 1minute. Add stock, thyme and carrots, stir, increase heat, bring to a boil, reduce temperature to low again and cook for 45 minutes. In a mortar and paste, mix liver with garlic, parsley, almonds and water and stir until you obtain a paste. Add this over rabbit pieces, stir and cook everything for 10 minutes more. Divide into bowls and serve with crusty bread on the side. Enjoy!

Nutrition: calories 500, fat 28, fiber 4, carbs 12, protein 56

Delicious Lamb Chops

Preparation time: 10 minutes
Cooking time: 6 minutes
Servings: 2

Ingredients:

- 1 red onion, thinly sliced
- Salt and black pepper to the taste
- 2 teaspoons brown sugar
- 6 lamb rib chops
- 1 teaspoon smoked paprika
- 6 mint leaves, chopped
- 1 tablespoons olive oil

Directions:

Put the onion in a bowl, add some cold water, leave aside for 5 minutes, drain and transfer to another bowl. Add lamb chops to the bowl, season with salt, pepper, mint, paprika and oil. Toss to coat and leave aside for 10 minutes. Heat up your kitchen grill over medium high heat, place lamb ribs on it, grill them for 3 minutes on each side and transfer to a platter. Serve with watermelon salad on the side. Enjoy!

Nutrition: calories 460, fat 31, fiber 1, carbs 18, protein 34

Spicy Steaks With Tasty Sauce

Preparation time: 10 minutes
Cooking time: 15 minutes
Servings: 4

Ingredients:

- 2 teaspoons chili powder
- 2 and ½ tablespoons olive oil
- Salt and black pepper to the taste
- 1 and ½ teaspoons onion powder
- 1 and ½ teaspoons garlic powder
- 1 tablespoon smoked paprika
- 1 red bell pepper, cut in halves
- 2 tomatoes, cut in halved
- 1 small red onion, cut into 6 wedges
- 4 beef steaks
- 2 teaspoons sherry vinegar
- 1 tablespoon oregano, chopped
- Hot sauce to the taste
- A pinch of cumin, ground
- 1/3 cup black olives, pitted and sliced

Directions:

In a bowl, mix chili powder with paprika, salt, pepper, garlic and onion powder. In another bowl, mix bell pepper with onion, tomatoes, 1 tablespoon spice mixture you've just made and ½ tablespoons oil and toss to coat. Mix steaks with the rest of the spice mix and toss to coat. Heat up your kitchen grill over medium high heat, add pepper and onion, cook for 4 minutes on each side and transfer to a plate. Add tomatoes, grill for 2 minutes and also transfer to the plate with the rest of the veggies. Place steaks on the grill, cook for 4 minutes on each side and transfer to a platter. In your blender, mix grilled veggies with cumin, the rest of the oil, vinegar, oregano, salt, pepper and hot sauce and blend until you obtain a sauce. Serve steaks with this sauce on top and with chopped olives. Enjoy!

Nutrition: calories 450, fat 23, fiber 2, carbs 8, protein 43

Delicious Sausage Kebabs

Preparation time: 1 hour
Cooking time: 13 minutes
Servings: 6

Ingredients:

- 1 yellow onion, chopped
- 1 pound ground pork
- 3 tablespoons parsley, chopped
- 1 tablespoon lemon juice
- 1 garlic clove, minced
  For the sauce:
- 2 tablespoons olive oil
- ¼ cup tahini sauce
- ¼ cup water
- 1 teaspoon oregano, dried
- 1 teaspoon mint, dried
- Salt and black pepper to the taste
- Vegetable oil

- 1 tablespoon lemon juice
- 1 garlic clove, minced
- Salt and cayenne pepper to the taste

Directions:

In a bowl, mix ground pork with onion, parsley, 1 garlic clove, 1 tablespoon lemon juice, mint, oregano, salt and pepper to the taste, stir well and divide into 6 portions. Shape your kebabs by squeezing each portion on a skewer, cover and keep them in the fridge for 1 hour. Heat up your kitchen grill over medium high heat, place kebabs on it, brush them with vegetable oil, cook them for 13 minutes, turning from time to time and transfer to plates. In your food processor, mix tahini with olive oil, 1 tablespoon lemon juice, 1 garlic clove, water, salt and cayenne pepper and blend well. Serve your kebabs with this sauce all over. Enjoy!

Nutrition: calories 250, fat 23, fiber 1, carbs 4, protein 14

Delicious Lamb With Artichokes, Beans And Yogurt

Preparation time: 4 hours
Cooking time: 35 minutes
Servings: 8

Ingredients:

- For the lamb:
- 6 tablespoons olive oil
- 2 racks of lamb, boneless and trimmed
- Zest from 1 lemon
- 10 garlic cloves, crushed
- For the veggies:
- 10 ounces shiitake mushrooms, sliced
- 2 tablespoons olive oil
- 1 tablespoon thyme, chopped
- 6 ounces jarred artichokes, drained
- 1 cup fava beans
- ½ cup chicken stock
- 6 tablespoons vermouth
- Juice of 1 lemon
- Salt and black pepper to the taste
- 2 rosemary sprigs
- ¼ teaspoon red pepper flakes, crushed
- 2 teaspoons lemon zest, grated
- 1 tablespoon butter
- A pinch of cayenne pepper
- Salt to the taste
- 2 cups Greek yogurts for serving
- 1 jar hot peppers in oil

Directions:

Put the lamb in a heatproof dish. Add 6 tablespoon oil, lemon zest and juice, 10 garlic cloves, rosemary sprigs, salt, pepper and red pepper flakes, toss to coat, cover and keep in the fridge for 4 hours. Take the lamb out of the fridge, discard lemon zest, rosemary and garlic, transfer meat to a pan heated over medium high heat, sear for 2 minutes on each side, return to baking dish, introduce in the oven at 400 degrees F and bake for 20 minutes. Take the lamb out of the oven, place on a cutting board, cool down, cut into separated chops and keep warm. Heat up a pan with 2 tablespoons oil over medium high heat, add artichokes, mushrooms, salt and pepper, stir and cook for 2 minutes. Add vermouth, stock, fava beans, stir and cook for 3 minutes. Reduce heat to medium-low, add butter, salt, cayenne pepper and 2 teaspoons lemon zest, stir and cook for 1 minute. In a bowl, whisk yogurt well and leave it aside for 10 minutes. Divide yogurt on serving plates and spread. Top yogurt with jarred peppers, add ¼ cup veggie mix on each plate on top of yogurt and peppers, place 2 lamb chops on each plate and serve. Enjoy!

Nutrition: calories 500, fat 23, fiber 3, carbs 23, protein 41

Grilled Lamb With Black Olives Puree

Preparation time: 1 hour
Cooking time: 15 minutes
Servings: 8

Ingredients:

- 4 and ½ pounds butterflied lamb leg
- 1 cup black olives, pitted
- ½ cup olive oil
- Salt and black pepper to the taste
- ½ cup mixed parsley with thyme and rosemary, finely chopped
- Salt and black pepper to the taste
- 4 garlic cloves, minced
- Juice of ½ lemon

Directions:

Mash olives with a fork until you obtain a paste, add 1 tablespoon mixed herbs, half of the olive oil, some salt and pepper and stir very well. In a bowl, mix the rest of the oil with the rest of the herbs mix and garlic and stir well. Rub lamb with this mix, cover and leave aside for 1 hour. Place lamb on heated grill over medium high heat, add salt and pepper to the taste, cook for 18 minutes flipping once and transfer to a cutting board. Add lemon juice over the meat, leave aside for 10 minutes, slice and arrange on a platter. Serve with olive puree on top. Enjoy!

Nutrition: calories 450, fat 23, fiber 1, carbs 3, protein 44

Lamb Meatballs

Preparation time: 10 minutes
Cooking time: 20 minutes
Servings: 4

Ingredients:

- 1 pound lamb shoulder, ground
- 1 tablespoon pine nuts
- 1 tablespoon ras el hanout
- 2 garlic cloves, minced
- Salt and black pepper to the taste
- 2 cups Greek yogurt
- ½ cup olive oil
- ¼ cup parsley, finely chopped

Directions:

Heat up a pan over medium heat, add pine nuts, toast for 4 minutes, transfer to a plate, cool them down and chop them. In a bowl, mix lamb with pine nuts, salt, pepper, ras el hanout and garlic and stir well. Shape 8 meatballs, place them on a lined baking sheet, introduce in the oven at 425 degrees F and bake for 17 minutes. Take meatballs out of the oven and leave them aside to cool down for 5 minutes. Meanwhile, in a bowl, mix yogurt with salt, pepper, oil and parsley and whisk well. Serve your meatballs with the yogurt sauce. Enjoy!

Nutrition: calories 96, fat 6, fiber 1, carbs 5, protein 6

Simple Pork Sandwiches

Preparation time: 10 minutes
Cooking time: 20 minutes
Servings: 4

Ingredients:

- 1 pork tenderloin, cut in half crosswise
- Salt and black pepper to the taste
- 3 tablespoons fennel seeds, crushed
- ¼ teaspoon allspice
- 1 tablespoon olive oil
- 4 sandwich rolls, toasted and cut in half
- 1/3 cup homemade mayonnaise
- ½ cup cucumber, sliced
- ½ cup dill, chopped

Directions:

In a bowl, mix half of the fennel seeds with half of the allspice, salt and pepper. Add oil, whisk and rub pork with this mix. Place pork on preheated grill over medium high heat, cook for 20 minutes, turning a few times, transfer to a cutting board and leave aside for a few minutes. In a bowl, mix mayo with the rest of the fennel seeds, allspice, salt and pepper. Spread this on sandwich rolls, add pork after you've sliced it, add cucumber slices and dill and serve. Enjoy!

Nutrition: calories 430, fat 21, fiber 2, carbs 23, protein 32

Delicious Turkey Cutlets

Preparation time: 10 minutes
Cooking time: 25 minutes
Servings: 4

Ingredients:

- 1 and ½ cups couscous
- ½ cup vegetable oil
- 1 cup breadcrumbs
- 2 cups chicken stock
- 1 tablespoons sesame seeds
- Salt and black pepper to the taste
- A pinch of paprika
- A pinch of cayenne pepper
- 2 eggs
- 4 turkey breast cutlets
- ¼ cup parsley, chopped
- 4 ounces feta cheese, crumbled
- ¼ cup red onion, chopped
- ½ cup white flour
- 4 lemon wedges

Directions:

Heat up a pan with 2 tablespoon oil over medium high heat, add couscous, stir and cook for 7 minutes. Add stock, bring to a boil, reduce heat to medium-low, simmer for 10 minutes, take off heat and keep warm. In a bowl, mix breadcrumbs with sesame seeds, cayenne, paprika, salt and pepper. Whisk eggs well in another bowl and put the flour in a third one. Dredge turkey cutlets in flour, eggs and breadcrumbs and arrange them on the plate. Heat up a pan with the rest of the oil over medium high heat, add cutlets, cook for 3 minutes flipping once and transfer them to paper towels in order to drain excess grease. Mix couscous with parsley onion, salt, pepper and feta cheese and stir. Divide turkey cutlets on plates, add couscous on the side and serve with lemon wedges. Enjoy!

Nutrition: calories 760, fat 20, fiber 4, carbs 34, protein 40

Slow Cooked Chicken

Preparation time: 10 minutes
Cooking time: 6 hours and 15 minutes
Servings: 4

Ingredients:

- 1 pound carrots, roughly chopped
- Zest from 1 lemon
- 30 apricots, dried
- ¼ cup white flour
- ¼ teaspoon cinnamon, ground
- A pinch of ginger, ground
- ¼ teaspoon coriander, ground
- A pinch of cardamom, ground
- Salt and black pepper to the taste
- A pinch of cayenne pepper
- 8 chicken thighs, bone-in and skinless
- 2 tablespoons vegetable oil
- 2 and ¼ cups yellow onion, chopped
- 2 tablespoons tomato paste
- 1 tablespoon butter
- 1 and ½ tablespoons garlic, minced
- ¼ cup lemon juice
- 1 cup apricot juice
- ½ cup chicken stock
- ¼ cup cilantro, chopped
- ¼ cup pine nuts, toasted

Directions:

Put lemon peel, apricots and carrots in your slow cooker. In a bowl, mix flour with salt, pepper, cayenne pepper, cinnamon, coriander, ginger and cardamom. Add chicken pieces and toss to coat well. Heat up a pan with the oil and the butter over medium high heat, add chicken pieces and brown them for 11 minutes. Transfer them to your slow cooker as well. Add garlic and onion to heated pan, stir and cook for 3 minutes. Add tomato paste, stock, nectar and lemon juice, stir, bring to a boil, simmer for 2 minutes and pour into your slow cooker. Cook everything for 6 hours, transfer to plates, garnish with nuts and cilantro on top. Enjoy!

Nutrition: calories 340, fat 3, fiber 4, carbs 12, protein 20

Wonderful Meatloaf

Preparation time: 10 minutes
Cooking time: 1 hour and 20 minutes
Servings: 8

Ingredients:

- 1 yellow onion, chopped
- 2 tablespoons olive oil
- 2 garlic cloves, minced
- ¾ cup red wine
- 4 ounces white bread, chopped
- 2 pounds lamb, ground
- 1 cup milk
- ¼ cup feta cheese, crumbled
- 2 eggs
- 1/3 cup kalamata olives, pitted and chopped
- 4 tablespoons oregano, chopped
- Salt and black pepper to the taste
- 2 tablespoons honey
- 1 tablespoon Worcestershire sauce
- 2 teaspoons lemon zest, grated

Directions:

Heat up a pan with 2 tablespoons oil over medium heat, add garlic and onion, stir and cook for 8 minutes. Add wine, stir, simmer for 5 minutes and transfer everything to a bowl. Put bread pieces in a bowl, add milk, leave aside for 10 minutes, squeeze bread a bit, chop and add it to onions mix. Add lamb, eggs, cheese, olives, lemon, zest, oregano, Worcestershire sauce, salt and pepper to onions mix and stir very well. Transfer meatloaf mix to a baking dish, spread honey all over, introduce in the oven at 375 degrees F and bake for 50 minutes. Take meatloaf out of the oven, leave aside for 5 minutes, slice and arrange on a platter. Enjoy!

Nutrition: calories 350, fat 23. fiber 1, carbs 17, protein 24

Simple And Tasty Braised Beef

Preparation time: 30 minutes
Cooking time: 3 hours and 30 minutes
Servings: 6

Ingredients:

For the ribs:

- 6 beef short ribs
- 1 tablespoon thyme, chopped
- Salt and black pepper to the taste
- 3 tablespoons olive oil
- 1 carrot, chopped
- 1 yellow onion, chopped
- 1 celery stalk, chopped

For the salsa:

- 1 cup parsley, chopped
- 1 teaspoons marjoram, chopped
- ¼ cup mint, chopped
- 1 garlic clove, minced
- 1 tablespoons capers, drained

- 1 and ½ cups ruby port
- 2 bay leaves
- 2 and ½ cups red wine
- 2 tablespoons balsamic vinegar
- 6 cups beef stock
- 4 parsley sprigs

- 1 anchovy
- ¾ cup olive oil
- Salt and black pepper to the taste
- ½ cup feta cheese, crumbled

Directions:

In a bowl, mix thyme with salt and pepper, add short ribs, toss to coat and leave aside for 30 minutes. Heat up a pot with the oil over high heat, add short ribs, sear for 3 minutes on each side and transfer them to a bowl. Heat up the pan again over medium heat, add celery, onion, carrot and bay leaves, stir and cook for 8 minutes. Add port, vinegar and wine, stir, bring to a boil and simmer for about 10 minutes. Add stock, return short ribs, parsley, salt and pepper, cover and bake in the oven at 325 degrees F for 3 hours. Take ribs out of the oven and leave aside for 30 minutes. In your food processor, mix 1 cup parsley with marjoram, mint, 1 garlic clove, capers, anchovy, ¾ cup olive oil, feta cheese, salt and pepper and pulse well. Divide short ribs into bowls, add some of the cooking liquid and toss with the salsa you've just made! Enjoy!

Nutrition: calories 450, fat 45, fiber 2, carbs 18, protein 43

Spanish Style Spareribs
Preparation time: 10 minutes
Cooking time: 1 hour and 30 minutes
Servings: 4

Ingredients:
For the ribs:
- 2 pork spareribs
- 2 teaspoons oregano, dried
- 2 teaspoons smoked paprika
For the sauce:
- 4 garlic cloves, minced
- 6 tablespoons sherry vinegar
- ¼ cup olive oil

- Salt and black pepper to the taste
- 2 teaspoons sugar

- 1 tablespoon oregano, dried
- Salt and black pepper to the taste

Directions:

In a bowl, mix salt with pepper, paprika, sugar, oregano and ribs. Heat up your grill over medium high heat, add spareribs, cover your grill and cook for 1 hour and 30 minutes flipping from time to time. Meanwhile, in a bowl, mix vinegar with garlic, oil, 1 tablespoon oregano, salt and pepper and whisk well. Transfer spareribs on a platter, leave aside for 5 minutes, drizzle the sauce you've just made all over them and serve. Enjoy!

Nutrition: calories 450, fat 34, fiber 1, carbs 2, protein 35

Tunisian-Style Short Ribs
Preparation time: 10 minutes
Cooking time: 3 hours
Servings: 6

Ingredients:
- 3 tablespoons vegetable oil
- 12 beef short ribs
- Salt and black pepper to the taste
- 1 cup onions, chopped
- 1 cup carrots, chopped
- 1 cup figs, dried and chopped
- 1 tablespoon ginger, grated
- 3-star anise

- 1 tablespoon garlic, minced
- 2 cinnamon sticks
- 1 cup canned tomatoes, crushed
- 1 cup red wine
- 1 cup chicken stock
- ¼ cup soy sauce
- 2 tablespoons mint, chopped
- 2 tablespoons parsley, chopped

Directions:

Heat up a pot with 2 tablespoons oil over medium high heat, add short ribs, season with salt and pepper to the taste, cook for 4 minutes on each side and transfer to a plate. Add the rest of the oil to your pot and heat up over medium high heat. Add onions and carrots, salt and pepper, stir and cook for 8 minutes. Add figs, ginger, garlic, cinnamon sticks, star anise, stir and cook for 1 minute. Add ½ cup wine, stir and cook for 1 minute. Return ribs to the pot, add tomatoes, soy sauce, the rest of the wine and stock, stir, bring to a simmer, cover and introduce in the oven at 325 degrees F. Bake for 2 hours and 50 minutes, stirring gently every 40 minutes. Add salt, pepper, parsley and mint, stir, divide into plates and serve. Enjoy!

Nutrition: calories 300, fat 23, fiber 4, carbs 23, protein 35

Delicious Mediterranean Chicken

Preparation time: 10 minutes
Cooking time: 1 hour and 20 minutes
Servings: 4

Ingredients:

- 8 chicken pieces, trimmed
- Salt and black pepper to the taste
- Zest and juice from 1 orange
- A pinch of cinnamon, ground
- 1 and ½ teaspoons thyme, dried
- 1 cup pomegranate juice
- 6 teaspoons canola oil
- 2 sweet potatoes, chopped
- ¾ cup chicken stock
- 2 parsnips, chopped
- 1 red onion, cut into medium wedges
- 1 cup walnuts, chopped

Directions:

Heat up a pan with the pomegranate juice and the orange juice, bring to a boil over medium heat and simmer for 15 minutes. Add ½ teaspoon thyme, cinnamon, salt and pepper and whisk well. Divide this into 2 bowls. Add 2 teaspoons oil to one bowl and chicken stock, salt and orange zest to the other one. Spread parsnips, onion wedges and potato pieces in a baking dish, add the rest of the thyme and the oil and toss to coat. Place chicken pieces on top, toss to coat everything, introduce in the oven at 400 degrees F and bake for 30 minutes. Take chicken out of the oven, pour the stock mix over it, add walnuts, introduce in the oven at 375 degrees F and bake for 30 minutes more. Take the chicken dish out of the oven, transfer it along with the veggies and walnuts on a platter and season with some more salt and pepper. Pour cooking liquid into a pan, heat up over medium heat, add pomegranate and oil mix from the remaining bowl, simmer for a few minutes and drizzle over chicken and veggies. Enjoy!

Nutrition: calories 546, fat 23, fiber 5, carbs 34, protein 44

Sautéed Chorizo

Preparation time: 10 minutes
Cooking time: 13 minutes
Servings: 4

Ingredients:

- 1 and 1.2 cups soft chorizo, sliced
- 3 tablespoons olive oil
- 1/3 cup dry red wine
- White bread, cubed

Directions:

Heat up a pan with the olive oil over medium high heat, add chorizo, stir and cook for 4 minutes. Stir again and cook for 5 minutes more. Add wine, stir and simmer for 3 minutes. Pour this into bowls and serve with cubed bread on top. Enjoy!

Nutrition: calories 340, fat 23, fiber 0, carbs 2, protein 21

Simple Pot Roast

Preparation time: 10 minutes
Cooking time: 3 hours
Servings: 6

Ingredients:

- 2 and ½ pounds shoulder roast, boneless
- 1 tablespoon olive oil
- Salt and black pepper to the taste
- 4 shallots, chopped
- 2 cups beef stock
- 1 and ½ cups red wine
- 2 teaspoons herbs de provender
- 1 red onion, cut into wedges
- 2/3 cup black olives, pitted
- 12 baby carrots
- 1 cup cherry tomatoes
- 1 zucchini, chopped

Directions:

Heat up a pot with the oil over medium high heat; add roast, salt and pepper, brown for 10 minutes and transfer to a plate. Add shallots to the pot, stir and sauté for 4 minutes. Add wine, stir and simmer until it reduces. Add herbs, stock and return roast, stir, cover, reduce heat to medium-low and cook for 2 hours and 30 minutes, turning roast from time to time. Take roast out of the pot, transfer to a platter, cover and keep warm. Add carrots, onion and olives to the pot, cover and cook for 10 minutes. Add tomatoes and zucchini, cook for 10 minutes and transfer all veggies next to the roast. Bring cooking liquid to a boil, cook for 5 minutes, add more salt and pepper and take off heat. Slice roast and divide between plates and drizzle the sauce on top. Enjoy!

Nutrition: calories 432, fat 12, fiber 2, carbs 13, protein 42

Simple Grilled Pork Chops

Preparation time: 30 minutes
Cooking time: 7 minutes
Servings: 4

Ingredients:

- 8 pork loin chops
- Salt and black pepper to the taste
- 1 tablespoon olive oil
- ¼ cup red wine vinegar
- 1 teaspoon oregano, dried
- 1 tablespoon garlic, minced
- ¼ cup sweet paprika

Directions:

In a bowl mix paprika with oregano, garlic, salt, pepper, olive oil and vinegar and whisk well. Spread this over pork chops, rub well and leave aside for 30 minutes. Heat up your kitchen grill over medium high heat, place pork chops on it, cook for 3 minutes on each side, transfer them to a platter and leave aside for 5 minutes. Serve right away with your favorite side salad. Enjoy!

Nutrition: calories 430, fat 23, fiber 2, carbs 4, protein 45

Mediterranean Diet Fish And Seafood Recipes

Tasty Linguine With Shrimp

Preparation time: 10 minutes
Cooking time: 15 minutes
Servings: 4

Ingredients:
- 3 tablespoons extra virgin olive oil
- 12 ounces linguine
- 1 tablespoon garlic, minced
- 30 big shrimp, peeled and deveined
- A pinch of red pepper flakes, crushed
- 1 cup green olives, pitted and chopped
- 3 tablespoons lemon juice
- 1 teaspoon lemon zest, grated
- ¼ cup parsley, chopped

Directions:

Put some water in a pot, add water, bring to a boil over medium high heat, add linguine, cook according to instructions, take off heat, drain and put in a bowl and reserve ½ cup cooking liquid. Heat up a pan with 2 tablespoons oil over medium high heat, add shrimp, stir and cook for 3 minutes. Add pepper flakes and garlic, stir and cook 10 seconds more. Add the rest of the oil, lemon zest and juice and stir well. Add pasta and olives, reserved cooking liquid and parsley, stir, cook for 2 minutes more, take off heat, divide between plates and serve. Enjoy!

Nutrition: calories 500, fat 20, fiber 5, carbs 45, protein 34

Amazing Steamed Mussels

Preparation time: 10 minutes
Cooking time: 25 minutes
Servings: 4

Ingredients:
- 1 tablespoon white wine vinegar
- 1 potato, chopped
- 5 ounces chorizo, chopped
- Salt and black pepper to the taste
- 2 tablespoons olive oil
- 1/3 cup parsley, finely chopped
- 1 tablespoon parsley, finely chopped
- 1 garlic clove, minced
- 1 sweet onion, chopped
- 4-pound mussels, scrubbed and debearded
- 1 cup white wine

Directions:

Put the potato in a pot, add some water to cover, vinegar and salt, bring to a boil over high heat, cook for 4 minutes, drain and transfer to a plate. Heat up a pot with the oil over medium high heat, add potato and chorizo and cook for 7 minutes. Stir and cook for 5 minutes more. Add ¼ cup parsley, salt and pepper, stir and transfer to a plate. Add onion to the pot, stir and cook for 3 minutes. Add mussels and wine, stir, cover and cook for 5 minutes. Discard unopened mussels, add chorizo and potato mix and the rest of the parsley, stir gently, divide into bowls and serve. Enjoy!

Nutrition: calories 345, fat 5, fiber 2, carbs 23, protein 27

Tasty Seafood Dish

Preparation time: 10 minutes
Cooking time: 35 minutes
Servings: 4
Ingredients:

- 12 clams, scrubbed and cleaned
- 3 dried chilies, soaked in hot water for 30 minutes, drained and chopped
- 1 lobster, tail separated and cut in half lengthwise
- ¼ cup water
- ¼ cup flour
- 3 tablespoons olive oil
- 1 and ½ pounds monkfish, skinless, boneless and cut in thin fillets
- Salt and black pepper to the taste
- 35 shrimp, unpeeled
- 1 onion, chopped
- 4 garlic cloves, minced
- 4 tomatoes, grated
- 1 baguette slice, toasted
- 30 hazelnuts, skinned
- 2 tablespoons parsley, chopped
- 1 cup fish stock
- ¼ teaspoon smoked paprika
- Lemon wedges for serving
- Crusty bread slices for serving

Directions:

Put the water in a pot, bring to a boil over high heat, add clams, cover, cook for 4 minutes, take off heat, discard unopened ones and keep warm for now. Heat up a pot with the oil over medium high heat. Put flour on a plate and mix with salt and pepper. Dredge fish in flour, place in the pan, cook for 3 minutes on each side and transfer to a plate. Add shrimp to the pan, cook for 2 minutes on each side and also transfer to a plate. Reduce heat to medium-low, add garlic to the pan, stir, cook for 1 minute and also transfer to a plate. Add onion, stir and sauté them for 3 minutes. Add tomatoes, stir and cook on a low heat for 15 minutes. In your blender, mix sautéed garlic with baguette slice, nuts, parsley and 2 tablespoons liquid from the clams and pulse well. Add chili peppers and stir well. Add this to the pan with the tomatoes and stir. Add fish, lobster, shrimp, clams and stock, stir, bring to a boil and cook for 2 minutes. Add salt and pepper to the taste, divide into bowls and serve with lemon wedges and crusty bread on the side. Enjoy!

Nutrition: calories 344, fat 14, fiber 4, carbs 14, protein 23

Delicious Oysters

Preparation time: 10 minutes
Cooking time: 6 minutes
Servings: 4

Ingredients:

- 2 tablespoons shallots, finely chopped
- ½ cup sherry vinegar
- A pinch of saffron threads
- ½ cup olive oil
- 1 tablespoon olive oil
- Salt and black pepper to the taste
- 1 pound chorizo sausage, chopped
- 1 pound fennel bulbs, thinly sliced lengthwise
- 24 oysters, shucked

Directions:

In a bowl, mix shallots with vinegar, saffron, salt, pepper and ½ cup olive oil and stir well. Heat up a pan with the rest of the oil over medium high heat, add sausage, cook for 4 minutes, transfer to a paper towel, drain grease and put on a plate. Add fennel on top, spoon vinaigrette into each oyster and place them on the platter as well, drizzle the rest of the vinaigrette on top and serve. Enjoy!

Nutrition: calories 113, fat 1, fiber 3, carbs 10, protein 7

Shrimp With Honeydew And Feta

Preparation time: 10 minutes
Cooking time: 4 minutes
Servings: 4

Ingredients:

- 30 big shrimp, peeled and deveined
- Salt and black pepper to the taste
- A pinch of cayenne pepper
- ¼ cup olive oil
- 2 tablespoons shallots, chopped
- 1 teaspoon lime zest
- 4 teaspoons lime juice
- ½ pound frisee, torn into small pieces
- 1 honeydew melon, peeled, seeded and chopped
- ¼ cup mint, chopped
- 8 ounces feta cheese, crumbled
- 1 tablespoon coriander seeds

Directions:

Heat up a pan with 2 tablespoons oil over medium high heat, add shrimp, cook for 1 minute and flip. Add lime zest, 1 teaspoon lime juice, shallots and some salt, stir, cook for 1 minute and take off heat. In a bowl, mix the rest of the oil with the rest of the lime juice, salt and pepper to the taste. Add honeydew and frisee, stir and divide into plates. Add shrimp, coriander seeds, mint and feta on top and serve. Enjoy!

Nutrition: calories 245, fat 23, fiber 3, carbs 23, protein 45

Delicious Mixed Shellfish Dish

Preparation time: 10 minutes
Cooking time: 22 minutes
Servings: 4

Ingredients:

- 2 tablespoons olive oil
- 12 cherry tomatoes
- 2 tablespoons butter
- ½ cup fennel, sliced
- 1 cup escarole leaves, sliced
- 3 garlic cloves, minced
- 1 cup fish stock
- 1 tablespoon amontillado sherry
- 16 clams, scrubbed
- 16 mussels, scrubbed
- 1 cup shrimp, peeled and deveined
- ¼ cup parsley, chopped
- A pinch of red pepper flakes, crushed
- 2 teaspoons lemon zest, grated
- ½ teaspoon rosemary, chopped
- Salt and black pepper to the taste
- 1 teaspoon lemon juice

Directions:

Heat up a pan with the butter for 3 minutes over medium high heat, transfer to a bowl and leave aside. Heat up another pan with the oil over medium high heat, add tomatoes, stir and cook for 3 minutes. Add garlic and fennel, stir and cook for 2 minutes. Add escarole, stir and cook for 1 minute. Add sherry, stir, increase heat and cook for 1 minute. Add fish stock, stir and simmer for 4 minutes. Add clams, stir, cover and cook for 2 minutes. Add mussels, stir and cook for 2 minutes more. Add shrimp, stir and cook for 1 minute. Transfer clams, mussels and shrimp to a bowl, cover and keep warm. Add pepper flakes and kale to the pan with the stock, stir and cook for 1 minute. Take off heat, add melted butter, parsley, rosemary, lemon juice, lemon zest, salt and pepper and stir well. Divide shellfish and shrimp on plates, add veggies and stock mix on top and serve. Enjoy!

Nutrition: calories 250, fat 5, fiber 2, carbs 10, protein 27

Classic Paella

Preparation time: 10 minutes
Cooking time: 25 minutes
Servings: 4

Ingredients:

- 1 yellow onion, chopped
- 1 teaspoon smoked paprika
- 1 teaspoon thyme, dried
- 3 tablespoons sherry
- 1 tablespoon extra-virgin olive oil
- 10 ounces risotto rice
- 12 ounces mixed shrimp and sea scallops, cooked and frozen
- 14 ounces canned tomatoes, chopped
- 1-quart chicken stock
- Juice of ½ lemon
- ½ lemon cut into wedges
- A handful parsley, chopped
- Salt and black pepper to the taste

Directions:

Heat up a pan with the oil over medium high heat, add onion, stir and cook for 5 minutes. Add thyme, rice and paprika, stir and cook for 1 minute. Add sherry, stir and cook for 1 minute more. Add tomatoes and stock and cook for 15 minutes stirring from time to time. Add salt and pepper to the taste, seafood mix and lemon juice, stir and cook for 5 minutes more. Sprinkle parsley, stir, divide into bowls and serve with lemon wedges on the side. Enjoy!

Nutrition: calories 430, fat 4, fiber 2, carbs 33, protein 25

Spicy Seared Mussels

Preparation time: 10 minutes
Cooking time: 15 minutes
Servings: 4

Ingredients:

- 1 and ½ cups green grapes, cut in quarters
- Zest from 1 lemon, chopped
- Juice of 1 lemon
- Salt and black pepper to the taste
- 2 scallions, chopped
- ¼ cup olive oil
- 2 tablespoons mint, chopped
- 2 tablespoons cilantro, chopped
- 1 teaspoon cumin, ground
- 1 teaspoon paprika
- ½ teaspoon ginger, ground
- ¼ teaspoon cinnamon, ground
- 1 teaspoon turmeric, ground
- ½ cup water
- 1 and ½ pounds sea scallops

Directions:

Heat up a pan with the water, some salt and the lemon zest over medium high heat and simmer for 10 minutes. Drain lemon zest and transfer to a bowl. Mix with grapes, 2 tablespoons oil, cilantro, mint and scallions and stir well. In another bowl, mix cumin with turmeric, paprika, cinnamon and ginger and stir. Season scallops with salt and pepper, coat with the spice mix and place them on a plate. Heat up a pan with the rest of the oil over medium high heat, add scallops, cook for 2 minutes on each side and transfer to a plate. Divide scallops on 4 plates, pour lemon juice over them and serve with grapes relish. Enjoy!

Nutrition: calories 320, fat 12, fiber 2, carbs 18, protein 28

Delicious Shrimp Dish

Preparation time: 10 minutes
Cooking time: 3 minutes
Servings: 4

Ingredients:

- 40 big shrimp, peeled and deveined
- 6 garlic cloves, minced
- Salt and black pepper to the taste
- 3 tablespoons olive oil
- ¼ teaspoon sweet paprika
- A pinch of red pepper flakes, crushed
- ¼ teaspoon lemon zest, grated
- 3 tablespoons sherry
- 1 and ½ tablespoons chives, sliced
- Juice of 1 lemon

Directions:

Heat up a pan with the oil over medium high heat, add shrimp, season with salt and pepper and cook for 1 minute. Add paprika, garlic and pepper flakes, stir and cook for 1 minute. Add sherry, stir and cook for 1 minute more. Take shrimp off heat, add chives and lemon zest, stir and transfer shrimp to plates. Add lemon juice all over and serve. Enjoy!

Nutrition: calories 140, fat 1, fiber 0, carbs 1, protein 18

Baked Orzo With Shrimp

Preparation time: 10 minutes
Cooking time: 25 minutes
Servings: 6

Ingredients:

- 1 pound shrimp, peeled and deveined
- 1 pound orzo
- 5 tablespoons olive oil
- Salt and black pepper to the taste
- 1 garlic clove, minced
- 5 ounces baby spinach
- 2 teaspoons thyme, chopped
- ¾ cup panko
- 6 ounces feta cheese, crumbled
- Zest from 1 lemon, grated

Directions:

Heat up a pan with 2 tablespoons oil over medium high heat, add shrimp, season with salt and pepper, stir and cook for 3 minutes. Add garlic, stir and cook for 30 seconds. Add spinach, stir again, cook for 1 minute more and take off heat. Put water in a pot, add salt, bring to a boil over medium high heat, add orzo, stir, cook according to package instructions, drain and add over shrimp mix. Also add cheese, 2 tablespoons oil, half of the thyme and lemon juice, stir and pour this into a greased baking dish. In a bowl, mix panko with the rest of the oil, the rest of the thyme, salt and pepper and stir. Spread this over orzo and shrimp mix, introduce in the oven at 425 degrees F and bake for 20 minutes. Leave orzo and shrimp mixture to cool down for a few minutes before dividing on plates and serving. Enjoy!

Nutrition: calories 345, fat 13, fiber 4, carbs 33, protein 22

Spicy Salmon With Lentils
Preparation time: 10 minutes
Cooking time: 1 hour
Servings: 4

Ingredients:
- 3 cups water
- 1 cup French lentils, rinsed
- Salt and black pepper to the taste
- 2 tablespoons olive oil
- 1/3 cup apricots, dried and chopped
- 1 yellow onion, chopped
- 1 tablespoon capers
- 1 tablespoon lemon juice
- ½ teaspoon lemon zest, grated
- ½ teaspoon paprika
- ½ teaspoon cumin, ground
- ¼ teaspoon cinnamon, ground
- A pinch of allspice, ground
- ¼ teaspoon ginger, ground
- ¼ teaspoon turmeric
- A pinch of cayenne pepper
- 4 salmon fillets, skinless
- Lemon wedges

Directions:
Put the water in a pot, add salt, bring to a boil over medium high heat, add lentils and apricots, stir, simmer for 45 minutes and drain. Heat up a pan with 1 tablespoons oil over medium high heat, add the onion, stir and cook for 8 minutes. Add lentils and apricots, lemon zest, lemon juice, capers, parsley, salt and pepper and stir. In a bowl, mix paprika with cumin, ginger, cinnamon, turmeric, cayenne, salt, pepper and allspice and stir. Rub salmon with this mix and place on a plate. Heat up a pan with the rest of the oil, add salmon, cook for 4 minutes, flip and cook for 3 minutes more. Divide salmon on plates, add lentils mix on the side and serve with lemon wedges. Enjoy!

Nutrition: calories 450, fat 12, fiber 15, carbs 40, protein 42

Black Sea Bass Dish
Preparation time: 10 minutes
Cooking time: 45 minutes
Servings: 4

Ingredients:
- 1 cup water
- 4 medium black sea bass fillets, skin on
- 2 tablespoons olive oil
- 2 teaspoons olive oil
- Salt and black pepper to the taste
- 1 yellow onion, sliced
- 2 red bell peppers, chopped
- 3 garlic cloves, minced
- 15 ounces canned tomatoes, chopped
- 2 bay leaves
- 1 cup white wine
- 1-pint cherry tomatoes, cut in halves
- ¼ cup parsley, chopped

Directions:
Season fish with salt, pepper and 2 teaspoons oil, rub well, place on a plate and leave aside. Heat up a pot with the rest of the oil over medium high heat, add onion, garlic and bell peppers, some salt and pepper, stir and cook for 5 minutes. Add wine, tomatoes, the water and bay leaves, stir, bring to a boil, reduce heat to medium-low and cook for 10 minutes. Add cherry tomatoes, stir and cook for 2 minutes. Add fish fillets, introduce everything in the oven at 350 degrees F and bake for 25 minutes. Take braized fish out of the oven, divide into plates, sprinkle parsley on top and serve. Enjoy!

Nutrition: calories 345, fat 12, fiber 4, carbs 15, protein 16

Delicious Cod Dish

Preparation time: 10 minutes
Cooking time: 15 minutes
Servings: 4

Ingredients:

- 4 cod fillets
- 2 tablespoons oil
- Salt and black pepper to the taste
- 2 ounces pancetta, chopped
- 1 teaspoon thyme, chopped
- 1 yellow onion, chopped
- ½ cup dry white wine
- ¼ teaspoon red pepper flakes, crushed
- 15 ounces canned tomatoes, chopped
- ½ cup green olives, pitted and chopped
- 1 cup artichoke hearts, marinated and chopped

Directions:

Heat up a pan with the oil over medium high heat, add pancetta, stir and cook for 3 minutes. Transfer to a paper towel, drain grease and leave aside for now. Heat up the pan again, add fish, season with salt and pepper to the taste, cook for 4 minutes, flip and transfer to a plate with the seared side up. Add onion, pepper flakes and thyme, stir and cook for 4 minutes. Add wine, stir and cook for 1 minute. Add tomatoes, olives and artichokes, stir and cook for 2 minutes. Reduce heat to medium-low, return fish to pan, cover and cook for 3 minutes. Divide into bowls, sprinkle pancetta all over and serve. Enjoy!

Nutrition: calories 340, fat 3, fiber 2, carbs 13, protein 32

Delicious Roasted Salmon

Preparation time: 10 minutes
Cooking time: 40 minutes
Servings: 4

Ingredients:

- 2 fennel bulbs, sliced into medium wedges
- 3 tablespoons extra virgin olive oil
- 1 small red onion, sliced
- Salt and black pepper to the taste
- 4 salmon fillets, skinless
- ½ cup pistachios, chopped
- ½ cup parsley, chopped
- 1 tablespoon lemon zest, grated
- 1 tablespoon garlic, minced

Directions:

In a bowl, mix fennel and onion with salt, pepper and oil, toss to coat, spread into a baking dish, introduce in the oven at 400 degrees F and bake for 25 minutes. Take veggies out of the oven, add salmon, season fish with salt and pepper, introduce in the oven again and bake for 15 minutes more. In a bowl, mix parsley with garlic, pistachios and lemon zest and stir well. Divide salmon and fennel on plates, top with parsley mixture and serve. Enjoy!

Nutrition: calories 430, fat 13, fiber 8, carbs 22, protein 45

Smoked Trout

Preparation time: 10 minutes
Cooking time: 5 minutes
Servings: 4

Ingredients:

- 12 ounces green beans
- ½ cup sunflower oil
- 2 cucumbers, chopped
- 4 cups cannellini beans, already cooked
- 1 cup black olives, pitted and chopped
- ¼ cup parsley, chopped
- ½ cup sunflower seeds, toasted
- ½ cup red onion, chopped
- 3 tablespoons lemon juice
- ¼ cup dill, chopped
- 3 tablespoons red wine vinegar
- 2 tablespoon marjoram, chopped
- 2 garlic cloves, minced
- 1 tablespoon water
- 1 tablespoon lemon zest, grated
- Salt and black pepper to the taste
- 10 ounces smoked trout fillet, skinless
- 1 cup Greek yogurt

Directions:

Heat up a pan with the oil over medium heat, add green beans and water, stir, cook for 5 minutes, transfer to a bowl and leave aside for 10 minutes. Add cannellini beans, olives, cucumber, onion, sunflower seeds, parsley, lemon juice, dill, vinegar, garlic, lemon zest, marjoram, salt and pepper and stir. Divide this between plates, add smoked trout on top, yogurt, more salt and pepper, toss to coat and serve. Enjoy!

Nutrition: calories 300, fat 12, fiber 8, carbs 21, protein 14

Tasty Swordfish With Creamy Sauce

Preparation time: 10 minutes
Cooking time: 2 hours and 30 minutes
Servings: 6

Ingredients:

- 28 ounces canned tomatoes, chopped
- 1 shallot, chopped
- 1 small fennel bulb, chopped
- 2 tablespoons tomato paste
- 1 tablespoon rosemary
- 1 teaspoon fennel seeds
- Salt and black pepper to the taste
- 1 teaspoon garlic, minced
- ¼ cup heavy cream
- 1 and ½ pounds swordfish steaks

Directions:

In your slow cooker, mix fennel with tomatoes, shallot, tomato paste, fennel seeds, rosemary, garlic, salt and pepper, stir, cover and cook on High for 2 hours. Add fish, season it with salt and pepper, cover it with some of the sauce and cook on High for 30 minutes more. Divide into bowls and serve. Enjoy!

Nutrition: calories 340, fat 14, fiber 5, carbs 15, protein 32

Cod With Tasty Polenta

Preparation time: 10 minutes
Cooking time: 40 minutes
Servings: 4

Ingredients:

- ½ teaspoon lemon zest
- 1 and ½ teaspoons coriander seeds
- 2 tablespoons lemon juice
- 1 lemon cut in wedges
- 1 cup cornmeal
- 4 cod pieces
- 3 ounces butter
- 3 cups water
- Salt and black pepper to the taste
- 2 tablespoons harissa paste
- 2 teaspoons cilantro, chopped

Directions:

Heat up a pan over medium high heat, add coriander seeds, stir and toast for 1 minute. Add the water, lemon zest, salt and pepper and bring to a boil. Add cornmeal, cook for 20 minutes stirring often and take off heat. Heat up another pan with the butter over medium high heat and melt it. Place fish in a baking dish, season with salt and pepper, add harissa, lemon juice and melted butter, stir, introduce in the oven at 400 degrees F and bake for 15 minutes. Take fish out of the oven, divide it between plates, top with cilantro and serve with the polenta you've made at the beginning and with lemon wedges on the side. Enjoy!

Nutrition: calories 450, fat 23, fiber 2, carbs 30, protein 30

Incredible Tuna Steaks

Preparation time: 10 minutes
Cooking time: 6 minutes
Servings: 4

Ingredients:

- 4 tuna steaks, boneless and skinless
- 2 tablespoons extra virgin olive oil
- Salt and black pepper to the taste
- 2 cups cherry tomatoes, yellow and red, cut in halves
- 1 shallot, chopped
- ½ cup green olives, pitted and chopped
- ½ tablespoon lemon juice
- 2 tablespoons basil, chopped

Directions:

Heat up a pan with the oil over medium high heat, add tuna steaks, season with salt and pepper, cook for about 4 minutes and transfer to a platter. Heat up the pan again over medium heat, add shallots, stir and cook for 1 minute. Add olives, tomatoes, basil, lemon juice, salt and pepper to the taste, stir and cook for 2 minutes. Divide this mix into serving plates, add tuna on the side and serve. Enjoy!

Nutrition: calories 300, fat 14, fiber 1, carbs 4, protein 42

Delicious Mahi Mahi

Preparation time: 10 minutes
Cooking time: 20 minutes
Servings: 4

Ingredients:

- 4 mahi-mahi fillets, skinless
- 2 tablespoons olive oil
- 1 yellow onion, chopped
- Salt and black pepper to the taste
- ¾ cup dry white wine
- 1 garlic clove, crushed
- 1 teaspoon oregano, dried
- ½ cup green olives, pitted and chopped
- 14 ounces canned tomatoes, chopped
- 1 tablespoon capers, drained
- ¼ cup parsley, chopped

Directions:

Heat up a pan with 1 tablespoon oil over medium high heat, add fish fillets, season with salt and pepper to the taste, cook for 5 minutes on each side and transfer to a platter. Add the rest of the oil to the pan and heat up over medium heat. Add onion, stir and cook for 3 minutes. Add garlic, stir and cook for 1 minute more. Add oregano and wine, stir, bring to a boil and simmer for 3 minutes. Add tomatoes, olives, capers, salt and pepper, stir, cook for 5 minutes and drizzle over fish. Sprinkle parsley at the end and serve. Enjoy!

Nutrition: calories 300, fat 11, fiber 2, carbs 7, protein 22

Delicious Pan Seared Char

Preparation time: 10 minutes
Cooking time: 15 minutes
Servings: 4

Ingredients:

- 4 red potatoes, sliced
- 4 char fillets
- Salt and black pepper to the taste
- 3 tablespoons olive oil
- ½ cup kalamata olives, pitted
- 2 rosemary sprigs
- 3 tablespoons parsley, chopped
- 4 lemon wedges
- 1 tablespoon balsamic vinegar

Directions:

Put water in a pot, add potatoes and salt, bring to a boil over medium heat, cook for 5 minutes, drain and leave aside. Heat up a pan with 1 and ½ tablespoons oil over medium high heat, add fish, salt and pepper, cook for 3 minutes, flip and cook for 3 more minutes and transfer to a platter. Add the rest of the oil to the pan and heat up over medium high heat as well. Add potatoes and rosemary and cook for 4 minutes. Add olives, salt, pepper, parsley and vinegar, stir gently and cook for 2 minutes more. Add this next to fish and serve with lemon wedges on the side. Enjoy!

Nutrition: calories 340, fat 21, fiber 2, carbs 13, protein 23

Special Salmon

Preparation time: 20 minutes
Cooking time: 10 minutes
Servings: 6

Ingredients:

- 3 tablespoons soft butter
- 3 tablespoons mustard
- 5 teaspoons honey
- ½ cup breadcrumbs
- ½ cup pecans, chopped
- 6 salmon fillets
- 3 teaspoons parsley, chopped
- Salt and pepper to the taste
- 6 lemon wedges

Directions:

In a bowl, mix mustard with honey and butter, stir and leave aside for now. In another bowl, mix pecans with parsley and bread crumbs and stir well. Season salmon fillets with salt and pepper to the taste, place on a baking sheet, brush with mustard mixture and top with breadcrumbs mix. Introduce in the oven at 400 degrees F and bake for 10 minutes per inch. Take out of the oven, transfer to serving plates and serve with lemon wedges. Enjoy!

Nutrition: calories 200, fat 4, fiber 2, carbs 5, protein 12

Glazed Salmon

Preparation time: 20 minutes
Cooking time: 30 minutes
Servings: 4

Ingredients:

- ¼ cup brown sugar
- 1 cup long-grain rice
- 2 tablespoons soy sauce
- 1 broccoli head, florets separated and chopped
- 4 pieces salmon fillets, skinless
- 1 big red onion cut in wedges
- 1 tablespoon olive oil
- Sea salt and black pepper to the taste

Directions:

In a small bowl, mix sugar with soy sauce, stir and leave aside. Cook rice according to instructions, add broccoli and onion during the last 3 minutes, take off heat, leave for 5 minutes, transfer to a platter and keep warm. Meanwhile, place salmon in a baking dish, drizzle olive oil on top, season with salt and pepper, place in preheated broiler over medium heat and cook for about 10 minutes. Add soy mix, stir, divide salmon and rice mix between plates and serve. Enjoy!

Nutrition: calories 200, fat 3, fiber 3, carbs 2, protein 3

Superb Salmon

Preparation time: 10 minutes
Cooking time: 10 minutes
Servings: 4

Ingredients:

- 1 tablespoon rice vinegar
- 1 teaspoon fresh thyme, chopped
- 1 tablespoon ginger, grated
- 4 tablespoons olive oil
- Sea salt and black pepper to the taste
- 2 red onions cut into wedges
- 3 peaches cut into medium wedges
- 4 salmon steaks

Directions:

In a small bowl, combine vinegar with ginger, thyme, 3 tablespoons olive oil, salt and pepper to the taste, stir and leave aside. In another bowl, mix onion with peaches, 1 tablespoon oil, salt and pepper to the taste, stir gently and leave aside. Season salmon with salt and pepper, place on preheated grill over medium heat, and cook for 6 minutes on each side. Transfer salmon to dishes and keep warm. Place peaches and onions on preheated grill over medium heat and cook for 4 minutes on each side. Arrange them on plates next to salmon, drizzle the vinegar mix you've prepared and serve right away! Enjoy!

Nutrition: calories 200, fat 2, fiber 2, carbs 3, protein 2

Simple Salmon Cakes

Preparation time: 10 minutes
Cooking time: 30 minutes
Servings: 4

Ingredients:

- 28 ounces canned pink salmon, drained, skinless and boneless
- 1 and ¼ cup breadcrumbs
- ¼ cup homemade mayonnaise
- 1 big egg, whisked
- 1 tablespoon Worcestershire sauce
- ¼ cup capers, drained
- 1 and ½ teaspoons tarragon, dried
- Sea salt and black pepper to the taste
- 2 cups instant brown rice
- 4 tablespoons olive oil
- 2 tablespoons parsley, chopped
- 1 tablespoon olive oil
- 1 tablespoon lemon juice
- 1 lemon cut in quarters

Directions:

In a bowl, mix canned salmon with mayonnaise, egg, ½ cup bread crumbs, Worcestershire sauce, tarragon, capers, salt and pepper to the taste and stir well. Shape 12 patties, coat in the rest of the breadcrumbs and leave aside for a few minutes. Cook rice according to instructions, remove from heat and keep warm until serving. Heat up a large pan with the olive oil over medium high heat, add patties, cook for 3 minutes on each side, drain excess grease, arrange on serving plates and leave aside. Serve with brown rice and lemon wedges, sprinkle parsley and drizzle olive oil and lemon juice on top. Enjoy!

Nutrition: Calories 142, fat 3, fiber 2, carbs 3, protein 3

Salmon And Black Bean Sauce

Preparation time: 10 minutes
Cooking time: 25 minutes
Servings: 4

Ingredients:
- 1 cup white rice
- 2 tablespoons soy sauce
- ½ cup olive oil
- 2 teaspoons sugar
- 2 teaspoons cornstarch
- 1 and ½ cup chicken stock
- 6 ounces salmon fillets
- 2 garlic cloves, minced
- 1 tablespoon ginger, grated
- 2 tablespoons jarred black bean sauce
- 2 teaspoons white wine vinegar
- ¼ cup radishes, grated
- ¼ cup carrots, grated
- ¼ cup scallions, chopped

Directions:

Cook rice according to instructions, take off heat and keep warm. Meanwhile, in a bowl, mix soy sauce with sugar and ¼ cup oil, whisk and leave aside. In another bowl, mix cornstarch with stock, stir and leave aside. Cut halfway into each salmon fish, place them in a baking dish, pour soy sauce all over and keep in the fridge for 10 minutes. Heat up a pan with the rest of the oil over medium heat, add garlic, ginger and black bean sauce, stir and cook for 3 minutes. Add vinegar, cornstarch mix, stir, bring to a boil, cook for 10 minutes, remove from heat and keep warm. Broil fish for 4 minutes on each side over medium high heat, divide among plates, garnish with rice, the black bean sauce and top with scallions, radishes and carrots. Enjoy!

Nutrition: calories 200, fat 1, fiber 2, carbs 4, protein 3

Smoked Salmon Salad

Preparation time: 10 minutes
Cooking time: 0 minutes
Servings: 6

Ingredients:
- 2 bunches watercress
- 1 pound smoked salmon, flaked
- 2 tablespoons already prepared horseradish
- 2 teaspoons mustard
- ¼ cup lemon juice
- ½ cup sour cream
- Salt and black pepper to the taste
- 1 big cucumber, sliced
- 2 tablespoons dill, chopped
- 1 lemon wedges

Directions:

Arrange salmon on 6 plates and add watercress on the side. In a bowl, mix horseradish with sour cream, mustard, salt, pepper and lemon juice, stir gently and reserve half in a small bowl. Add cucumber to the other half of the dressing and toss to coat. Divide this next to salmon and watercress and sprinkle dill on top. Serve right away with the reserved dressing and lemon wedges. Enjoy!

Nutrition: calories 132, fat 2, fiber 3, carbs 4, protein 3

Salmon And Asparagus Salad

Preparation time: 10 minutes
Cooking time: 10 minutes
Servings: 8

Ingredients:

- 1 pound fresh asparagus, chopped
- ½ cup pecans
- 2 red lettuce heads, torn
- ½ cup peas
- ¼ pound smoked salmon, cut into small chunks
- ¼ cup olive oil
- 1 teaspoon Dijon mustard
- 2 tablespoon lemon juice
- Sea salt and black pepper to the taste

Directions:

Put some water in a pot, bring to a boil over medium heat, add asparagus, cook for 5 minutes, drain and leave aside for now. Heat up a pan over medium heat, add pecans, toast for 5 minutes and take off heat. In a large bowl, mix asparagus with lettuce, pecans, peas and salmon and stir gently. In another bowl, mix olive oil with mustard, salt, pepper and lemon juice, whisk well, add to salad, toss and serve. Enjoy!

Nutrition: calories 253, fat 3, fiber 2, carbs 5, protein 3

Salmon And Avocado Salad

Preparation time: 10 minutes
Cooking time: 20 minutes
Servings: 4

Ingredients:

- 2 medium salmon fillets
- ¼ cup melted butter
- 4 ounces mushrooms, sliced
- Sea salt and black pepper to the taste
- 12 cherry tomatoes, halved
- 2 tablespoons olive oil
- 8 ounces lettuce leaves, torn
- 1 avocado, pitted, peeled and cubed
- 1 jalapeno pepper, chopped
- 5 cilantro sprigs, chopped
- 2 tablespoons white wine vinegar
- 1 ounce feta cheese, crumbled

Directions:

Place salmon on a lined baking sheet, brush with 2 tablespoons melted butter, season with salt and pepper, broil for 15 minutes over medium heat and then keep warm. Meanwhile, heat up a pan with the rest of the butter over medium heat, add mushrooms, stir and cook for a few minutes. Put tomatoes in a bowl, add salt, pepper and 1 tablespoon olive oil and toss to coat. In a salad bowl, mix salmon with mushrooms, lettuce, avocado, tomatoes, jalapeno and cilantro. Add the rest of the oil, vinegar, salt and pepper, sprinkle cheese on top and serve. Enjoy!

Hearty Salmon Salad

Preparation time: 10 minutes
Cooking time: 15 minutes
Servings: 4

Ingredients:

- ¼ cup tomato ketchup
- 2 tablespoon lime juice
- 3 tablespoons teriyaki sauce
- 2 tablespoons olive oil
- 2 tablespoons brown sugar
- 8 cups packed salad greens
- 14 ounces canned salmon, skinless, boneless and flaked
- 1 cup cucumber, sliced
- 1 cup carrot, sliced
- ¼ radish, sliced
- ¼ cup cilantro, chopped
- 1 teaspoon sesame seeds, toasted

Directions:

In a bowl, mix ketchup with teriyaki sauce, lime juice, brown sugar and sesame oil, whisk well and leave aside. Place salad green in a large bowl, add salmon, carrot, cucumber, radish, coriander and stir gently. Add salad dressing, toss to coat and sprinkle sesame seeds on top. Enjoy!

Nutrition: calories 253, fat 3, fiber 2, carbs 5, protein 4

Salmon And Greek Yogurt Sauce

Preparation time: 10 minutes
Cooking time: 20 minutes
Servings: 2

Ingredients:

- 2 medium salmon fillets
- 1 tablespoon basil, chopped
- 6 lemon slices
- Sea salt and black pepper to the taste
- 1 cup Greek yogurt
- 2 teaspoons curry powder
- A pinch of cayenne pepper
- 1 garlic clove, minced
- ½ teaspoon cilantro, chopped
- ½ teaspoon mint, chopped

Directions:

Place each salmon fillet on a parchment paper piece, do 3 splits in each and stuff them with basil. Season with salt and pepper, top each fillet with 3 lemon slices, fold parchment, seal edges, introduce in the oven at 400 degrees F and bake for 20 minutes. Meanwhile, in a bowl, mix yogurt with cayenne pepper, salt to the taste, garlic, curry, mint and cilantro and whisk well. Transfer fish to plates, drizzle the yogurt sauce you've just prepared on top and serve right away! Enjoy!

Nutrition: calories 242, fat 1, fiber 2, carbs 3, protein 3

Salmon And Tahini Sauce

Preparation time: 20 minutes
Cooking time: 10 minutes
Servings: 4

Ingredients:

- ½ cup couscous
- 1 and ½ cups water
- 1 tablespoon olive oil
- 4 salmon fillets, skinless and boneless
- 4 tablespoons tahini paste
- Juice of 1 lemon
- 1 lemon, cut into wedges
- ½ cucumber, chopped
- Seeds from 1 pomegranate
- A small bunch of parsley, chopped

Directions:

Put couscous in a bowl, add water, cover and leave aside for 8 minutes. Meanwhile, heat up a pan with the oil over medium heat, add salmon, cook for 5 minutes on one side, flip, cook for 2 more minutes, remove from heat and leave aside. In a bowl, mix tahini with lemon juice and a splash of water and whisk well. Drain couscous, add cucumber, parsley and pomegranate seeds and toss to coat. Divide salmon between plates and serve with couscous, lemon wedges on the side and tahini sauce on top. Enjoy!

Nutrition: calories 254, fat 3, fiber 1, carbs 3, protein 4

Flavored Salmon

Preparation time: 10 minutes
Cooking time: 30 minutes
Servings: 6

Ingredients:

- 2 cups whole bread croutons
- 3 red onions, cut into wedges
- ¾ cup green olives, pitted
- 3 red bell peppers, cut into 6 pieces
- ½ teaspoon smoked paprika
- Salt and black pepper to the taste
- 5 tablespoons olive oil
- 6 -6 ounces salmon fillets, skinless and boneless
- 2 tablespoons parsley, chopped

Directions:

Spread croutons, peppers, onions and olives on a lined baking sheet, add smoked paprika, salt, pepper and 3 tablespoons olive oil, toss to coat, introduce in the oven at 375 degrees F, bake for 15 minutes and leave aside for now. Rub salmon fillets with the rest of the olive oil, a place among croutons, introduce in the oven again and bake for 12 more minutes. Take salmon out of the oven, divide everything between plates, sprinkle parsley on top and serve. Enjoy!

Nutrition: calories 321, fat 2, fiber 3, carbs 5, protein 8

Green Tea Salmon

Preparation time: 10 minutes
Cooking time: 25 minutes
Servings: 2

Ingredients:

- ½ cup basmati rice
- 2 medium salmon fillets, skinless and boneless
- Salt and pepper to the taste
- 1 green tea bag
- 2 teaspoons olive oil
- 1 garlic clove, minced
- 12 ounces mixed salad veggies (chopped carrots, tomato, cucumber)
- 1 small mango, peeled and chopped
- 1 red chili, chopped
- 1 small piece ginger, grated
- Juice from 1 lime
- 1 teaspoon sesame seeds
- A splash of soy sauce

Directions:

Cook rice according to instructions, drain and leave aside. Season salmon fillets with salt and pepper to the taste, sprinkle tea bag and rub them with oil and with garlic slices. Place on a lined baking sheet, introduce in the oven at 350 degrees F and bake for 25 minutes. Place mixed veggies in a bowl, add mango, lime juice and soy sauce and toss to coat. Add chili and mix gently again. Heat up a pan with 1 teaspoon oil over medium high heat, add garlic and cook for 2 minutes. Add rice, stir and take off heat. Arrange veggie salad on plates, add salmon and rice and serve. Enjoy!

Nutrition: calories 200, fat 3, fiber 3, carbs 2, protein 2

Salmon And Olives Sauce

Preparation time: 10 minutes
Cooking time: 15 minutes
Servings: 4

Ingredients:

- 4 medium salmon fillets, skinless and boneless
- 1 fennel bulb, chopped
- Salt and black pepper to the taste
- ¼ cup dry white wine
- ¼ cup water
- 1 cup Greek yogurt
- ¼ cup green olives pitted and chopped
- ¼ cup fresh chives, chopped
- 1 tablespoon olive oil
- 1 tablespoon lemon juice

Directions:

Arrange the fennel in a baking dish, add salmon fillets, season with salt and black pepper, add wine and water, introduce in the microwave and cook on High for 8 minutes. Drain excess grease, arrange on a platter and leave aside for now. In a bowl, mix yogurt with chives, olives, lemon juice, olive oil, salt and black pepper and whisk well. Transfer salmon to plates, top with the baked fennel and pour olives and yogurt sauce on top. Enjoy!

Nutrition: calories 342, fat 2, fiber 2, carbs 2, protein 3

Creamy Salmon

Preparation time: 10 minutes
Cooking time: 10 minutes
Servings: 6

Ingredients:

- 1 tablespoon lemon zest
- 1 tablespoon lemon juice
- 1 lemon cut in wedges
- Salt and black pepper to the taste
- 1 cup low fat cream
- 1 pound asparagus
- 18 ounces fresh fettuccine
- Water for boiling
- 20 ounces salmon, skinless and boneless
- 1 ounce parmesan cheese, grated

Directions:

Put water in a pot, add a pinch of salt, bring to a boil over medium heat, add asparagus and cook for 1 minute. Add pasta and cook according to instructions. Drain pasta and asparagus and reserve cooking liquid. Heat up the pot with the water again over medium heat, add salmon, cook for 5 minutes and also drain. In a bowl, mix lemon peel with cream and lemon juice, whisk well and leave aside Heat up a pan over medium high heat, add pasta, asparagus, cream mix, salt and pepper, cook for 1 more minute, divide between plates, add salmon on top and serve with grated parmesan and lemon wedges. Enjoy!

Nutrition: calories 354, fat 2, fiber 2, carbs 2, protein 4

Amazing Salmon

Preparation time: 10 minutes
Cooking time: 20 minutes
Servings: 4

Ingredients:

- 4 medium salmon fillets, skinless and boneless
- 1 tablespoon olive oil
- 8 ounces canned tomatoes, chopped with ¼ cup juice reserved
- 1 yellow onion, chopped
- ¼ cup kalamata olives, pitted and chopped
- 1 tablespoon capers
- 3 zucchinis, sliced
- 2 tablespoons water
- 1 tablespoon lemon juice
- Salt and black pepper to the taste

Directions:

Heat up a pan with the oil over medium high heat, season salmon with salt and pepper to the taste, add it to the pan, cook for 3 minutes on each side and transfer to a plate. Heat up the same pan over medium heat, add onion, stir and cook for 5 minutes stirring all the time. Add tomatoes, reserved tomato juice, bring to a boil and cook for 2 minutes. Add olives and capers, toss to coat and keep warm until serving as well. Place zucchini slices in a microwave-safe bowl, add the water, cover and cook in your microwave on High for 5 minutes. Dain water, add lemon juice and stir gently. Divide salmon on plates, add tomato, capers and olives sauce and the zucchini slices on the side. Enjoy!

Nutrition: calories 275, fat 2, fiber 2, carbs 1, protein 3

Salmon And Brussels Sprouts Delight

Preparation time: 10 minutes
Cooking time: 20 minutes
Servings: 6

Ingredients:

- 2 tablespoons brown sugar
- 1 teaspoon onion powder
- 1 teaspoon garlic powder
- 1 teaspoon smoked paprika
- 3 tablespoons olive oil
- 1 and ¼ pounds Brussels sprouts, halved
- 10 medium salmon fillets
- Chopped chives for serving

Directions:

In a bowl, mix sugar with onion powder, garlic powder, smoked paprika and 2 tablespoon olive oil and whisk well. Spread Brussels sprouts on a lined baking sheet, drizzle the rest of the olive oil, toss to coat, season with salt and pepper, introduce in the oven at 450 degrees F and bake for 5 minutes. Arrange salmon fillets on another lined baking sheet, season with salt, brush with sugar mix you've prepared, introduce in the oven next to Brussels sprouts and bake for 15 minutes. Transfer salmon and sprouts to plates, sprinkle chives on top and serve right away! Enjoy!

Nutrition: calories 312, fat 3, fiber 3, carbs 5, protein 4

Special Salmon

Preparation time: 10 minutes
Cooking time: 25 minutes
Servings: 4

Ingredients:

- 1 pound medium beets, sliced
- 6 tablespoons olive oil
- 1 and ½ pounds salmon fillets, skinless and boneless
- Salt and pepper to the taste
- 1 tablespoon chives, chopped
- 1 tablespoon parsley, chopped
- 1 tablespoon fresh tarragon, chopped
- 3 tablespoon shallots, chopped
- 1 tablespoon grated lemon zest
- ¼ cup lemon juice
- 4 cups mixed baby greens

Directions:

In a bowl, mix beets with ½ tablespoon oil and toss to coat. Season them with salt and pepper, arrange them on a baking sheet, introduce in the oven at 450 degrees F and bake for 20 minutes. Take beets out of the oven, add salmon on top, brush it with the rest of the oil and season with salt and pepper. In a bowl, mix chives with parsley and tarragon and sprinkle 1 tablespoon of this mix over salmon. Introduce in the oven again and bake for 15 minutes. Meanwhile, in a bowl with shallots with lemon peel, salt, pepper and lemon juice and the rest of the herbs mixture and stir gently. Combine 2 tablespoons of shallots dressing with mixed greens and toss gently. Take salmon out of the oven, arrange on plates, add beets and greens on the side, drizzle the rest of the shallot dressing on top and serve right away. Enjoy!

Nutrition: calories 312, fat 2, fiber 2, carbs 2, protein 4

Healthy Halibut Dish

Preparation time: 10 minutes
Cooking time: 10 minutes
Servings: 4

Ingredients:

- 4 halibut fillets, skinless
- 1 eggplant, cut into rounds
- 2 tablespoons soy sauce
- 2 tablespoons olive oil
- Salt and black pepper to the taste
- 1 teaspoon ginger, grated
- 2 tablespoons rice vinegar
- ½ cup cilantro, chopped
- 1 jalapeno chili, sliced

Directions:

In a bowl, mix oil with 1 tablespoon soy sauce and stir well. Brush eggplant rounds with this mix and add salt and pepper to the taste. Brush your kitchen grill with some oil, heat up over medium high heat, add eggplant slices and halibut and cook them all for 5 minutes on each side. Meanwhile, in a bowl, mix ginger with vinegar, the rest of the soy sauce, cilantro and jalapeno and stir well. Divide eggplant slices and halibut on serving plates, drizzle the vinegar mix on top and serve them. Enjoy!

Nutrition: calories 200, fat 4, fiber 4, carbs 6, protein 12

Salmon And Amazing Sweet Potatoes

Preparation time: 10 minutes
Cooking time: 25 minutes
Servings: 4

Ingredients:

- 2 lemongrass stalks, tender parts finely chopped
- 1 sweet potato, sliced
- 2 garlic cloves, minced
- 1 inch ginger, chopped
- 1 teaspoon olive oil
- ½ cup vegetable stock
- ½ cup coconut milk
- lime leaves
- 1 red chili, chopped
- 4 medium salmon fillets
- Soy sauce to the taste

Directions:

Arrange potato slices in a roasting pan. In a bowl, mix sesame oil with stock, lemongrass, garlic, ginger and chili and stir well. Pour this over potatoes and toss to coat. Add lime leaves, introduce pan in the oven at 374 degrees F and bake for 15 minutes. Take potatoes out of the oven, add salmon fillets and bake for 10 more minutes. Drizzle soy sauce over salmon and potatoes and serve! Enjoy!

Nutrition: calories 170, fat 5, fiber 3, carbs 8, protein 12

Delicious Shrimp

Preparation time: 10 minutes
Cooking time: 15 minutes
Servings: 4
Ingredients:

- 2 carrots, cut into matchsticks
- ½ cucumber, cut into matchsticks
- ½ cup snow peas finely, sliced
- 7 ounces broccoli florets
- Juice from 2 limes
- 1 lime cut in wedges

For the sauce:

- 2-inch ginger piece, chopped
- 3 garlic cloves, sliced
- 2 spring onions, sliced
- 2 tablespoons hot chili sauce

- 2 tablespoons sesame seeds
- ½ tablespoon olive oil
- 16 big shrimp
- 1 red chili, chopped
- 2 spring onions, sliced
- 1 bunch coriander, chopped

- 1 cup apple juice
- 1 tablespoon sweet miso
- 2 tablespoon honey

Directions:

Heat up a pan over medium temperature, add 3 garlic cloves and 2-inch ginger piece, stir and for 1-2 minutes. Add 2 spring onions, hot chili sauce, the apple juice, miso and honey, stir well, cook for 3 minutes, take off heat and keep warm. Heat up a pan with the oil over medium heat, add broccoli, carrot, cucumber and snow peas, stir and cook for 2 minutes. Add 3 tablespoons sauce you've made and lime juice, stir and cook for 2 more minutes. Add 2 spring onions, coriander and red chili , stir and cook for 1-2 minutes. Meanwhile, heat up another pan over medium high heat, add sesame seeds and toast them for 2 minutes. Heat up the third pan with a drizzle of oil, add shrimp and cook for 2 minutes on each side. Transfer veggies mix on plates, add shrimp and sesame seeds on top and drizzle the rest of the sauce over them! Add lime wedges on the side and serve! Enjoy!

Nutrition: calories 190, fat 5, fiber 5, carbs 10, protein 14

Simple Shrimp

Preparation time: 10 minutes
Cooking time: 15 minutes
Servings: 4

Ingredients:

- 1 pound shrimp, deveined and peeled
- 2 teaspoons extra virgin olive oil
- 6 tablespoons lemon juice
- 3 tablespoons dill, chopped
- 1 tablespoon oregano, chopped
- 2 garlic cloves, chopped
- Salt and black pepper to the taste

- ¾ cup Greek yogurt
- ½ pounds cherry tomatoes
- 2 cucumbers, sliced
- 4 whole wheat flatbreads
- 1 red onion, sliced
- lettuce leaves

Directions:

Pat dry shrimp, put in a bowl and mix with 2 tablespoons lemon juice, 1 tablespoon dill, 1 tablespoon oregano and 1 teaspoon oil. Stir, cover and leave aside for 10 minutes. Meanwhile, in another bowl, mix ¼ cup yogurt with 1 tablespoon dill, half of the garlic, 2 tablespoons lemon juice, cucumber, salt and pepper and toss. In another bowl, mix ½ cup yogurt with the rest of the lemon juice, the rest of the garlic and the rest of the dill and whisk well. In a bowl, mix tomatoes with onion and 1 teaspoon olive oil in a bowl. Heat up your kitchen grill over medium high heat, grill tomatoes and shrimp for 5 minutes, divide between plates, add cucumber salad, onions, tomatoes, shrimp and lettuce leaves on top and serve. Enjoy!

Nutrition: calories 353, fat 6, fiber 6, carbs 10, protein 31

Hash

Preparation time: 10 minutes
Cooking time: 10 minutes
Servings: 4

Ingredients:

- 1 and ½ pounds potatoes, chopped
- 1 tablespoon olive oil
- 4 ounces smoked salmon, chopped
- 1 tablespoon chives, chopped
- 2 teaspoons already prepared horseradish
- ¼ cup sour cream
- Salt and black pepper to the taste

Directions:

Heat up a pan with the oil over medium heat, add potatoes and cook until they are tender enough and take off heat. In a bowl, mix sour cream with salt, pepper, horseradish and chives and stir well. Mix salmon with potatoes, add cream mix, toss to coat and serve right away. Enjoy!

Nutrition: calories 233, fat 6, fiber 5, carbs 9, protein 12

Cod With Capers Sauce

Preparation time: 10 minutes
Cooking time: 15 minutes
Servings: 4

Ingredients:

- 4 medium cod fillets, skinless and boneless
- 2 tablespoons mustard
- 1 tablespoon tarragon, chopped
- 1 tablespoon capers, drained
- 4 tablespoons olive oil+ 1 teaspoon
- Salt and black pepper to the taste
- 2 cups lettuce leaves, torn
- 1 small red onion, sliced
- 1 small cucumber, sliced
- 2 tablespoons lemon juice
- 2 tablespoons water

Directions:

In a bowl, mix mustard with 2 tablespoons olive oil, tarragon, capers and water, whisk well and leave aside. Heat up a pan with 1 teaspoon oil over medium high heat, season fish with salt and pepper to the taste, add to pan and cook for 6 minutes on each side. In a bowl, mix cucumber with onion, lettuce, lemon juice, 2 tablespoons olive oil, salt and pepper to the taste. Take cod off heat, arrange on plates, drizzle mustard sauce you've made and serve with the cucumber salad on the side. Enjoy!

- **Nutrition:** calories 278, fat 12, fiber 1, carbs 5, protein 28

Mediterranean Shrimp Dip

Preparation time: 10 minutes
Cooking time: 30 minutes
Servings: 20

Ingredients:

- ounces cream cheese, soft
- ½ pound shrimp, already cooked, peeled, deveined and chopped
- 1 cup mayonnaise
- ½ cup mozzarella cheese, shredded
- 3 garlic cloves, minced
- 1 tablespoon Worcestershire sauce
- ¼ teaspoon hot sauce
- 1 tablespoon lemon juice
- Olive oil spray
- ½ cup scallions, finely sliced

Directions:

In a bowl, mix cream cheese with mozzarella, mayo, Worcestershire sauce, hot sauce, garlic and lemon juice and whisk well. Add scallions and shrimp, stir again, pour everything into a baking dish which you've sprayed with some olive oil, introduce in the oven at 350 degrees F and bake for 30 minutes. Transfer dip to bowls and serve. Enjoy!

Nutrition: calories 175, fat 3, fiber 2, carbs 2, protein 3

Crab Dip

Preparation time: 10 minutes
Cooking time: 30 minutes
Servings: 10

Ingredients:

- ½ pound crab meat, flaked
- ounces cream cheese, soft
- 1 tablespoon dill, chopped
- 1 teaspoon lemon juice

Directions:

In a bowl, mix crab meat with dill, cream cheese and lemon juice and stir well. Pour this into a baking dish, introduce in the oven at 350 degrees F and bake for 30 minutes. Transfer to a bowl and serve right away. Enjoy!

Nutrition: calories 321, fat 2, fiber 3, carbs 5, protein 4

Smoked Salmon Dip

Preparation time: 1 hour and 5 minutes
Cooking time: 0 minutes
Servings: 8

Ingredients:

- 2 ounces goat cheese
- 4 ounces cream cheese
- 3 tablespoons beet horseradish, already prepared
- 1 pound smoked salmon, skinless, boneless and flaked
- 2 teaspoons lemon zest, grated
- 2 radishes, chopped
- ½ cup capers, drained and chopped
- 1/3 cup red onion, chopped
- 3 tablespoons chives, chopped

Directions:

In your food processor, mix cream cheese with horseradish, goat cheese and lemon zest and blend very well. Spread 1/3 salmon on the bottom of a lined spring form pan, press well, add half the cheese mixture and spread evenly. In a bowl, mix onion with radishes, stir and spread over cream mix in the pan. Layer half of the remaining salmon and sprinkle the capers. Spread the rest of the cheese mix and top the rest of the salmon. Cover this and keep in the fridge for 1 hour. Transfer to a plate by removing the ring mold, top dip with chives and serve. Enjoy!

Nutrition: calories 254, fat 2, fiber 1, carbs 2, protein 2

Smoked Trout Dip

Preparation time: 6 minutes
Cooking time: 0 minutes
Servings: 8

Ingredients:

- 4 ounces smoked trout, skinless, boneless and flaked
- ¼ cup sour cream
- 1 tablespoon lemon juice
- 1/3 cup Greek yogurt
- 1 and ½ tablespoon dill, chopped
- 3 tablespoons chives, chopped
- Salt and black pepper to the taste
- A drizzle of olive oil

Directions:

In a bowl mix trout with yogurt, sour cream, salt, pepper to the taste, chives, lemon juice and 1 tablespoon dill and stir well. Drizzle some olive oil at the end and sprinkle the rest of the dill before serving! Enjoy!

Nutrition: calories 254, fat 2, fiber 2, carbs 2, protein 3

Anchovy Dip

Preparation time: 5 minutes
Cooking time: 0 minutes
Servings: 6

Ingredients:

- 8 ounces anchovies in oil, drained
- 1 tablespoon red wine vinegar
- ½ cup olive oil
- 2 garlic cloves, minced

Directions:

In your food processor, mix anchovies with garlic and mix until you obtain a paste. Transfer to a bowl, add olive oil gradually stirring all the time and the vinegar at the end. Stir again well and serve right away! Enjoy!

Nutrition: calories 200, fat 2, fiber 3, carbs 2, protein 3

Roasted Salmon And Tomatoes

Preparation time: 10 minutes
Cooking time: 20 minutes
Servings: 4

Ingredients:

- 1-pint grape tomatoes, halved
- 2 tablespoon olive oil
- Salt and black pepper to the taste
- 3 anchovy fillets
- ½ cup kalamata olives, pitted
- 1 pound green beans
- 2 garlic cloves, minced
- 1 salmon fillet, skinless

Directions:

Spread tomatoes, garlic, beans, olives and anchovies on a lined baking sheet, sprinkle pepper and 1 tablespoon oil, toss, introduce in the oven at 425 degrees F and roast for 15 minutes. Heat up a pan with the rest of the oil over medium high heat, add salmon, season with salt and pepper to the taste and cook for 5 minutes on each side. Transfer salmon to a platter, add roasted veggies on the side and serve. Enjoy!

Nutrition: calories 200, fat 2, fiber 3, carbs 5, protein 4

Shrimp Salad

Preparation time: 15 minutes
Cooking time: 0 minutes
Servings: 5

Ingredients:

- 3 tablespoons Dijon mustard
- 3 tablespoons white wine vinegar
- 3 tablespoons white sugar
- 6 tablespoons homemade mayonnaise
- 4 cucumbers, peeled and cubed
- 1 mango, peeled and cubed
- 3 tablespoons dill, finely chopped
- 1 pound shrimp, peeled, deveined and already cooked
- Some hot pepper sauce
- lettuce leaves
- Salt to the taste

Directions:

In a bowl, mix sugar with vinegar and stir well. Add mayo and mustard, stir well again and keep in the fridge for now. In a salad bowl, mix cucumbers with shrimp, dill and mango. Add salt and hot pepper sauce and stir. Also add dressing you've made and toss to coat. Divide lettuce leaves on serving plates, add cucumber and shrimp salad on top and serve. Enjoy!

Nutrition: calories 174, fat 3, fiber 2, carbs 4

Special Salmon Tartar

Preparation time: 10 minutes
Cooking time: 0 minutes
Servings: 4

Ingredients:

- 2 tablespoons scallions, chopped
- 2 tablespoons sweet onion, chopped
- 1 and ½ teaspoons lime juice
- 1 tablespoon chives, minced
- 1 teaspoon sesame oil
- 1 tablespoon olive oil
- 2 tablespoons pressed caviar
- ½ pound salmon, skinless and diced
- cherry tomatoes, halved
- Salt and black pepper to the taste
- 12 parsley sprigs

Directions:

Put the onion in a bowl and mix with scallions, lime juice, chives, sesame oil and 1 tablespoon olive oil and whisk. Roll out caviar, dice it and add to onions mix. Add salt and pepper to the taste and salmon and toss everything to coat. Arrange tartar on serving plates, drizzle some olive oil over them, top with parsley sprigs and cherry tomatoes and serve. Enjoy!

Nutrition: calories 200, fat 1, fiber 3, carbs 6, protein 6

Salmon Salad

Preparation time: 10 minutes
Cooking time: 10 minutes
Servings: 4
Ingredients:
For the salad dressing:

- 3 tablespoons balsamic vinegar
- tablespoons olive oil
- 1/3 cup kalamata olives, pitted and minced
- 1 garlic clove crushed and finely chopped

For the salad:

- ½ pound green beans, chopped
- ¾ pound small red potatoes, cut into quarters
- ½ pound cherry tomatoes, halved
- Salt and black pepper to the taste
- ½ fennel bulb, sliced
- Salt and black pepper to the taste
- ½ teaspoons red pepper flakes, crushed
- ½ teaspoon lemon zest, grated
- ½ red onion, sliced
- 2 cups baby arugula
- ¾ pound cedar planked salmon, skinless, boneless and cut into 4 pieces

Directions:

In a bowl, mix vinegar with garlic, olives, oil, red pepper flakes, lemon zest, salt and pepper to the taste, whisk very well and leave aside for now. Put potatoes in a pot, add water to cover, add salt, bring to a boil over medium high heat, cook for 5 minutes, drain, reserve liquid and put in a bowl. Mix potatoes with 2 tablespoons salad dressing, add salt and pepper to the taste, toss to coat and leave aside for now. Return reserved water to heat, bring to a boil over medium heat, add green beans, blanch for 2 minutes, drain and put them in a bowl filled with ice water. Drain beans again and add them potatoes. Also add onion, tomatoes, fennel and stir. Add almost all the dressing, more salt and pepper, the arugula and toss everything to coat. Transfer salad to a platter, add salmon on top, drizzle the rest of the salad dressing and serve right away. Enjoy!

Nutrition: calories 312, fat 3, fiber 3, carbs 6, protein 4

Mediterranean Shrimp

Preparation time: 10 minutes
Cooking time: 30 minutes
Servings: 4
Ingredients:

- 1 teaspoon lemon juice
- Salt and black pepper to the taste
- ½ cup mayo
- ½ teaspoon paprika
- A pinch of cayenne pepper
- 3 tablespoons olive oil
- 1 fennel bulb, chopped
- 1 yellow onion, chopped
- 3 thin strips orange zest
- garlic cloves, minced
- A pinch of cloves, ground
- ½ cup dry white wine
- 1 cup clam juice
- 1 cup water
- 1 cup canned tomatoes chopped
- 1 and ½ pounds big shrimp, peeled and deveined
- ¼ teaspoon saffron crumbled

Directions:

Put 2 garlic cloves in a bowl, add salt and stir very well. Add lemon juice, mayo, cayenne and black pepper and paprika and stir well again. Add 1 tablespoon oil, whisk and leave aside for now. Heat up a pan with the rest of the oil over medium high heat, add onion and fennel, stir and cook for 7 minutes. Add 4 garlic cloves, ground cloves and orange zest, stir and cook 1 minute. Add wine, stir and cook for 5 more minutes. Add clam juice, saffron, tomatoes and 1 cup water, bring to a boil, add salt and pepper and simmer for 10 minutes. Add shrimp, stir gently and simmer for 4 more minutes. Discard orange zest, stir gently the whole mix, divide between plates and serve. Enjoy!

Nutrition: calories 310, fat 2, fiber 1, carbs 3, protein 4

Crab Gazpacho

Preparation time: 4 hours and 10 minutes
Cooking time: 0 minutes
Servings: 4

Ingredients:

- ¼ cup basil, chopped
- 2 pounds tomatoes
- 5 cups watermelon, cubed
- ¼ cup red wine vinegar
- 1/3 cup olive oil
- 2 garlic cloves, minced
- 1 zucchini, chopped
- Salt and black pepper to the taste
- 1 cup crabmeat

Directions:

In your food processor, mix tomatoes with basil, vinegar, 4 cups watermelon, garlic, 1/3 cup oil salt and black pepper to the taste and pulse very well. Pour this into a bowl, cover and keep in the fridge for 4 hours. Divide soup into bowls, top with the rest of the watermelon, zucchini, crab and basil and serve. Enjoy!

Nutrition: calories 231, fat 3, fiber 3, carbs 6, protein 6

Wonderful Shrimp

Preparation time: 10 minutes
Cooking time: 30 minutes
Servings: 4

Ingredients:

- 1 pound shrimp, peeled and deveined
- Salt and black pepper to the taste
- 3 garlic cloves, minced
- 1 tablespoon olive oil
- ½ teaspoon oregano, dried
- 1 yellow onion, chopped
- 2 cups chicken stock
- 2 ounces orzo
- ½ cup water
- 4 ounces canned tomatoes, chopped
- Juice of 1 lemon
- ¼ cup parmesan, grated
- ½ cup peas

Directions:

Put shrimp in a bowl, mix with salt and pepper to the taste and leave aside for now. Heat up a pan with the oil over medium high heat, add onion, garlic and oregano, stir and cook for 4 minutes. Add orzo, stir and cook for 2 more minutes. Add stock and ½ cup water, bring to a boil, cover, reduce heat to low and cook for 12 minutes. Add peas, lemon juice, tomatoes and shrimp and stir gently. Sprinkle parmesan on top, introduce in the oven at 400 degrees F and bake for 14 minutes. Take out of the oven and serve right away. Enjoy!

Nutrition: calories 298, fat 4, fiber 3, carbs 7, protein 8

Shrimp Delight

Preparation time: 1 hour
Cooking time: 25 minutes
Servings: 24

Ingredients:

- 24 medium shrimp, cooked, peeled and deveined
- 24 baguette slices, toasted
- ½ cup raisins
- 4 cups yellow onion, chopped
- 2 tablespoons olive oil
- 2 tablespoons capers, chopped
- 2 tablespoons dill, chopped
- Salt and black pepper to the taste

Directions:

Place raisins in a bowl, cover with boiling water and leave aside for 30 minutes. Meanwhile, heat up a large pan with the oil over medium high heat, add onions, stir and cook for 10 minutes. Cover the pan and cook for another 10-15 minutes. Drain raisins, chop, add to onions and stir well. Also add capers, salt, pepper and dill, stir and cook for 6 minutes more Transfer this mixture to a bowl and leave aside for 20-30 minutes. Scoop this mixture on each baguette slice, add 1 shrimp on each and serve right away. Enjoy!

Nutrition: calories 200, fat 2, fiber 2, carbs 6, protein 4

Sardines Appetizer

Preparation time: 10 minutes
Cooking time: 15 minutes
Servings: 12

Ingredients:

- 4 ounces canned and smoked sardines in olive oil, skinless, boneless and crushed
- 2 teaspoons olive oil
- 2 tablespoons mint, chopped
- Salt to the taste
- slices whole grain baguette
- 1 small tomato, chopped
- 1 tablespoon yellow onion, sliced

Directions:

In a bowl, mix sardines with olive oil, salt and mint and stir well. Cut each slice of bread into 4 triangles, place them all on a lined baking sheet, introduce in the oven at 350 degrees F and bake for 15 minutes. Divide tomato pieces on each, add 1 and ½ teaspoons of sardines mixture on and top with onion slices. Enjoy!

Nutrition: calories 200, fat 3, fiber 1, carbs 5, protein 5

Salmon Rolls

Preparation time: 15 minutes
Cooking time: 0 minutes
Servings: 16

Ingredients:

- 8 slices smoked salmon
- 1 cup cream cheese,
- 1 and ½ teaspoons lemon rind, grated
- 3 teaspoons dill, chopped
- 3 ounces Greek style crepes
- 1 small red onion, sliced
- Salt and pepper to the taste

Directions:

In a bowl, mix cream cheese with lemon rind, dill, salt and pepper and whisk. Place 1 crepe on a working surface, spread 1 tablespoon cream mixture, add 1 slice salmon, add some sliced onion, roll, cut in half and secure with a toothpick. Repeat this with the rest of the crepes, arrange on a platter and serve. Enjoy!

Nutrition: calories 200, fat 3, fiber 3, carbs 6, protein 3

Scallops Appetizer

Preparation time: 10 minutes
Cooking time: 6 minutes
Servings: 12

Ingredients:

- 2 pounds scallops
- 1 pound prosciutto, sliced and then cut into halves lengthwise
- A drizzle of olive oil
- 2 lemons, cut in wedges
- Salt and black pepper to the taste

Directions:

Wrap each scallop in a prosciutto slice, sprinkle salt and pepper, drizzle some oil, place on preheated grill over medium high heat, cook for 3 minutes on each side and transfer them all to a platter. Serve right away with the rest of the lemon wedges. Enjoy!

Nutrition: calories 173, fat 2, fiber 5, carbs 4, protein 7

Crazy Mediterranean Mussels

Preparation time: 10 minutes
Cooking time: 30 minutes
Servings: 4

Ingredients:
- 3 tablespoons olive oil
- 2 pounds mussels, scrubbed
- 4 ounces dried chorizo, chopped
- Salt and black pepper to the taste
- 3 cups canned tomatoes, crushed
- 1 big shallot, chopped
- 2 garlic cloves, minced
- ¼ teaspoon red pepper flakes, crushed
- 2 cups dry white wine
- 1/3 cup parsley, chopped

Directions:

Heat up a large pan with the olive oil over medium high heat, add shallot, stir and cook for 3 minutes. Add garlic, red pepper flakes and cook for another 3 minutes. Add wine, bring to a boil, add crushed tomatoes and chorizo, stir and cook for 15 minutes. Add salt and pepper to the taste and stir again. Add mussels, cover the pan and boil for another 10 minutes. Add parsley at the end, stir and serve right away as an appetizer. Enjoy!

Nutrition: calories 210, fat 2, fiber 3, carbs 5, protein 6

Scallops Salad

Preparation time: 15 minutes
Cooking time: 35 minutes
Servings: 6

Ingredients:
- 12 ounces dry sea scallops
- 4 tablespoons olive oil+ 2 teaspoons
- 4 teaspoons soy sauce
- 1 and ½ cup quinoa, rinsed
- 2 teaspoons garlic, minced
- A pinch of salt
- 3 cups water
- 1 cup snow peas, sliced
- 1 teaspoon sesame oil
- 1/3 cup rice vinegar
- 1 cup scallions, sliced
- 1/3 cup red bell pepper, chopped
- ¼ cup cilantro, chopped

Directions:

In a bowl, mix scallops with 2 teaspoons soy sauce, toss and leave aside for now. Heat up a pan with 1 tablespoon olive oil over medium heat, add quinoa, stir and cook for 8 minutes. Add garlic, stir and cook for 1 more minute. Add water and a pinch of salt, bring to a boil, stir, cover and cook for 15 minutes. Add snow peas, cover and leave for 5 more minutes. Meanwhile, in a bowl, mix 3 tablespoons olive oil with 2 teaspoons soy sauce, vinegar and sesame oil and whisk well. Add quinoa and snow peas to this mixture and stir again. Add scallions, bell pepper and stir again. Pat dry the scallions and discard marinade. Heat up another pan with 2 teaspoons olive oil over medium high heat, add scallions and cook for 1 minute on each side. Add scallops to quinoa salad, stir gently and serve with chopped cilantro on top. Enjoy!

Nutrition: calories 201, fat 5, fiber 2, carbs 5, protein 8

Kale And Salmon Salad

Preparation time: 7 minutes
Cooking time: 18 minutes
Servings: 4

Ingredients:

- 2/3 cup cider vinegar+ 2 tablespoons
- ½ cup water
- 1 cup red onion, sliced
- 1 tablespoon honey
- 4 golden beets, trimmed
- 2 tablespoons olive oil
- Salt and black pepper to the taste
- 1 teaspoon, mustard
- 4 cups curly kale,
- 10 ounces canned salmon, skinless, boneless and drained
- ¼ cup almonds, toasted

Directions:

In a small pan, mix 2/3 cup vinegar with ½ cup water and 2 teaspoons honey, stir and bring to a boil over medium heat. Add onion, boil for 1 more minute and leave aside for 10 minutes and drain. Wrap beets in parchment paper pieces and introduce in the microwave for 7 minutes. Peel, cut beets in wedges and leave aside. In a bowl, mix 2 tablespoons vinegar with 1 teaspoon honey, oil, mustard, salt and pepper to the taste and whisk well. Add kale and beets, stir gently and divide between plates. Top each serving with salmon, the onion and almonds and serve right away! Enjoy!

Nutrition: calories 242, fat 3, fiber 1, carbs 4, protein

Easy Shrimp Salad

Preparation time: 1 hour and 10 minutes
Cooking time: 0 minutes
Servings: 4

Ingredients:

- 4 cups shrimp, cooked, peeled, deveined and chopped
- 5 tablespoons rice vinegar
- 2 tablespoons garlic chili sauce
- 1 and ½ tablespoons olive oil
- 1 tablespoon lime rind, rind
- ¼ cup lime juice
- ½ teaspoon paprika
- ½ teaspoon cumin, ground
- 2 garlic cloves, minced
- A pinch of salt
- 4 cups baby spinach
- 1 cup radishes, sliced
- 1 cup mango, peeled and chopped
- ½ cup green onions, chopped
- 2 tablespoon pumpkin seeds
- ¼ cup avocado, pitted, peeled and sliced

Directions:

In a bowl, mix 2 tablespoons vinegar with garlic chili sauce and whisk well. Add shrimp, stir, cover and keep in the fridge for 1 hour. Meanwhile, in another bowl, mix 3 tablespoons vinegar with oil, lime rind, lime juice, paprika, cumin , garlic cloves and a pinch of salt and whisk. Divide spinach between plates, top each with shrimp salad, add ¼ cup mango on each, ¼ cup radishes, 1 tablespoon avocado, 2 tablespoons onions and 1 and ½ teaspoons pumpkin-seed kernels. Drizzle with 2 tablespoons vinegar and lime vinaigrette all over and serve right away! Enjoy!

Nutrition: calories 194, fat 3, fiber 2, carbs 4, protein 4

Squid And Shrimp Salad

Preparation time: 10 minutes
Cooking time: 15 minutes
Servings: 4

Ingredients:

- ounces squid, cut into medium pieces
- ounces shrimp, peeled and deveined
- 1 red onion, sliced
- 1 cucumber, chopped
- 2 tomatoes, cut into medium wedges
- 2 tablespoons cilantro, chopped
- 1 hot jalapeno pepper, cut in rounds
- 3 tablespoons rice vinegar
- 3 tablespoons olive oil
- 1 teaspoon salt
- ¼ teaspoon pepper

Directions:

In a bowl, mix onion with cucumber, tomatoes, pepper, cilantro, shrimp and squid and stir well. Divide seafood mixture into parchment paper pieces, fold , seal edges, place on a baking sheet and introduce in the oven at 400 degrees F for 15 minutes. Meanwhile, in a small bowl mix olive oil with vinegar, salt and pepper and whisk very well. Unwrap parchment papers, divide seafood mix between plates, drizzle the dressing all over and serve. Enjoy!

Nutrition: calories 210, fat 2, fiber 3, carbs 5, protein 6

Traditional Mediterranean Seafood Salad

Preparation time: 2 hours
Cooking time: 1 hour and 30 minutes
Servings: 4

Ingredients:

- 1 big octopus, cleaned and head on
- 1 pound mussels
- 2 pounds clams
- 1 big squid, cut into rings
- 3 garlic cloves, minced
- 1 celery rib, cut crosswise into thirds
- ½ cup celery rib, sliced
- 1 carrot, cut crosswise into 3 pieces
- 1 small white onion, chopped
- 1 bay leaf
- ¾ cup white wine
- 2 cups radicchio, sliced
- 1 red onion, sliced
- 1 cup parsley, chopped
- 1 cup olive oil
- 1 cup red wine vinegar
- Salt and black pepper to the taste

Directions:

Place the octopus in a large pot with celery rib cut in thirds, garlic, carrot, bay leaf, white onion and white wine. Add water to cover the octopus, cover with a lid, bring to a boil over high heat, reduce heat to low and simmer for 1 and ½ hours. Drain octopus, reserve boiling liquid and leave aside to cool down. Put ¼ cup octopus cooking liquid in another pot, add mussels, cook over medium heat until they open, transfer to a bowl and leave aside. Add clams to this pan, cover, cook over medium high heat until they open as well, transfer to the bowl with mussels and leave aside. Add squid to the pan, cover and cook over medium high heat for 3 minutes, transfer to the bowl with mussels and clams. Meanwhile, slice octopus into small pieces and mix with the rest of the seafood. Add sliced celery, radicchio, red onion, vinegar, olive oil, parsley, salt and pepper, stir gently and leave aside for 2 hours. Serve and enjoy!

Nutrition: calories 210, fat 3, fiber 3, carbs 6, protein 8

Shrimp Salad Delight

Preparation time: 25 minutes
Cooking time: 25 minutes
Servings: 2

Ingredients:

- 8 medium shrimp, peeled and deveined
- 12 ounces package mixed salad leaves
- 10 cherry tomatoes, halved
- 2 green onions, sliced
- 2 medium mushrooms, sliced
- 1/3 cup rice vinegar
- ¼ cup toasted sesame seeds
- 1 tablespoon soy sauce
- 2 teaspoons ginger, minced
- 2 teaspoons garlic, minced
- 2/3 cup olive oil
- 1/3 cup sesame oil

Directions:

In a bowl, mix vinegar with sesame seeds, soy sauce, garlic, ginger and whisk well. Transfer this to your kitchen blender, add olive oil and sesame oil, blend very well and leave aside. Brush shrimp with 3 tablespoons of the ginger dressing you've prepared, place them on preheated grill over medium heat, cook for 3 minutes on each side and transfer to a bowl filled with mixed salad leaves. Add mushrooms, green onions and tomatoes, drizzle ginger dressing on top and serve right away! Enjoy!

Nutrition: calories 198, fat 4, fiber 3, carbs 6, protein 4

Shrimp And Scallops Salad

Preparation time: 25 minutes
Cooking time: 15 minutes
Servings: 4

Ingredients:

- ¾ pound shrimp, peeled and deveined
- ½ pounds sea scallops, halved
- 1 celery stalk, quartered
- 2 celery stalks, sliced
- 3 garlic cloves, minced
- Salt and black pepper to the taste
- Juice of 1 lemon
- 4 ounces baby carrots cut in halves
- 1 small avocado, peeled, pitted and chopped
- 2 romaine lettuces, shredded
- 1 tablespoon capers
- 1 tablespoon capers brine
- 1 tablespoon homemade mayonnaise
- cups water

Directions:

In a large pan, mix 1 quartered celery, 2 garlic cloves, 10 cups water, salt and pepper to the taste and half of the lemon juice, stir, bring to a simmer over medium high heat and boil for 2 minutes. Add shrimp, cook for 4 minutes, transfer carrots and shrimp to a bowl and leave them aside. Bring the water to a boil again over medium heat, add scallops, cook for 2 minutes, rinse with cold water and also leave aside. In a bowl, mix half of the avocado with chopped celery, lettuce and capers. Add scallops, shrimp and baby carrots to this mixture. In your blender, mix the rest of the avocado with some of the cooking liquid from boiling the seafood, the rest of the lemon juice, caper brine, mayo, the rest of the garlic, salt and pepper to the taste and blend again. Add this dressing to your seafood salad, toss and serve right away. Enjoy!

Nutrition: calories 214, fat 3, fiber 3, carbs 6, protein 4

Mediterranean Squid Salad

Preparation time: 1 hour
Cooking time: 15 minutes
Servings: 8

Ingredients:

- 1 pound baby squid, washed, body and tentacles chopped
- ½ teaspoon lemon zest, grated
- ½ teaspoon orange zest, grated
- ½ teaspoon lime zest, grated
- 1 cup olive oil
- 1 and ¼ teaspoon red pepper flakes, crushed
- 2 cups parsley, chopped
- 2 anchovy fillets
- 4 garlic cloves, minced
- 1 shallot, chopped
- 2 tablespoons capers
- 2 tablespoons red wine vinegar
- Salt and black pepper to the taste
- 2 tablespoons lemon juice
- 4 ounces baby arugula
- 3 cups cantaloupe, cubed
- 2 celery ribs, sliced
- 1 red-hot chili pepper, sliced

Directions:

In a bowl, mix squid pieces with grated lemon zest, lime zest, orange zest, 1 teaspoon red pepper flakes and ¼ cup oil, toss and keep in the fridge for 1 hour. Meanwhile, in another bowl mix parsley with garlic, anchovies, capers, shallots and ½ cup olive oil and whisk well. Add vinegar and ¼ teaspoon pepper flakes and whisk again. Place squid pieces on your preheated grill over medium high heat, season with some salt and cook for 5 minutes. Transfer squid to a bowl, add half of the dressing you've made earlier, toss and leave aside. In another bowl, mix ¼ cup olive oil with the lemon juice and some salt and stir. Add arugula, celery, fresh chili pepper and melon and stir. Add squid, stir and divide between plates. Top with the rest of the salad dressing and serve right away! Enjoy!

Nutrition: calories 253, fat 3, fiber 1, carbs 5, protein 3

Amazing Salmon Soup

Preparation time: 15 minutes
Cooking time: 15 minutes
Servings: 6

Ingredients:

- 2 tablespoon butter
- 1 leek, chopped
- 1 red onion, chopped
- Salt and white pepper to the taste
- 3 potatoes, peeled and cubed
- 2 carrots, chopped
- 4 cups fish stock
- 4 ounces salmon skinless cut in cubes
- ½ cup heavy cream
- 1 tablespoon dill, chopped

Directions:

Heat up a pan with the butter over medium heat, add leek and onion, stir and cook for 7 minutes. Add salt and pepper, add carrots, potatoes and stock, stir, bring to a boil and cook for 8 more minutes. Add salmon, boil for 3 more minutes. Add cream, dill, stir and boil for 3 minutes. Ladle into bowls and serve. Enjoy!

Nutrition: calories 132, fat 3, fiber 4, carbs 5, protein 5

Mediterranean Diet Poultry Recipes

Delicious Roasted Duck

Preparation time: 10 minutes
Cooking time: 4 hours and 10 minutes
Servings: 4

Ingredients:

- 1 medium young duck
- 1 celery rib, chopped
- 2 yellow onions, chopped
- 2 teaspoons thyme, dried
- 8 garlic cloves, minced

For the sauce:

- Duck organs
- 1 tablespoon tomato paste
- 1 yellow onion, chopped
- ½ teaspoon sugar
- ½ cup white wine

- 2 bay leaves
- ¼ cup parsley, chopped
- A pinch of salt and black pepper
- 1 teaspoon herbs de Provence

- 3 cups water
- 1 cup chicken stock
- 1 and ½ cups black olives, pitted and chopped
- ¼ teaspoon herbs de Provence

Directions:

In a baking dish, spread thyme, parsley, garlic and 2 onions. Add duck, season with salt, 1 teaspoon herbs de Provence and pepper, introduce in the oven at 475 degrees F and roast for 10 minutes. Cover the dish, reduce heat to 275 degrees F and roast duck for 3 hours and 30 minutes. Meanwhile, heat up a pan over medium heat, add duck organs, cover and brown for a few minutes. Add 1 yellow onion, stir and cook for 10 minutes. Add tomato paste, stock, sugar, ¼ teaspoon herbs de Provence, olives and water, cover, reduce heat to low and cook for 1 hour. Transfer duck to a working surface, carve, discard bones and divide between plates. Drizzle the sauce all over and serve Enjoy!

Nutrition: calories 254, fat 3, fiber 3, carbs 8, protein 13

Tasty Duck Breast

Preparation time: 10 minutes
Cooking time: 20 minutes
Servings: 4

Ingredients:

- 4 duck breasts, boneless
- Salt and black pepper to the taste
- ¼ teaspoon cinnamon, ground
- ¼ teaspoon coriander, ground
- 5 tablespoons apricot preserves
- 3 tablespoons chives, chopped

- 2 tablespoons parsley, chopped
- A drizzle of olive oil
- 3 tablespoons apple cider vinegar
- 2 tablespoons red onions, chopped
- 1 cup apricots, chopped
- ¾ cup blackberries

Directions:

Season duck breasts with salt, pepper, coriander and cinnamon, place them on preheated grill over medium high heat, cook for 2 minutes, flip them and cook for 3 minutes more. Flip duck breasts again, add 3 tablespoons apricot preserves, cook for 1 minute, transfer them to a cutting board, leave aside for 2-3 minutes and slice. Heat up a pan over medium heat, add vinegar, onion, 2 tablespoons apricot preserves, apricots, blackberries and chives, stir and cook for 3 minutes. Divide sliced duck breasts between plates and serve with apricot sauce drizzled on top. Enjoy!

Nutrition: calories 275, fat 4, fiber 4, carbs 7, protein 12

Mediterranean Duck Breast Salad

Preparation time: 10 minutes
Cooking time: 20 minutes
Servings: 4

Ingredients:
- 3 tablespoons white wine vinegar
- 2 tablespoons sugar
- 2 oranges, peeled and cut into segments
- 1 teaspoon orange zest, grated
- 1 tablespoons lemon juice
- 1 teaspoon lemon zest, grated
- 3 tablespoons shallot, minced
- tablespoons canola oil
- Salt and black pepper to the taste
- 2 duck breasts, boneless but skin on, cut into 4 pieces
- 1 head of frisee, torn
- 2 small lettuce heads washed, torn into small pieces
- 2 tablespoons chives, chopped

Directions:
Heat up a small pot over medium high heat, add vinegar and sugar, stir and boil for 5 minutes and take off heat. Add orange zest, lemon zest and lemon juice, stir and leave aside for a few minutes. Add shallot, salt and pepper to the taste and the oil, whisk very well and leave aside for now. Pat dry duck pieces, score skin, trim and season with salt and pepper. Heat up a pan over medium high heat for 1 minute, arrange duck breast pieces skin side down, brown for 8 minutes, reduce heat to medium and cook for 4 more minutes. Flip pieces, cook for 3 minutes, transfer to a cutting board and cover them with foil. Put frisee and lettuce in a bowl, stir and divide between plates. Slice duck, arrange on top, add orange segments, sprinkle chives and drizzle the vinaigrette you've made at the beginning. Enjoy!

Nutrition: calories 320, fat 4, fiber 4, carbs 6, protein 14

Special Duck Dish

Preparation time: 10 minutes
Cooking time: 5 hours
Servings: 6

Ingredients:

- 2 medium ducks, fat trimmed, necks, hearts and gizzards reserved
- 1 tablespoon olive oil
- 1 cup water
- Salt and black pepper to the taste
- 2 tomatoes, chopped
- 2 carrots, chopped
- 2 celery ribs, chopped
- 1 leek, chopped
- 2 garlic cloves, minced
- 1 yellow onion, chopped
- 2 bay leaves
- 3 tablespoons white flour
- 1 teaspoon thyme, dried
- 2 tablespoons tomato paste
- 1-quart chicken stock
- Thin zest strips from 1 orange
- Juice from 2 oranges
- 3 oranges, peeled and cut into segments
- 1/3 cup sugar
- 2 tablespoons currant jelly
- 1/3 cup cider vinegar
- 2 tablespoons cold butter

Directions:

Prick ducks, season them with salt and pepper inside and out, arrange in a roasting pan, add 1 cup water, introduce in the oven at 450 degrees F and bake for 20 minutes. Reduce heat to 350 degrees F, turn ducks and bake them for 30 minutes more. Turn ducks again and roast them for 30 minutes more. Meanwhile, heat up a pan with the oil over high heat, add duck hearts, necks, gizzards and joints, season with salt and pepper, stir and cook for 10 minutes. Add carrots, celery, leek, tomatoes, garlic, onion, thyme and bay leaves, stir and cook for 5 minutes. Add tomato paste, flour, wine and stock gradually, bring to a boil, reduce heat to medium low, simmer for 50 minutes, take off heat and strain sauce into a bowl. Put orange zest strips in a pot filled with boiling water, boil over medium high heat for 1 minute, drain zest and pat dry it. Heat up a small pan over medium high heat, add vinegar and sugar, stir and cook for 4 minutes. Add orange juice and currant jelly, stir and bring to a boil. Add strained sauce, salt and pepper, stir and cook for 8 minutes. Add butter gradually and stir very well again. Take ducks out of the oven, turn them again, introduce in the oven again and cook for 40 more minutes. Take ducks out of the oven again, introduce them in preheated broiler and broil them for 3 minutes. Transfer ducks to a platter and keep them warm for now. Heat up juices from the pan in a pot over medium heat, take off heat and strain them into a bowl. Add this to orange sauce and stir. Arrange orange segments next to the ducks, add blanched orange zest and serve with orange sauce on top. Enjoy!

Nutrition: calories 342, fat 3, fiber 4, carbs 7, protein 12

Duck Breast And Special Sauce

Preparation time: 10 minutes
Cooking time: 25 minutes
Servings: 4

Ingredients:
- 4 duck breasts
- 2 tablespoons balsamic vinegar
- 3 tablespoons sugar
- Salt and black pepper to the taste
- 1 and ½ cups water
- 4 ounces lingonberries
- ¼ cup chicken stock
- 1 tablespoon butter
- 2 teaspoons corn flour

Directions:

Pat dry duck breasts with paper towels, score the skin, season with salt and pepper to the taste, place on a plate and leave them aside for 30 minutes. Put breasts skin side down in a pan, heat up over medium temperature and cook for 8 minutes. Flip breasts and cook for 30 more seconds. Transfer duck breasts in a baking dish skin side up, introduce in the oven at 425 degrees F and bake for 15 minutes. Take the breasts out of the oven and leave them aside to cool down for 10 minutes before you cut and serve them. Meanwhile, put sugar in a pan, heat up over medium temperature and melt it stirring all the time. Take pan off the heat, add water, chicken stock, balsamic vinegar and almost all lingonberries. Heat up this mix to medium temperature and cook until sauce is reduced to half. Transfer sauce to another pan, add corn flour mixed with water, heat up again and cook until it thickens. Add the rest of the lingonberries, salt and pepper and the butter and stir well. Slice duck breasts, arrange on serving plates and serve with the lingonberries sauce on top. Enjoy!

Nutrition: calories 320, fat 5, fiber 5, carbs 7, protein 12

Braised Duck Legs

Preparation time: 12 hours
Cooking time: 1 hour and 50 minutes
Servings: 4

Ingredients:
- 4 duck legs, trimmed
- ½ pound shallots, chopped
- 1 cup miso+ 1 tablespoon miso
- 3 carrots, chopped
- 2 tablespoons mirin
- 1 tablespoon ginger, chopped
- 2 sprigs rosemary
- ½ teaspoon red pepper flakes, crushed
- 3 cups chicken stock
- ½ cup scallions, sliced

Directions:

In a bowl, mix 1 cup miso with duck legs, cover and keep in the fridge for 12 hours. Pat dry duck legs, arrange them in a pot, heat up over medium high heat and cook for 7 minutes. Transfer duck legs to a plate, discard fat, transfer them to the pot again, add carrots, sake, shallots, ginger, mirin, stock, rosemary and pepper flakes, bring to a boil, introduce in the oven at 250 degrees F and bake for 1 and ½ hours. Transfer duck legs and veggies to a platter, cover and keep them warm. Strain the liquid from the pot into a bowl and leave aside for 5 minutes. Transfer liquid to a pot, bring to a boil over medium high heat and cook for 5 minutes. Add 1 tablespoon mirin to this sauce, stir and pour over veggies. Sprinkle scallions on top and serve. Enjoy!

Nutrition: calories 257, fat 4, fiber 6, carbs 8, protein 12

Smoked Duck

Preparation time: 10 minutes
Cooking time: 50 minutes
Servings: 4

Ingredients:
- ¼ cup peanuts, roasted

For the smoked duck:
- Zest from 1 orange
- ¼ cup lychee tea
- ¼ cup jasmine rice

For the salad:
- 1 tablespoon fish sauce
- 1 tablespoon lime juice
- 1 garlic clove, minced
- 1 red Serrano chili, chopped
- 1 small shallot, sliced

- ¼ cup brown sugar
- 2 big duck breasts boneless
- Salt and black pepper to the taste

- 1 tablespoon brown sugar
- 2 mangos, peeled and sliced
- ¼ cup basil, chopped
- Salt to the taste

Directions:

Spread orange zest in the middle an aluminum foil. Add rice, tea and sugar, fold foil and form a packet. Heat up your grill over medium high heat, rub it with oil and tea, wait 10 minutes and when there's enough smoke coming out, add duck breasts seasoned with salt and pepper. Smoke duck breasts for 17 minutes and remove from grill. Heat up a pan over medium low heat, add duck breasts skin side down and cook them for 15 minutes. Transfer to a cutting board, slice, divide between plates and leave aside for now. In a bowl, mix fish sauce with garlic, lime juice, chili, sugar and shallot. Also add basil, mango slices and toss to coat. Add the salad next to the duck slices and serve. Enjoy!

Nutrition: calories 320, fat 4, fiber 4, carbs 6, protein 12

Roasted Turkey

Preparation time: 10 minutes
Cooking time: 2 hours and 20 minutes
Servings: 8

Ingredients:
- 1 cup hot water
- 12 black tea bags
- 2/3 cup brown sugar
- 2 tablespoons butter
- ½ cup cranberry sauce
- 1 big turkey

- 1 onion, cut into 4 wedges
- 1 lemon, cut into 4 wedges
- 2 tablespoons cornstarch
- 1 cup chicken stock
- Salt and black pepper to the taste

Directions:

Put the hot water in a bowl, add tea bags, leave aside covered for 5 minutes and discard bags. Heat up a pan with the butter over medium high heat, add sugar and cranberry, stir and cook until sugar is dissolved. Add tea, stir and cook for 15 minutes. Stuff turkey with lemon and onion pieces, place it in a roasting pan and brush it with the tea glaze. Introduce in the oven at 350 degrees F and roast for 2 hours, flipping and basting the turkey with the glaze every 20 minutes. Put chicken stock in a pot and heat up over medium heat. Add cornstarch, salt and pepper, stir and cook for 1 minute. Carve turkey and divide it between plates. Strain gravy and drizzle it over your turkey. Enjoy!

Nutrition: calories 500, fat 13, fiber 1, carbs 20, protein 7

Herb And Citrus Turkey

Preparation time: 30 minutes
Cooking time: 4 hours
Servings: 10

Ingredients:

- 1 whole turkey, neck and giblets removed
- Zest and juice from 1 lemon
- ½ cup butter
- ½ shallot, chopped
- 2 sage leaves
- 1 tablespoon rosemary, dried
- 2 tablespoon thyme, chopped
- 1 garlic clove, minced
- 1 yellow onion, roughly chopped
- 2 carrots, roughly chopped
- 2 celery ribs, chopped
- 1 cup dry white wine
- 1 cup chicken stock
- ¼ cup whole wheat flour

Directions:

Place lemon zest and juice in your food processor, add butter, shallot, sage, thyme, rosemary and garlic and pulse. Lift skin from turkey breast without detaching it, rub it with 3 tablespoons of the herb butter under the skin and secure with toothpicks. Season the cavity and the whole turkey with salt and pepper to the taste and place in a baking dish. Add onion, carrots and celery ribs, tie ends of turkey legs together, rub the turkey with the rest of herb butter, add wine and stock to the pan, introduce in the oven and bake at 425 degrees F for 30 minutes. Reduce heat to 325 degrees F and bake for 2 hours and 30 minutes. Transfer to a platter, pour veggie drippings through a strainer and reserve 2 and ½ cups of drippings. Heat up a pan with the reserved chilled herb butter over medium heat, add flour, stir well and cook for 2 minutes. Add reserved pan drippings, bring to a boil, reduce the temperature and cook for 5 minutes stirring occasionally. Cut turkey and serve with the gravy you've just prepared. Enjoy!

Nutrition: calories 287, fat 4, fiber 7, carbs 9, protein 12

Wonderful Mediterranean Chicken Breast

Preparation time: 10 minutes
Cooking time: 15 minutes
Servings: 6

Ingredients:

- ¼ cup breadcrumbs
- ¼ teaspoon garlic powder
- ½ cup pecorino cheese, grated
- 1 teaspoon basil, dried
- 3 tablespoons olive oil
- A pinch of salt and black pepper
- 6 chicken breast halves, skinless and boneless

Directions:

In a bowl, mix breadcrumbs with garlic powder, cheese, basil, salt and pepper and stir. Rub chicken with half of the oil, dip in breadcrumbs mix and place on a plate. Heat up a pan with the rest of the oil over medium high heat, add chicken breast halves, cook for 7 minutes, flip and cook for 8 minutes more. Drain excess grease with paper towels if needed, arrange chicken on plates and serve. Enjoy!

Nutrition: calories 212, fat 2, fiber 1, carbs 3, protein 18

Super Special Chicken

Preparation time: 10 minutes
Cooking time: 40 minutes
Servings: 6

Ingredients:

- 6 chicken breast halves, skinless and boneless
- 2 teaspoons olive oil
- ½ cup white wine+ 2 tablespoons
- 1 tablespoon basil, chopped
- 2 teaspoons thyme, chopped
- ½ cup yellow onion, chopped
- 3 garlic cloves, minced
- ½ cup kalamata olives, pitted and sliced
- ¼ cup parsley, chopped
- 3 cups tomatoes, chopped

Directions:

Heat up a pan with the oil and 2 tablespoons wine over medium heat, add chicken, cook for 6 minutes on each side and transfer to a plate. Heat up the same pan over medium heat, add garlic, stir and cook for 1 minute. Add onion, stir and cook for 3 minutes. Add tomatoes and the rest of the wine, stir, bring to a simmer and cook for 10 minutes. Add basil and thyme, stir and cook for 5 minutes more. Add chicken, stir, cover pan and cook for 10 minutes more. Add parsley, olives, salt and pepper, stir, divide between plates and serve. Enjoy!

Nutrition: calories 221, fat 2, fiber 4, carbs 7, protein 19

Unbelievable Chicken Dish

Preparation time: 10 minutes
Cooking time: 50 minutes
Servings: 4

Ingredients:

- 1 tablespoon olive oil
- 4 teaspoons garlic, minced
- A pinch of salt and black pepper
- ¼ teaspoon thyme, dried
- 12 small red potatoes, halved
- Olive oil cooking spray
- 2 pounds chicken breast, skinless, boneless and cubed
- 1 cup red onion, sliced
- ¾ cup white wine
- ¾ cup chicken stock
- ½ cup pepperoncini peppers, chopped
- 2 cups tomato, chopped
- ¼ cup kalamata olives, pitted and halved
- 2 tablespoons basil, chopped
- 14 ounces canned artichokes, chopped
- ½ cup parmesan, grated

Directions:

In a baking dish, mix potatoes with 2 teaspoons garlic, olive oil, thyme, salt and pepper and toss. Introduce in the oven at 400 degrees F and roast for 30 minutes. Heat up a pot with some cooking spray over medium high heat, add chicken, season with a pinch of salt and black pepper, cook for 5 minutes on each side and transfer to a plate. Heat up the pot again over medium heat, add onion, stir and cook for 5 minutes. Add wine, stir and cook for 2 minutes. Add stock, return chicken, add olives, pepperoncini and roasted potatoes, stir and cook for 3 minutes. Add the rest of the garlic, artichokes, basil, tomato and some more black pepper, stir and cook for 3 minutes more. Divide between plates and serve with cheese sprinkled on top. Enjoy!

Nutrition: calories 271, fat 2, fiber 3, carbs 10, protein 17

Divine Chicken Dish

Preparation time: 10 minutes
Cooking time: 25 minutes
Servings: 4

Ingredients:

- 8 chicken breast halves, skinless and boneless
- 6 tablespoons olive oil
- 1 and ½ pounds oyster mushrooms
- 1 and ½ cups chicken stock
- A pinch of salt and black pepper
- 3 plum tomatoes, chopped
- 2/3 cup kalamata olives, pitted and sliced
- 1 tablespoon shallot, chopped
- 3 garlic cloves, minced
- 1 tablespoon capers
- 2 tablespoons butter
- 1 cup cherry tomatoes, red and yellow
- 3 tablespoons pine nuts
- 3 tablespoons parsley, chopped

Directions:

Heat up a pan with 3 tablespoons oil over medium high heat, add chicken, season with some salt and pepper, cook for 3 minutes on each side and transfer to a plate. Discard grease from the pan, add the rest of the oil, heat up over medium high heat, add mushrooms, stir and cook for 3 minutes. Add stock, stir and cook for 5 minutes more. Add plum tomatoes, shallot, garlic, olives and capers, stir and cook for 7 minutes. Add a pinch of salt and black pepper, also add butter and cherry tomatoes, stir and cook for a few minutes more. Divide chicken on plates, add mushroom mix on the side, sprinkle parsley and pine nuts on top and serve. Enjoy!

Nutrition: calories 241, fat 4, fiber 5, carbs 6, protein 16

Easy And Very Simple Chicken

Preparation time: 8 hours and 10 minutes
Cooking time: 30 minutes
Servings: 8

Ingredients:

- 1 whole chicken, cut into medium pieces
- A pinch of salt and black pepper
- ½ cup olive oil
- 1 tablespoon rosemary, chopped
- 3 garlic cloves, minced
- 1 tablespoon thyme, chopped
- 1 tablespoon oregano, chopped
- Juice from 2 lemons

Directions:

In a bowl, mix oil with salt, pepper, garlic, rosemary, thyme, oregano and lemon juice and whisk well. Add chicken, toss well and keep in the fridge for 8 hours. Place chicken pieces on preheated grill over medium heat, cook for 15 minutes on each side, divide between plates and serve with a side salad. Enjoy!

Nutrition: calories 287, fat 3, fiber 1, carbs 4, protein 20

Healthy Greek Chicken

Preparation time: 2 hours and 10 minutes
Cooking time: 30 minutes
Servings: 5

Ingredients:

- 1 and ½ pounds chicken breast, skinless and boneless
- ½ cup olive oil
- 1 tablespoon mustard
- ¼ cup red wine vinegar
- 2 garlic cloves, minced
- ½ teaspoon basil, dried
- ½ teaspoon oregano, dried
- ½ teaspoon onion powder
- A pinch of salt and black pepper
- 1 red onion, sliced
- 1-pint cherry tomatoes, halved
- Feta cheese, crumbled for serving
- Black olives, pitted and sliced for serving

Directions:

In a bowl, mix oil with vinegar, mustard, oregano, basil, garlic, salt, pepper and onion powder and whisk well. In a bowl, mix chicken with half of this mix, stir, cover and leave aside for 1 hour. In another bowl, mix onion and tomatoes with the rest of the marinade, toss and keep in the fridge for 1 more hour. Combine veggies and chicken in a baking dish, toss them gently, introduce in the oven at 375 degrees F and bake for 30 minutes. Divide chicken and veggies on plates, sprinkle feta cheese and olives on top and serve. Enjoy!

Nutrition: calories 300, fat 4, fiber 2, carbs 7, protein 30

Easy Chicken Bowls

Preparation time: 20 minutes
Cooking time: 10 minutes
Servings: 4

Ingredients:
For the chicken:
- ¼ cup olive oil
- 2 pounds chicken breasts, skinless and boneless
- 3 tablespoons garlic, minced
- 1/3 cup lemon juice

For the salad:
- 2 cucumbers, sliced
- 2 tablespoons olive oil
- 1/3 cup lemon juice

For the sauce:
- 1 tablespoon garlic, minced
- 1 cucumber, chopped
- 1 cup Greek yogurt
- ½ tablespoon dill, chopped

For serving:
- ½ cup red onion, sliced
- 1 and ½ pounds cherry tomatoes, halved

- 1 tablespoon oregano, dried
- 1 tablespoon red wine vinegar
- 1/3 cup Greek yogurt
- A pinch of salt and black pepper

- 1 tablespoon red vinegar
- ½ teaspoon oregano, dried
- ½ tablespoon garlic, minced

- ½ teaspoon mint, chopped
- 1 teaspoon lemon zest, grated
- 1 tablespoon lemon juice

- 3 cups brown rice, already cooked

Directions:
In a bowl, mix chicken with 3 tablespoons garlic, 1/3 cup lemon juice, 1 tablespoon vinegar, 1 tablespoon oregano, 1/3 cup Greek yogurt, salt and pepper and ½ cup oil, toss really well, cover and keep in the fridge for 20 minutes. Heat up a pan with ½ cup oil over medium high heat, add chicken, cook for 4 minutes on each side, transfer to a plate and keep warm for now. In a salad bowl, mix 2 cucumbers with 2 tablespoons oil, 1 tablespoon vinegar, 1/3 cup lemon juice, ½ teaspoon oregano and ½ teaspoon garlic and toss well. In a small bowl, mix 1 cucumber with 1 tablespoon garlic, ½ tablespoon dill, ½ teaspoon mint, 1 tablespoon lemon juice, 1 teaspoon lemon zest and 1 cup yogurt and whisk well. Divide brown rice into bowls, add salad on the side and top with chicken. Add red onions, cherry tomatoes and drizzle the cucumber sauce you've made. Enjoy!

Nutrition: calories 298, fat 4, fiber 5, carbs 7, protein 18

The Best Chicken Ever

Preparation time: 10 minutes
Cooking time: 1 hour
Servings: 8

Ingredients:

- 3 pounds potatoes, peeled and roughly chopped
- 2 green bell peppers, chopped
- 1 yellow onion, chopped
- 4 garlic cloves, minced
- ½ cup black olives, pitted and sliced
- 14 ounces canned tomatoes, chopped
- 16 chicken drumsticks, skinless
- 1 tablespoon mixed herbs, dried
- 3 ounces feta cheese, crumbled
- ½ cup parsley, chopped

Directions:

Put potatoes in a pot, add water to cover, bring to a boil over medium heat, cook for a couple of minutes, drain and transfer to a big roasting pan. Add green bell pepper, onion, garlic, tomatoes, olives and herbs and toss. Add chicken, some salt and pepper, toss again, introduce in the oven at 400 degrees F and roast for 40 minutes. Toss everything again and roast for 20 minutes more. Divide on plates, sprinkle parsley and feta on top and serve. Enjoy!

Nutrition: calories 298, fat 3, fiber 3, carbs 7, protein 16

Marvellous Chicken And Mustard Sauce

Preparation time: 10 minutes
Cooking time: 30 minutes
Servings: 4

Ingredients:

- 8 bacon strips, chopped
- 1/3 cup mustard
- Salt and black pepper to the taste
- 1 cup yellow onion, chopped
- 1 tablespoon olive oil
- 1 and ½ cups chicken stock
- 4 chicken breasts, skinless and boneless
- ¼ teaspoon sweet paprika

Directions:

In a bowl, mix paprika with mustard, salt and pepper and stir well. Spread this on chicken breasts and massage. Heat up a pan over medium high heat, add bacon, stir, cook until it browns and transfer to a plate. Heat up the same pan with the oil over medium high heat, add chicken breasts, cook for 2 minutes on each side and also transfer to a plate. Heat up the pan once again over medium high heat, add stock, stir and bring to a simmer. Add bacon and onions, salt and pepper and stir. Return chicken to pan as well, stir gently and simmer over medium heat for 20 minutes, turning meat halfway. Divide chicken on plates, drizzle the sauce over it and serve. Enjoy!

Nutrition: calories 223, fat 8, fiber 1, carbs 3, protein 26

Delicious And Easy Chicken

Preparation time: 10 minutes
Cooking time: 1 hour
Servings: 6

Ingredients:

- 8 ounces mushrooms, chopped
- 1 pound Italian sausage, chopped
- 2 tablespoons avocado oil
- 6 cherry peppers, chopped
- 1 red bell pepper, chopped
- 1 red onion, sliced
- 2 tablespoons garlic, minced
- 2 cups cherry tomatoes, halved
- 4 chicken thighs
- Salt and black pepper to the taste
- ½ cup chicken stock
- 1 tablespoon balsamic vinegar
- 2 teaspoons oregano, dried
- Some chopped parsley for serving

Directions:

Heat up a pan with half of the oil over medium heat, add sausages, stir, brown for a few minutes and transfer to a plate. Heat up the pan again with the rest of the oil over medium heat, add chicken thighs, season with salt and pepper, cook for 3 minutes on each side and transfer to a plate. Heat up the pan again over medium heat, add cherry peppers, mushrooms, onion and bell pepper, stir and cook for 4 minutes. Add garlic, stir and cook for 2 minutes. Add stock, vinegar, salt, pepper, oregano and cherry tomatoes and stir. Add chicken pieces and sausages ones, stir gently, transfer everything to the oven at 400 degrees and bake for 30 minutes. Sprinkle parsley, divide between plates and serve. Enjoy!

Nutrition: calories 340, fat 33, fiber 3, carbs 4, protein 20

Mediterranean Orange Chicken

Preparation time: 10 minutes
Cooking time: 15 minutes
Servings: 4

Ingredients:

- 2 pounds chicken thighs, skinless, boneless and cut into pieces
- Salt and black pepper to the taste

For the sauce:

- 2 tablespoons fish sauce
- 1 and ½ teaspoons orange extract
- 1 tablespoon ginger, grated
- ¼ cup orange juice
- 2 teaspoons stevia
- 1 tablespoon orange zest

- 3 tablespoons coconut oil
- ¼ cup coconut flour

- ¼ teaspoon sesame seeds
- 2 tablespoons scallions, chopped
- ½ teaspoon coriander, ground
- 1 cup water
- ¼ teaspoon red pepper flakes
- 2 tablespoons gluten free soy sauce

Directions:

In a bowl, mix coconut flour and salt and pepper and stir. Add chicken pieces and toss to coat well. Heat up a pan with the oil over medium heat, add chicken, cook until they are golden on both sides and transfer to a bowl. In your blender, mix orange juice with ginger, fish sauce, soy sauce, stevia, orange extract, water and coriander and blend well. Pour this into a pan and heat up over medium heat. Add chicken, stir and cook for 2 minutes. Add sesame seeds, orange zest, scallions and pepper flakes, stir cook for 2 minutes and take off heat. Divide between plates and serve. Enjoy!

Nutrition: calories 423, fat 20, fiber 5, carbs 6, protein 45

Great Mediterranean Chicken Bites

Preparation time: 10 minutes
Cooking time: 10 minutes
Servings: 4

Ingredients:

- 20 ounces canned pineapple slices
- A drizzle of olive oil
- 3 cups chicken thighs, boneless, skinless and cut into medium pieces
- 1 tablespoon smoked paprika

Directions:

Heat up a pan over medium high heat, add pineapple slices, cook them for a few minutes on each side, transfer to a cutting board, cool them down and cut into medium cubes. Heat up another pan with a drizzle of oil over medium high heat, rub chicken pieces with paprika, add them to the pan and cook for 5 minutes on each side. Arrange chicken cubes on a platter, add a pineapple piece on top of each and stick a toothpick in each. Serve right away!

Nutrition: calories 120, fat 3, fiber 1, carbs 5, protein 2

Incredible Chicken Salad

Preparation time: 10 minutes
Cooking time: 30 minutes
Servings: 4

Ingredients:

- 1 whole chicken, chopped
- 4 scallions, chopped
- 2 celery ribs, chopped
- 1 cup mandarin orange, chopped
- ¼ cup homemade mayo
- ½ cup yogurts
- 1 cup cashews, toasted and chopped
- A pinch of salt and black pepper

Directions:

Put chicken pieces in a pot, add water to cover, add a pinch of salt, bring to a boil over medium heat and cook for 25 minutes. Transfer chicken to a cutting board, leave aside to cool down, discard bones, shred meat and put it in a bowl. Add celery, orange pieces, cashews, scallion and toss. Add salt, pepper, mayo and yogurt, toss to coat well and keep in the fridge until you serve it. Enjoy!

Nutrition: calories 150, fat 3, fiber 3, carbs 7, protein 6

Incredible Chicken Mix

Preparation time: 10 minutes
Cooking time: 1 hour and 10 minutes
Servings: 6

Ingredients:
- 1 cup white flour
- Salt and black pepper to the taste
- 4 pounds chicken breast, skinless, boneless and cubed
- 4 ounces olive oil
- 4 ounces celery, chopped
- 1 tablespoon garlic, minced
- 8 ounces onion, chopped
- 5 ounces red bell pepper, chopped
- 7 ounces poblano pepper, chopped
- ¼ teaspoon cumin, ground
- 2 cups corn
- A pinch of cayenne pepper
- 1-quart chicken stock
- 1 teaspoon chili powder
- 16 ounces canned beans, drained
- ¼ cup cilantro, chopped

Directions:
Dredge chicken pieces in flour. Heat up a pan with the oil over medium high heat, add chicken, cook for 5 minutes on each side, transfer to a bowl and leave aside. Heat up the pan again over medium high heat, add onion, celery, garlic, bell pepper, poblano pepper and corn, stir and cook for 2 minutes more. Add stock, cumin, chili powder, beans, cayenne, cumin, salt, pepper and chicken pieces, stir, bring to a simmer, reduce heat to medium low, cover and cook for 1 hour. Add cilantro, stir, divide into bowls and serve. Enjoy!

Nutrition: calories 345, fat 12, fiber 3, carbs 9, protein 4

Smoked Chicken Delight

Preparation time: 10 minutes
Cooking time: 0 minutes
Servings: 6

Ingredients:
- ½ cup hot water
- 1 celery rib, chopped
- ½ cup mayonnaise
- 1 red apple, cored and chopped
- ½ cup smoked chicken breast, skinless, boneless, cooked and shredded
- 1 teaspoon thyme, chopped
- 1 cucumber, sliced
- 12 whole grain bread slices, toasted
- Sunflower sprouts

Directions:
In a bowl, mix chicken with celery, apple, thyme, cucumber and mayo and stir well. Divide this into 6 bread slices, add sunflower sprouts on each, top with the other bread slices, cut each sandwich into quarters and serve. Enjoy!

Nutrition: calories 160, fat 7, fiber 2, carbs 10, protein 5

The Best Chicken And Peaches

Preparation time: 10 minutes
Cooking time: 1 hour and 10 minutes
Servings: 4

Ingredients:

- 1 whole chicken, cut into medium pieces
- ¾ cup water
- 1/3 cup honey
- Salt and black pepper to the taste
- ¼ cup olive oil
- 4 peaches, halved

Directions:

Put the water in a pot, bring to a simmer over medium heat, add pepper and honey, whisk really well and leave aside. Rub chicken pieces with the oil, season with salt and pepper, place on preheated grill over medium high heat, brush with honey mixture and cook for 15 minutes. Brush chicken with more honey mix, cook for 15 minutes more and then flip again. Brush one more time with the honey mix, cover and cook for 20 minutes more. Divide chicken pieces on plates and keep warm. Brush peaches with what's left of the honey marinade, place them on your grill and cook for 4 minutes. Flip again and cook for 3 minutes more. Divide between plates next to chicken pieces and serve. Enjoy!

Nutrition: calories 500, fat 14, fiber 3, carbs 15, protein 10

Mediterranean Glazed Chicken

Preparation time: 10 minutes
Cooking time: 1 hour and 10 minutes
Servings: 4

Ingredients:

- ½ cup apricot preserves
- ½ cup pineapple preserves
- 1 cup hot water
- 6 black tea bags
- 1 tablespoon soy sauce
- 1 onion, chopped
- ¼ teaspoon red pepper flakes
- 1 tablespoon vegetable oil
- Salt and black pepper to the taste
- 6 chicken legs

Directions:

Put the hot water in a bowl, add tea bags, leave aside covered for 10 minutes, discard bags at the end and transfer tea to another bowl. Add soy sauce, pepper flakes, apricot and pineapple preserves and whisk really well. Heat up a pan with the oil over medium high heat, add chicken pieces, cook them for 5 minutes on each side and transfer to a bowl. Spread onion on the bottom of a baking dish and add chicken pieces on top. Season with salt, pepper, drizzle the tea glaze on top, cover dish, introduce in the oven at 350 degrees F and bake for 30 minutes. Uncover dish and bake for 20 minutes more. Divide chicken on plates and keep warm. Pour cooking juices into a pan, heat up over medium high heat, cook until sauce is reduced and drizzle it over chicken pieces. Enjoy!

Nutrition: calories 298, fat 14, fiber 1, carbs 4, protein 30

Easy Chicken Soup

Preparation time: 10 minutes
Cooking time: 1 hour and 10 minutes
Servings: 6

Ingredients:

- 3 and ½ pounds small tomatoes, halved
- 2 tablespoons extra virgin olive oil + some more for frying
- 2 yellow onions, cut into wedges
- 1 chicken, cut into pieces
- 3 garlic cloves, chopped
- 3 red chili peppers, chopped
- 1 tablespoon coriander seeds, crushed
- ounces canned black beans, drained
- 4 tablespoons chipotle paste
- Zest from 1 lime
- Juice from 1 lime
- Salt and black pepper to the taste
- A handful coriander, chopped
- 2 avocados, pitted, peeled and chopped
- 3 ounces sour cream

Directions:

Arrange tomatoes in a baking dish, add onions and chicken pieces, season with salt and pepper, add 1 tablespoon olive oil, toss to coat, introduce in the oven at 350 degrees F and bake for 50 minutes. Transfer chicken to a bowl, cover with foil to keep warm and reserve cooking juices from the baking dish. Transfer baked onions and tomatoes to your blender and pulse well. Heat up a pot with the rest of the oil over medium high heat, add chilies, garlic and coriander, stir and cook for 3 minutes. Discard bones and skin from chicken pieces, shred meat and add to pan. Also add lime zest, beans and chipotle paste and stir well. Add tomatoes mix and cooking juices from the baking dish, stir and cook for 5 minutes. Ladle soup into bowls, add salt and pepper to the taste, add some sour cream and lime juice on top, sprinkle coriander and avocado pieces and serve. Enjoy!

Nutrition: calories 253, fat 4, fiber 2, carbs 4, protein 4

Mediterranean Chicken And Tomato Dish

Preparation time: 10 minutes
Cooking time: 20 minutes
Servings: 4

Ingredients:

- 5 chicken thighs
- 1 tablespoon olive oil
- 1 tablespoon thyme, chopped
- 2 garlic cloves, minced
- 1 teaspoon red pepper flakes, crushed
- ½ cup heavy cream
- ¾ cup chicken stock
- ½ cup sun dried tomatoes in olive oil, drained and chopped
- Salt and black pepper to the taste
- ¼ cup parmesan cheese, grated
- Basil leaves, chopped for serving

Directions:

Heat up a pan with the oil over medium high heat, add chicken, salt and pepper to the taste, cook for 3 minutes on each side, transfer to a plate and leave aside for now. Return pan to heat, add thyme, garlic and pepper flakes, stir and cook for 1 minute. Add stock, tomatoes, salt and pepper, heavy cream and parmesan, stir and bring to a simmer. Add chicken pieces, stir, introduce in the oven at 350 degrees F and bake for 15 minutes. Take pan out of the oven, leave chicken aside for 2-3 minutes, divide between plates and serve with basil sprinkled on top. Enjoy!

Nutrition: calories 212, fat 4, fiber 3, carbs 3, protein 3

Incredible Chicken Dish

Preparation time: 10 minutes
Cooking time: 30 minutes
Servings: 4

Ingredients:

- 14 ounces canned tomatoes, crushed
- 1 pound chicken breast, boneless and skinless
- 2 tablespoons olive oil
- Salt and black pepper to the taste
- 2 red bell peppers, sliced
- 1 small yellow onion, sliced
- 2 garlic cloves, minced
- 2 zucchinis, chopped
- ½ teaspoon oregano, dried
- 1 cup chicken stock
- ¼ cup basil leaves, torn

Directions:

Heat up a pan with the oil over medium high heat, add chicken breasts, salt and pepper, cook for 6 minutes on each side, transfer to a plate and leave aside for now. Return pan to heat, add peppers and onion, stir and cook for 5 minutes. Add zucchini, stir and cook for 3 minutes. Add garlic and oregano, stir and cook for 1 minute. Add tomatoes and stock, stir, bring to a boil, reduce heat and simmer for 10 minutes. Add chicken breasts, toss to coat, cook for 1 minute, transfer to plates, sprinkle basil and serve. Enjoy!

Nutrition: calories 253, fat 3, fiber 2, carbs 3, protein 3

Creamy Chicken Salad

Preparation time: 10 minutes
Cooking time: 0 minutes
Servings: 6

Ingredients:

- 20 ounces chicken meat, already cooked and chopped
- ½ cup pecans, chopped

For the creamy cucumber salad dressing:

- 1 cup Greek yogurt
- 1 cucumber, chopped
- 1 garlic clove, chopped
- 1 cup green grapes, seedless and cut in halves
- ½ cup celery, chopped
- ounces canned mandarin oranges, drained

- Salt and white pepper to the taste
- 1 teaspoon lemon juice

Directions:

In a bowl, mix cucumber with salt, pepper to the taste, lemon juice, garlic and yogurt and stir very well. In a salad bowl, mix chicken meat with grapes, pecans, oranges and celery. Add cucumber salad dressing, toss to coat and keep in the fridge until you serve it. Enjoy!

Nutrition: calories 200, fat 3, fiber 1, carbs 2, protein 4, protein 8

Amazing Chicken Salad

Preparation time: 30 minutes
Cooking time: 20 minutes
Servings: 4

Ingredients:

- 4 medium chicken breasts, boneless and skinless
- 2 eggplants, sliced
- Salt and black pepper to the taste
- 1 tablespoon ginger, grated
- 1 tablespoon garlic, minced

For the vinaigrette:

- 1 teaspoon ginger, grated
- 2 teaspoons rice vinegar
- 2 teaspoons Dijon mustard
- 1 teaspoon brown sugar

For serving:

- ½ lettuce head, leaves torn
- 1 pound cucumbers, sliced
- ¾ cup cilantro, chopped
- ½ cup scallions, sliced

- 2 tablespoons soy sauce
- 1 teaspoon sesame oil
- 3 tablespoons roasted peanut oil
- 2 tablespoons rice wine
- ¼ teaspoon chili paste

- 3 tablespoons roasted peanut oil
- 1 teaspoon sesame oil
- Salt to the taste
- 1 tablespoon lime juice

- 1 jalapeno, sliced
- 2 tablespoons sesame seeds, toasted
- Lime wedges

Directions:

In a bowl, mix 1 tablespoon grated ginger with 1 tablespoon minced garlic, 2 tablespoons soy sauce, 3 tablespoons peanut oil, 1 teaspoon sesame oil, 2 tablespoon rice wine and ½ teaspoon chili paste and whisk very well. Put eggplant slices in a bowl, add half of the mix you've just made and toss to coat. Put chicken breasts in another bowl, add the rest of the ginger mix, also toss to coat and leave everything aside for 30 minutes. Heat up your kitchen grill over medium high heat, add eggplant slices, cook for 3 minutes on each side and transfer them to a bowl. Arrange chicken breasts on grill, cook for 5 minutes, flip and cook for 2 more minutes, transfer them to a cutting board, leave aside for 4 minutes and then slice them. Arrange lettuce leaves on a platter, add chicken slices, grilled eggplant slices, cucumbers and scallions and some salt. In a bowl, mix 2 teaspoons rice vinegar with 1 teaspoon grated ginger, brown sugar, mustard, 1 teaspoon sesame oil, 3 tablespoons roasted peanut oil, salt to the taste and lime juice and stir very well. Spread 1 tablespoon of this vinaigrette over eggplant and chicken salad. Add cilantro, sesame seeds, jalapeno slices on top and serve with lime wedges on the side. Enjoy!

Nutrition: calories 264, fat 4, fiber 2, carbs 4, protein 4

Delicious Chicken Soup

Preparation time: 10 minutes
Cooking time: 1 hour
Servings: 8

Ingredients:

- cups eggplant, diced
- Salt and black pepper to the taste
- ¼ cup olive oil+ 1 tablespoon
- 1 cup yellow onion, chopped
- 2 tablespoons garlic, minced
- 1 red bell pepper, chopped
- 2 tablespoons hot paprika+ 2 teaspoons
- ¼ cup parsley, chopped
- 1 teaspoon turmeric
- 1 and ½ tablespoons oregano, chopped
- 4 cups chicken stock
- 1 pound chicken breast, skinless, boneless and cut into small pieces
- 1 cup half and half
- 1 and ½ tablespoons cornstarch
- 2 egg yolks
- ¼ cup lemon juice
- Lemon wedges for serving

Directions:

In a bowl, mix eggplant pieces with ¼ cup oil, salt and pepper to the taste and toss to coat. Spread eggplant on a lined baking sheet, introduce in the oven at 400 degrees F, bake for 10 minutes, flip, cook for 10 minutes more and leave aside to cool down. Heat up a pot with 1 tablespoon oil over medium heat, add garlic and onion, cover pot and cook for 10 minutes. Add bell pepper stir and cook uncovered for 3 minutes. Add hot and sweet paprika, ginger and turmeric and stir well. Also add stock, chicken, eggplant pieces, oregano and parsley, stir, bring to a boil and simmer for 12 minutes. In a bowl, mix cornstarch with half and half and egg yolks and stir well. Add 1 cup soup, stir again and pour gradually into soup. Stir soup, add salt and pepper to the taste and lemon juice. Ladle into soup bowls and serve with lemon wedges on the side. Enjoy!

Nutrition: calories 242, fat 3, fiber 2, carbs 5, protein 3

Mediterranean Chicken And Lentils Soup

Preparation time: 10 minutes
Cooking time: 1 hour and 10 minutes
Servings: 8

Ingredients:

- 4 tablespoons butter
- 2 celery stalks, chopped
- 2 carrots, chopped
- 1 yellow onion, chopped
- 2 tablespoons tomato paste
- 2 garlic cloves, chopped
- cups chicken stock
- 2 cups French lentils
- 1 pound chicken thighs, skinless and boneless
- Salt and black pepper to the taste
- Grated parmesan for serving

Directions:

Heat up a Dutch oven with the butter over medium high heat, add onion, garlic, carrots and celery, stir and cook for 6 minutes. Add salt and pepper to the taste, stir and cook for 4 more minutes. Add tomato paste, stir and cook for 2 minutes. Add lentils, chicken stock and chicken thighs, stir, bring to a boil, cover pot and cook for 1 hour. Transfer chicken thighs to a plate and leave aside to cool down. Transfer soup to your food processor, add more salt and pepper if needed and blend. Return soup to pot, shred chicken meant and also add to pot. Stir, ladle into soup bowls, sprinkle cheese on top and serve. Enjoy!

Nutrition: calories 231, fat 2, fiber 2, carbs 5, protein 3

Classic Mediterranean Chicken Soup

Preparation time: 15 minutes
Cooking time: 1 hour and 20 minutes
Servings: 4

Ingredients:

- 1 big chicken
- 3 tablespoons salt
- 4 cups water
- 1 leek, cut in quarters
- 2 bay leaves
- 1 carrot, cut into quarters
- 3 tablespoons olive oil
- 2/3 cup rice
- 2 cups yellow onion, chopped
- 2 eggs
- ½ cup lemon juice
- 1 teaspoon black pepper

Directions:

Put chicken in a pot, add water and 2 tablespoons salt, bring to a boil over medium high heat, reduce heat and skim foam. Add carrot, bay leaves and leek and simmer for 1 hour. Heat up a pan with the oil over medium high heat, add onion, stir and cook for 6 minutes, take off heat and leave aside for now. Transfer chicken to a cutting board and leave aside to cool down. Strain soup into another pot and return to pot. Add sautéed onion and rice, bring again to a boil over high heat, reduce temperature to low and simmer for 20 minutes. Discard chicken bones and skin, dice into big chunks and return to boiling soup. Meanwhile, in a bowl, mix lemon juice with eggs and black pepper and stir well. Add 2 cups boiling soup and whisk again well. Pour this into the soup and stir well. Add the rest of the salt, stir, take off heat, transfer to soup bowls and serve right away. Enjoy!

Nutrition: calories 242, fat 3, fiber 2, carbs 3, protein 3

Rich Chicken Soup

Preparation time: 10 minutes
Cooking time: 50 minutes
Servings: 6

Ingredients:

- 4 chicken things, bone-in and skin on
- 1 tablespoon olive oil
- Salt and black pepper to the taste
- 2 celery stalks, chopped
- 2 carrots, chopped
- 1 yellow onion, chopped
- cups chicken stock
- ½ cup parsley, chopped
- ½ cup barley
- 1 teaspoon lemon zest, grated

Directions:

Heat up a pot with the oil over medium high heat, add chicken, season with salt and pepper to the taste, stir and cook for 8 minutes, take off heat and transfer to a plate. Return pot to medium heat, add onion, celery, carrots, salt and pepper, stir and cook for 5 minutes. Add stock, barley and return chicken to pot. Stir, bring to a boil, reduce heat, cover and simmer for 40 minutes. In a small bowl, mix parsley with a pinch of salt, pepper and lemon zest and stir very well. Take chicken out of the pot, discard bones and skin, shred and return to pot again. Ladle soup into bowls, top with parsley mixture and serve right away. Enjoy!

Nutrition: calories 213, fat 2, fiber 2, carbs 4, protein 5

Divine Chicken

Preparation time: 20 minutes
Cooking time: 40 minutes
Servings: 4

Ingredients:

- 3 and ½ pounds chicken, cut into 10 medium pieces
- 2 yellow onions, chopped
- 2 tablespoons olive oil
- 1 garlic clove, minced
- ¼ pint chicken stock, warm
- 1 tablespoon white flour
- 2 teaspoons mixed dried herbs (parsley and basil)
- ounces canned tomatoes, chopped
- Salt and black pepper to the taste

Directions:

Heat up a pot with the oil over medium high heat, add chicken meat, stir and brown it for 5 minutes, take off heat, transfer to a plate and leave aside for now. Return pot to heat, add garlic and onion, stir and cook for 3 minutes. Add flour and stir well. Add herbs, tomatoes and stock, stir, bring to a boil and season with salt and pepper to the taste. Add chicken pieces, stir, reduce heat to medium and simmer the stew for 45 minutes. Transfer to plates and serve right away. Enjoy!

Nutrition: calories 200, fat 4, fiber 3, carbs 7, protein 12

Chicken And Mediterranean Veggies

Preparation time: 10 minutes
Cooking time: 30 minutes
Servings: 4

Ingredients:

- 4 chicken things, bone-in
- Salt and black pepper to the taste
- 1 tablespoon olive oil
- 1 cup chicken stock
- 6 radishes, halved
- 1 teaspoon sugar
- 3 carrots, cut into thin sticks
- 2 tablespoon chives, chopped

Directions:

Heat up a Dutch oven with the oil over medium high heat, add chicken, salt and pepper to the taste, stir and brown for 7 minutes on each side and discard excess grease. Add stock, carrots, sugar and radishes, stir gently, reduce heat to medium, cover pot partly and simmer for 20 minutes. Take off heat, allow the chicken to cool down for 2-3 minutes, transfer to plates and serve with chopped chives sprinkled on top. Enjoy!

Nutrition: calories 237, fat 10, fiber 3, carbs 9, protein 29

Chicken And Tasty Slaw

Preparation time: 10 minutes
Cooking time: 6 minutes
Servings: 4

Ingredients:

- 3 medium chicken breasts, skinless, boneless and cut into thin strips
- 4 ounces broccoli slaw
- 5 tablespoon extra virgin olive oil
- Salt and black pepper to the taste
- 2 tablespoons sherry vinegar
- 1 and ½ cups peaches, pitted and sliced
- 1 tablespoon chives, chopped
- ¼ cup feta cheese, crumbled
- ¼ cup barbeque sauce
- 2 bacon slices, cooked and crumbled

Directions:

In a bowl, mix 4 tablespoon oil with vinegar, salt and pepper to the taste and stir very well. Add peaches and broccoli slaw, toss to coat and leave aside for now. Season chicken with salt and pepper, heat up a pan with the rest of the oil over medium high heat, add chicken, cook for 6 minutes, take off heat, transfer to a bowl and mix well with barbeque sauce. Arrange salad on serving plates, add chicken strips, sprinkle cheese, chives and crumbled bacon and serve right away. Enjoy!

Nutrition: calories 200, fat 15, fiber 3, carbs 10, protein 33

Zucchini And Chicken Delight

Preparation time: 10 minutes
Cooking time: 15 minutes
Servings: 4

Ingredients:

- 1 pound chicken breasts, cut into medium chunks
- 12 ounces zucchini, sliced
- 2 tablespoons olive oil
- 2 garlic cloves, minced
- 2 tablespoons parmesan, grated
- 1 tablespoon parsley, chopped
- Salt and black pepper to the taste

Directions:

In a bowl, mix chicken pieces with 1 tablespoon oil, some salt and pepper and toss to coat. Heat up a pan over medium high heat, add chicken pieces, brown for 6 minutes on all sides, transfer to a plate and leave aside. Heat up the pan with the rest of the oil over medium heat, add zucchini slices and garlic, stir and cook for 5 minutes. Return chicken pieces to the pan, add parmesan on top, stir, take off heat, divide between plates and serve with some parsley on top. Enjoy!

Nutrition: calories 212, fat 4, fiber 3, carbs 4, protein 7

Mediterranean Surprise

Preparation time: 10 minutes
Cooking time: 10 minutes
Servings: 4

Ingredients:

- 1 and ½ cups instant brown rice
- 1 and ½ tablespoons sugar
- 1 cup chicken stock
- 2 tablespoon soy sauce
- ounces chicken breast boneless, skinless and cut into small pieces
- 1 egg
- 2 egg whites
- A few scallions, sliced

Directions:

Cook the instant rice according to instructions, place in a bowl and leave aside until you serve it. Put stock in a pot, heat up over medium low heat, add soy sauce and sugar, stir and bring to a boil. In a bowl, mix the egg with egg whites and stir very well. Add chicken to stock, also add eggs mix, sprinkle scallions on top and cook for 3 minutes without stirring. Divide rice in 4 bowls, add chicken soup on top and serve. Enjoy

Nutrition: calories 231, fat 3, fiber 2, carbs 3, protein 4

Wonderful Chicken Soup

Preparation time: 10 minutes
Cooking time: 30 minutes
Servings: 4

Ingredients:

- 1 yellow onion, chopped
- 1 tablespoon butter
- 2 celery stalks, chopped
- 1 big garlic clove, minced
- 2 carrots chopped
- Salt and black pepper to the taste
- 1 tablespoon thyme, chopped
- 1 pound red potatoes, cut into quarters
- 1 qtr. chicken stock
- 4 ounces Bella mushrooms, sliced
- 1 bay leaf
- 1 cup heavy cream
- 4 cups rotisserie chicken, shredded
- 2 tablespoons chives, chopped

Directions:

Heat up a Dutch oven with the butter over medium heat, add onions, celery, garlic, carrot and thyme, stir and cook for 5 minutes. Add salt, potatoes, stock, mushrooms and bay leaf, stir, bring to boil and simmer for 20 minutes. Add chicken, heavy cream and black pepper, cook for 5 more minutes and discard bay leaf. Ladle into bowls serve with chives sprinkled on top. Enjoy!

Nutritional value: calories 267, fat 6, fiber 4, carbs 7, protein 4

Healthy Mediterranean Chicken

Preparation time: 5 minutes
Cooking time: 6 hours and 10 minutes
Servings: 6

Ingredients:

- 2 pounds chicken breasts, boneless and skinless
- 28 ounces canned tomatoes, chopped
- 28 ounces canned artichoke hearts, drained
- 1 and ½ cups chicken stock
- 1 yellow onion, chopped
- ¼ cup white wine vinegar
- ½ cup kalamata olives, pitted and chopped
- 1 tablespoon curry powder
- 2 teaspoons thyme
- 2 teaspoons basil
- Salt and black pepper to the taste
- ¼ cup parsley, chopped

Directions:

Put chicken breasts in your slow cooker. Add tomatoes, artichoke hearts, onion and olives and stir. Add stock, vinegar, curry powder, thyme, basil, salt and black pepper to the taste. Cover and cook on Low for 6 hours. Uncover, add more salt and pepper if needed, add parsley and stir gently. Transfer to plates and serve! Enjoy!

Nutrition: calories 342, fat 3, fiber 3, carbs 5, protein 4

Special Slow Cooked Chicken

Preparation time: 10 minutes
Cooking time: 6 hours
Servings: 4

Ingredients:

- 3 already chicken breasts, already browned
- 56 ounces canned plum tomatoes and their juice
- 16 ounces canned chickpeas
- 2 garlic cloves, minced
- 1 yellow onion, chopped
- 1 cup Mediterranean olives, pitted
- 2 cups chicken stock
- 2 tablespoons capers
- 1 cup brown rice, cooked
- ¼ cup oregano, chopped
- Salt and black pepper to the taste
- Feta cheese for serving

Directions:

Put chicken breasts in your slow cooker lined with slow cooker liner. Add tomatoes and their juice and stir gently. Add chickpeas, garlic, onion, olives, capers, chicken stock, some salt and pepper, cover and cook on Low for 6 hours. Uncover, add more salt and pepper, add oregano and stir gently. Transfer to plates and serve with brown rice on the side and crumbled feta cheese on top. Enjoy!

Nutrition: calories 300, fat 2, fiber 3, carbs 5, protein 4

Mediterranean Chicken Thighs

Preparation time: 10 minutes
Cooking time: 4 hours
Servings: 12

Ingredients:

- 1 tablespoon olive oil
- 12 chicken thighs
- Salt and black pepper to the taste
- 1 yellow onion, chopped
- 1 and ½ cups mushrooms, cut in quarters
- 2 zucchinis, chopped
- 15 ounces canned chickpeas
- 15 ounces canned tomatoes, chopped
- ½ cup sun dried tomatoes, chopped
- 1 cup kalamata olives, pitted
- 2 tablespoons lemon juice
- 3 garlic cloves, minced
- 2 tablespoons capers
- 1 teaspoon oregano, dried

Directions:

Heat up a pan with the olive oil over medium high heat, add chicken, season with salt and pepper, brown it on both sides, remove and leave aside for now. Put mushrooms, zucchini and onion in your slow cooker. Add chicken thighs, chickpeas, tomatoes, sundried tomatoes, garlic, olives, lemon juice and oregano. Add capers on top, cover and cook on High for 4 hours. Divide between plates and serve right away! Enjoy!

Nutrition: calories 264, fat 4, fiber 3, carbs 4, protein 5

Chicken Wings Delight

Preparation time: 10 minutes
Cooking time: 1 hour and 50 minutes
Servings: 6

Ingredients:

- 12 chicken wings, halved
- 2 garlic cloves, minced
- Juice of 1 lemon
- Zest from 1 lemon
- 2 tablespoons olive oil
-
- 1 teaspoon cumin, ground
- Salt and pepper to the taste
- A small bowl full of olives
- A small bowl full of dates
- A small bowl full of pickled chilies

Directions:

In a bowl, mix lemon zest with lemon juice, garlic, olive oil, cumin, salt and pepper and stir well. Add chicken wings, toss to coat and keep in the fridge for 1 hour. Put chicken wings on a baking tray, introduce in the oven and bake for 50 minutes at 350 degrees F. Take chicken wings out of the oven, transfer to a platter and serve with small bowls full of olives, dates and pickled chilies and flatbreads on the side. Enjoy!

Nutrition: calories 321, fat 3, fiber 4, carbs 6, protein 8

Roasted Chicken And Special Sauce

Preparation time: 10 minutes
Cooking time: 40 minutes
Servings: 4

Ingredients:

- 4 chicken thighs
- 2 tablespoons olive oil
- ½ teaspoon sweet paprika
- 1 teaspoon cumin, ground
- 5 ounces hot chicken stock
- 6 ounces walnuts, chopped
- 1 yellow onion, chopped
- 2 garlic cloves, minced
- 1 and ½ tablespoons heavy cream
- A handful coriander, chopped
- Juice of 1 lemon
- Salt and pepper to the taste

Directions:

Put chicken thighs in a baking dish, add paprika, cumin, salt, pepper and 1 tablespoon olive oil and toss. Introduce in the oven at 350 degrees F and bake for 40 minutes. Heat up a pan over medium high heat, add walnuts, cook for 3 minutes and leave aside. Heat up another pan with the rest of the oil over medium high heat, add onion and garlic, stir and for 3-4 minutes. Transfer onion to your food processor, add walnuts and pulse well. Add the chicken stock and pulse until you obtain a paste. Transfer this paste to the pan and heat it up over medium heat. Add lemon juice, salt and pepper, coriander and the cream, stir and pour into a bowl. Take chicken out of the oven, arrange on a platter and serve with the sauce drizzled all over. Enjoy!

Nutrition: calories 253, fat 4, fiber 5, carbs 7, protein 8

The Best Chicken Salad

Preparation time: 10 minutes
Cooking time: 20 minutes
Servings: 2

Ingredients:

- 2 tablespoons olive oil
- 2 ounces quinoa
- 2 ounces cherry tomatoes, cut in quarters
- 3 ounces sweet corn
- A handful coriander, chopped
- Lime juice from 1 lime
- Lime zest from 1 lime, grated
- Salt and black pepper to the taste
- 2 spring onions, chopped
- 1 small red chili pepper, chopped
- 1 avocado, pitted, peeled and chopped
- 7 ounces chicken meat, roasted, skinless, boneless and chopped

Directions:

Put some water in a pan, bring to a boil over medium high heat, add quinoa, stir and cook for 12 minutes. Meanwhile, put corn in a pan, heat up over medium high heat, cook for 5 minutes and leave aside for now. Drain quinoa, transfer to a bowl, add tomatoes, corn, coriander, onions, chili, lime zest, olive oil, salt and black pepper to the taste and toss. In another bowl, mix avocado with lime juice and stir well. Add this to quinoa salad, also add chicken, toss to coat and serve. Enjoy!

Nutrition: calories 320, fat 4, fiber 4, carbs 5, protein 7

Healthy Chicken Dish

Preparation time: 10 minutes
Cooking time: 12 minutes
Servings: 4

Ingredients:

- 4 chicken breast halves, skinless and boneless
- Salt and black pepper to the taste
- 4 teaspoons olive oil
- 1 small cucumber, sliced
- 3 teaspoons cilantro, chopped
- 4 Greek whole wheat tortillas
- 4 tablespoons peanut sauce

Directions:

Heat up your grill over medium high heat, season chicken with salt and pepper, rub with the oil, add to the grill, cook for 6 minutes on each side, transfer to a cutting board, leave to cool down for 5 minutes, slice and leave aside. In a bowl, mix cilantro with cucumber and stir. Heat up a pan over medium heat, add each tortilla, heat up for 20 seconds and transfer them to a working surface. Spread 1 tablespoon peanut sauce on each tortilla, divide chicken and cucumber mix on each, fold, arrange on plates and serve. Enjoy!

Nutrition: calories 321, fat 3, fiber 4, carbs 7, protein 9

Mediterranean Chicken And Salsa

Preparation time: 10 minutes
Cooking time: 43 minutes
Servings: 4

Ingredients:

- 1 pound chicken breast, boneless and skinless
- 16 ounces Greek salsa Verde
- Salt and black pepper to the taste
- 1 tablespoon olive oil
- 1 and ½ cups goat cheese, crumbled
- ¼ cup cilantro, chopped
- White rice for serving
- Juice from 1 lime

Directions:

In a bowl, mix chicken with salt, pepper, and oil and toss to coat. Spread salsa in a baking dish, add chicken on top, introduce in the oven at 400 degrees F and bake for 40 minutes. Take chicken out of the oven, add cheese, introduce everything in preheated broiler and broil for 3 minutes. Add lime juice, divide between plates, sprinkle cilantro and serve with white rice. Enjoy!

Nutrition: calories 300, fat 3, fiber 4, carbs 6, protein 7

Chicken And Mushrooms

Preparation time: 10 minutes
Cooking time: 50 minutes
Servings: 8

Ingredients:

- 3 tablespoons butter
- 8 chicken thighs, bone in, skin-on
- Salt and black pepper to the taste
- 3 garlic cloves, minced
- 8 ounces mushrooms, halved
- ½ teaspoons thyme, dried
- 1 cup chicken stock
- ¼ cup heavy cream
- ½ teaspoon basil, dried
- ½ teaspoon oregano, dried
- 1 tablespoon mustard
- ¼ cup parmesan, grated

Directions:

Heat up a pot with 2 tablespoons butter over medium high heat, add chicken thighs, salt and pepper to the taste, cook for 3 minutes on each side, take off heat and transfer to a plate. Return pot to medium heat, add the rest of the butter, add mushroom and garlic, stir and cook for 6 minutes. Add salt, pepper to the taste, stock, oregano, thyme and basil and stir. Add chicken, stir and bake in the oven at 400 degrees F for 30 minutes. Take pot off heat, transfer chicken to plates and heat up pan juices on the stove over medium heat. Add cream, mustard and parmesan, stir, bring to a boil, reduce heat to low and simmer for 10 minutes. Pour over chicken and serve right away. Enjoy!

Nutrition: calories 290, fat 5, fiber 3, carbs 6, protein 7

Mediterranean Diet Vegetable Recipes

Easy Lentils Salad

Preparation time: 15 minutes
Cooking time: 0 minutes
Servings: 4

Ingredients:

- 14 ounces canned lentils, drained
- 1 tomato, chopped
- 1 small red onion, chopped
- 1 green onion, chopped
- ½ red bell pepper, chopped
- 1 birds eye chili, chopped
- 1 tablespoon fresh lime juice
- 1/3 cup coriander, chopped
- 2 teaspoon fish sauce

Directions:

Put lentils in a salad bowl. Add onion, tomato, green onion, capsicum and chili. Add fish sauce, lime juice and coriander, toss everything to coat and serve right away! Enjoy!

Nutrition: calories 200, fat 2, fiber 3, carbs 6, protein 9

Cabbage Salad

Preparation time: 15 minutes
Cooking time: 0 minutes
Servings: 6

Ingredients:

- 1 cabbage head, shredded
- 1 carrot, chopped

For the dressing:

- 2 Serrano chilies, chopped
- 1 teaspoon sugar
- 1 garlic clove, minced
- 2 tablespoons coriander, chopped
- ½ cup cashews, halved
- A pinch of salt
- 3 tablespoons fish sauce
- 2 tablespoons balsamic vinegar

Directions:

In a mortar, mix chili with sugar, garlic and salt and mash well. Transfer this into a bowl, add fish sauce and vinegar and whisk well. In a salad bowl, mix cabbage with carrot, coriander and cashew halves. Add salad dressing, toss to coat and serve right away! Enjoy!

Nutrition: calories 210, fat 3, fiber 2, carbs 5, protein 8

Pomegranate Salad

Preparation time: 10 minutes
Cooking time: 0 minutes
Servings: 3

Ingredients:

- 3 big pears, cored and cut with a spiralizer
- ¾ cup pomegranate seeds

For the vinaigrette:
- 1 tablespoon sesame oil
- 1 tablespoon olive oil
- 1 tablespoon maple syrup
- 1 teaspoon white sesame seeds
- 2 tablespoons apple cider vinegar
- 5 ounces arugula
- ¾ cup walnuts, chopped

- 1 tablespoon soy sauce
- 1 garlic clove, minced
- A pinch of sea salt
- Black pepper to the taste

Directions:

In a bowl, mix sesame oil with olive oil, maple syrup, sesame seeds, vinegar, garlic, soy sauce, salt and pepper and whisk very well. In a salad bowl, mix pear noodles with arugula, walnuts and pomegranate seeds. Add vinaigrette, toss to coat well and serve right away. Enjoy!

Nutrition: calories 200, fat 2, fiber 4, carbs 6, protein 9

Intense Bulgur And Veggie Salad

Preparation time: 15 minutes
Cooking time: 0 minutes
Servings: 6

Ingredients:

- 1 and ½ cups hot water
- 1 cup bulgur
- Juice from 1 lime
- 4 tablespoons cilantro, chopped
- ½ cup cranberries, dried
- 1 lime, cut into wedges
- A pinch of cumin, ground
- 1 and ½ teaspoons curry powder
- 1/3 cup almonds, sliced
- ¼ cup green onions, chopped
- ½ cup red bell peppers, chopped
- ½ cup carrots, grated
- 4 tablespoons pepitas
- 1 tablespoon olive oil
- A pinch of sea salt
- Black pepper to the taste

Directions:

Put bulgur into a bowl, add boiling water to it, stir, cover and leave aside for 15 minutes. Fluff bulgur with a fork and transfer to a salad bowl. Add lime juice, cilantro, cranberries, almonds, bell peppers, onions and carrots and stir. Add cumin, curry powder and pepitas and stir again. Add oil, a pinch of salt and black pepper, stir and serve right away with lime wedges on the side. Enjoy!

Nutrition: calories 160, fat 3, fiber 3, carbs 7, protein 10

Mediterranean Black Bean Salad

Preparation time: 15 minutes
Cooking time: 0 minutes
Servings: 4

Ingredients:
- 1 and ½ cups cooked black beans
- ½ teaspoon garlic powder
- ½ teaspoon smoked paprika
- 2 teaspoons chili powder
- A pinch of sea salt
- Black pepper to the taste
- 1 teaspoon cumin
- A pinch of cayenne pepper
- 1 and ½ cups chickpeas, cooked
- ¼ teaspoon cinnamon
- 1 lettuce head, chopped
- 1 red bell pepper, chopped
- 2 tomatoes, chopped
- 1 avocado, pitted, peeled and chopped
- 1 cup corn kernels, chopped

For the salad dressing:
- 2 tablespoons lemon juice
- ¾ cup cashews, soaked for a couple of hours and drained
- ½ cup water
- 1 garlic clove, minced
- 1 tablespoon apple cider vinegar
- ½ teaspoon onion powder
- 1 teaspoon chives, chopped
- ½ teaspoon oregano, dried
- 1 teaspoon dill, dried
- 1 teaspoon cumin
- ½ teaspoon smoked paprika

Directions:

In your blender, mix cashews with water, 2 tablespoons lemon juice, 1 tablespoon vinegar, 1 garlic clove, ½ teaspoon onion powder, dill, oregano, chives, 1 teaspoon cumin, a pinch of salt and ½ teaspoon paprika, blend really well and leave aside for now. In a salad bowl, mix black beans with chili powder, ½ teaspoon garlic powder, ½ teaspoon paprika, 1 teaspoon cumin, cayenne, chickpeas, cinnamon, a pinch of salt and black pepper to the taste and stir really well. Add lettuce leaves, tomatoes, corn, avocado and bell peppers and stir everything. Drizzle the salad dressing all over your salad, toss to coat and serve right away. Enjoy!

Nutrition: calories 300, fat 4, fiber 1, carbs 6, protein 13

Lentils Salad

Preparation time: 10 minutes
Cooking time: 0 minutes
Servings: 2

Ingredients:
- 1 pita bread, cubed
- 1/3 cup canned and cooked green lentils, drained
- 2 teaspoons olive oil
- 1 carrot, grated
- 4 cups arugula
- 2 celery stalks, chopped
- 1 cucumber, sliced
- ¼ cup dates, pitted and chopped
- 1 radish, sliced
- 2 tablespoons sunflower seeds

For the vinaigrette:
- 1 tablespoon maple syrup
- 1 tablespoon Dijon mustard
- 2 tablespoons balsamic vinegar
- 2 tablespoons olive oil

Directions:

In a bowl, mix maple syrup with mustard, vinegar and olive oil and whisk well. In a salad bowl, mix green lentils with bread cubes, carrot, arugula, celery, cucumber, dates, radish and sunflower seeds. Add 2 teaspoons oil and toss to coat. Add the vinaigrette you've made, toss again and serve. Enjoy!

Nutrition: calories 179, fat 4, fiber 3, carbs 6, protein 12

Greek Chickpeas Salad

Preparation time: 15 minutes
Cooking time: 0 minutes
Servings: 2

Ingredients:
- 16 ounces canned chickpeas, drained
- 1 handful raisins
- 1 handful baby spinach leaves
- 1 tablespoon maple syrup
- ½ tablespoon lemon juice
- 4 tablespoons olive oil
- 1 teaspoon cumin, ground
- A pinch of sea salt
- Black pepper to the taste
- ½ teaspoon chili flakes

Directions:

In a bowl, mix maple syrup with lemon juice, oil, cumin, a pinch of salt, black pepper and chili flakes and whisk well. In a salad bowl, mix chickpeas with spinach and raisins and stir. Add salad dressing, toss to coat and serve. Enjoy!

Nutrition: calories 300, fat 3, fiber 6, carbs 12, protein 9

Great Greek Salad

Preparation time: 10 minutes
Cooking time: 0 minutes
Servings: 4

Ingredients:
- 1 handful kalamata olives, pitted and sliced
- 1 punnet cherry tomatoes, halved
- 4 tomatoes, chopped
- 1 and ½ cucumbers, sliced

For the salad dressing:
- 1 teaspoon sugar
- 2 tablespoons balsamic vinegar
- ¼ cup olive oil
- 1 garlic clove, minced
- 1 red onion, chopped
- 2 tablespoons oregano, chopped
- 1 tablespoon mint, chopped

- 2 teaspoons Italian herbs, dried
- 1 teaspoon soy sauce
- A pinch of sea salt
- Black pepper to the taste

Directions:

In a salad bowl, mix cherry tomatoes with tomatoes, olives, cucumbers, onion, mint and oregano and stir. In another bowl, mix sugar with vinegar, oil, garlic, dried Italian herbs, soy sauce, a pinch of salt and black pepper and whisk well. Add this to salad, toss to coat and serve. Enjoy!

Nutrition: calories 140, fat 2, fiber 3, carbs 6, protein 12

Fast Salad

Preparation time: 10 minutes
Cooking time: 0 minutes
Servings: 4

Ingredients:

- 15 ounces canned chickpeas, drained
- 15 ounces canned great northern beans, drained
- 2 tablespoons olive oil
- ½ cup spinach, chopped
- ½ cup cucumber, sliced
- 1 tablespoon basil, chopped
- 1 tablespoon parsley, chopped
- sun dried tomatoes, chopped
- A pinch of sea salt
- 2 tablespoon vinegar

Directions:

In a bowl, mix chickpeas with beans, spinach, cucumber, tomatoes, basil and parsley. Add salt, vinegar and oil, toss to coat well and serve. Enjoy!

Nutrition: calories 140, fat 5, fiber 6, carbs 9, protein 15

Beans And Avocado Salad

Preparation time: 10 minutes
Cooking time: 0 minutes
Servings: 4

Ingredients:

- 15 ounces canned white beans, drained
- 1 tomato, chopped
- 1 avocado, pitted, peeled and chopped
- ¼ sweet onion, chopped
- A pinch of sea salt
- Black pepper to the taste
- ¼ cup lemon juice
- 1 and ½ tablespoons olive oil
- A handful basil, chopped
- 1 teaspoon garlic, minced
- 1 teaspoon mustard

Directions:

In a salad bowl, mix beans with tomato, avocado and onion. Add a pinch of salt and black pepper and stir gently everything. In a bowl, mix oil with lemon juice, basil, mustard and garlic and whisk well. Add this to the salad, toss to coat and serve. Enjoy!

Nutrition: calories 150, fat 3, fiber 2, carbs 6, protein 14

Corn And Avocado Salad

Preparation time: 10 minutes
Cooking time: 0 minutes
Servings: 4

Ingredients:
- 2 avocados, pitted, peeled and cubed
- 1 pint mixed cherry tomatoes, halved

For the salad dressing:
- 2 tablespoons olive oil
- 1 tablespoon lime juice
- ½ teaspoon lime zest, grated

- 2 cups fresh corn
- 1 red onion, chopped

- A pinch of salt
- Black pepper to the taste
- ¼ cup cilantro, chopped

Directions:
In a salad bowl, mix avocados with onion, corn and tomatoes. In a smaller bowl, mix oil with lime juice and zest, a pinch of salt and some black pepper and whisk well. Add this over salad, sprinkle cilantro on top, toss to coat and serve. Enjoy!

Nutrition: calories 120, fat 3, fiber 2, carbs 6, protein 9

Greek Beans And Cucumber Salad

Preparation time: 10 minutes
Cooking time: 0 minutes
Servings: 4

Ingredients:
- 1 cucumber, cut into chunks
- 15 ounces canned black beans, drained
- 1 cup corn
- 1 cup cherry tomatoes, halved
- 1 small red onion, chopped
- 3 tablespoons olive oil

- 4 and ½ teaspoons orange marmalade
- 1 teaspoon agave nectar
- Salt and black pepper to the taste
- ½ teaspoon cumin
- 1 tablespoon lemon juice

Directions:
In a bowl, mix beans with cucumber, corn, onion and tomatoes. In another bowl, mix marmalade with oil, agave nectar, lemon juice, salt, pepper to the taste and cumin and stir very well. Pour this dressing over salad, toss to coat and serve right away. Enjoy!

Nutrition: calories 110, fat 0, fiber 3, carbs 6, protein 8

Corn Salad

Preparation time: 10 minutes
Cooking time: 0 minutes
Servings: 4

Ingredients:

- 1 and ½ teaspoons agave nectar
- 2 tablespoons lime juice
- 1 jalapeno, chopped
- ¼ cup olive oil
- ¼ teaspoon cumin, ground
- A pinch of sea salt
- Black pepper to the taste
- 4 cups fresh corn kernels
- ½ cup parsley, chopped
- 6 radishes, thinly sliced
- 1 red onion, chopped

Directions:

In your blender, mix agave nectar with lime juice, jalapeno, cumin, oil, salt and pepper and blend well. In a salad bowl, mix corn with onion, radishes and parsley. Add salad dressing, toss to coat and serve. Enjoy!

Nutrition: calories 100, fat 0.4, fiber 0.8, carbs 1, protein 6

Different Greek Corn Salad

Preparation time: 10 minutes
Cooking time: 0 minutes
Servings: 4

Ingredients:

- 1 red bell pepper, thinly sliced
- 2 cups corn
- Juice of 1 lemon
- Zest from 1 lemon, grated
- 8 cups arugula
- A pinch of sea salt
- Black pepper to the taste

Directions:

In a salad bowl, mix arugula with corn and bell pepper. Add salt, pepper, lemon zest and juice, toss to coat and serve. Enjoy!

Nutrition: calories 90, fat 0, fiber 1, carbs 1, protein 5

Corn And Bulgur Salad

Preparation time: 30 minutes
Cooking time: 0 minutes
Servings: 4

Ingredients:
- 1 cup bulgur
- 2 cups hot water
- A pinch of sea salt
- Black pepper to the taste
- 2 cups corn
- 1 cucumber, chopped
- 2 tablespoons lemon juice
- 2 tablespoons balsamic vinegar
- ¼ cup olive oil

Directions:

In a bowl, mix bulgur with the water, cover, leave aside for 25 minutes, fluff with a fork and transfer to a salad bowl. Add corn and cucumber and stir. In a small bowl, mix oil with lemon juice, vinegar, salt and pepper and whisk well. Add this to your salad, toss to coat well and serve. Enjoy!

Nutrition: calories 100, fat 0.5, fiber 2, carbs 2, protein 6

Fattoush Salad

Preparation time: 10 minutes
Cooking time: 15 minutes
Servings: 6

Ingredients:
- 3 tablespoons olive oil
- 2 loaves pita bread
- 1 cucumber, chopped
- 1 heart lettuce, chopped
- 5 medium tomatoes, chopped

For the dressing:
- 1/3 cup olive oil
- Juice from 1 and ½ limes
- Salt and black pepper to the taste
- ½ teaspoon sumac
- 5 green bell peppers, chopped
- 1 cup parsley, chopped
- 5 radishes, sliced

- 1 teaspoon sumac
- ½ teaspoon cinnamon powder
- ¼ teaspoon allspice, ground

Directions:

Heat up a pan with 3 tablespoons olive oil over medium heat, break pita, place in pan, brown for 1-2 minutes, add salt, pepper and ½ teaspoon sumac, transfer to paper towels and leave aside. In a bowl, mix lettuce with cucumber, onion, tomatoes, radishes and parsley and leave aside as well. In another bowl, mix 1/3 cup olive oil with lime juice, salt, pepper, 1 teaspoon sumac, cinnamon and all spice and stir very well. Mix salad with this dressing, toss to coat and top with toasted pita. Serve right away! Enjoy!

Nutrition: calories 201, fat 3, fiber 2, carbs 5, protein 8

Summer Mediterranean Salad

Preparation time: 30 minutes
Cooking time: 0 minutes
Servings: 6

Ingredients:

- 1 pound tomatoes, chopped
- ¾ pound cucumbers, chopped
- 1 long green pepper, chopped
- 1 red onion, soaked in cold water and sliced
- 1 tablespoon dill, chopped
- ¼ cup parsley, chopped
- 2 tablespoons mint, chopped
- 1 teaspoon sumac
- Salt and black pepper to the taste
- 3 tablespoons olive oil
- 3 tablespoons lemon juice
- 2 ounces feta cheese, crumbled
- 10 big black olives, pitted
- Pita bread for serving

Directions:

In a large salad bowl mix tomatoes with cucumber, green pepper, red onion and some salt and stir well. Add black pepper, sumac, dill, parsley and mint and stir everything. Add lemon juice, olive oil and cheese and toss to coat. Introduce in the fridge for 30 minutes and then serve with black olives on top and with pita bread. Enjoy!

Nutrition: calories 241, fat 3, fiber 2, carbs 5, protein 6

Lentil And Rice Salad

Preparation time: 10 minutes
Cooking time: 15 minutes
Servings: 4

Ingredients:

- 1 cup green lentils
- ½ cup rice
- 4 tablespoons olive oil
- 1 yellow onion, sliced
- 1 carrot, grated
- 3 green onions, chopped
- 1 cup parsley, chopped
- ½ cup mint, chopped
- Juice of 1 lemon
- ½ cup corn
- Salt and black pepper to the taste

Directions:

Boil rice and lentils in separate pots, drain water and cool them down. Heat up a pan with the oil over medium high heat, add onions and cook for 5 minutes. Add carrots and cook for 8 more minutes. Put lentils and rice in a bowl, add sautéed onions and carrots, add green onions as well and toss. Add mint, parsley, corn, salt, pepper and lemon juice, toss to coat and serve right away! Enjoy!

Nutrition: calories 200, fat 3, fiber 3, carbs 5, protein 7

Easy Couscous Salad

Preparation time: 10 minutes
Cooking time: 20 minutes
Servings: 6

Ingredients:

- 1 pound couscous
- 3 tablespoons olive oil
- 2 carrots, cubed
- ½ cup sweet peas
- ¼ cup parsley, chopped
- ½ cup sweet corn
- 1 tablespoon mint, chopped
- Salt to the taste
- 1 red bell pepper, cut into strips

Directions:

Place couscous in a bowl, cover with water and leave aside for 10 minutes. Drain, add olive oil and stir well. Put some water and salt in a pot, add carrots and sweet peas, bring to a boil over medium heat, boil for 4 minutes, drain water and put into the same bowl with the couscous. Add corn, parsley and salt and toss gently. Serve cold with red bell pepper strips on top. Enjoy!

Nutrition: calories 210, fat 2, fiber 2, carbs 4, protein 7

Fresh Cucumber Salad

Preparation time: 1 hour and 10 minutes
Cooking time: 0 minutes
Servings: 6

Ingredients:

- 2 garlic cloves, minced
- Salt to the taste
- 1 tablespoon wine vinegar
- 1 and ½ cups Greek yogurt
- 1 tablespoon dill, chopped
- 3 medium cucumbers, sliced
- 1 tablespoon olive oil
- 1 tablespoon mint, chopped

Directions:

In a bowl, mix vinegar with salt, yogurt, dill and garlic and whisk well. Combine cucumbers with yogurt dressing, introduce in the fridge for 1 hour and then serve with olive oil drizzled on top and mint leaves sprinkled all over. Enjoy!

Nutrition: calories 210, fat 1, fiber 2, carbs 5, protein 8

Greek Potato Soup

Preparation time: 10 minutes
Cooking time: 25 minutes
Servings: 2

Ingredients:

- 2 medium potatoes, peeled and cut into cubes
- 1 yellow onion, chopped
- 2 tablespoons butter
- 1 small carrot, cubed
- 1 and ½ tablespoon flour
- 1 bay leaf
- 2 and ½ cups chicken stock
- Salt and black pepper to the taste

Directions:

Heat up a pot with the butter over medium high heat, add onion and carrot, stir and cook for 3-4 minutes. Add potatoes and cook for 5 more minutes. Add flour, stir well and cook for 1 minute. Add chicken stock, salt, pepper and bay leaf and cook for 15-20 minutes. Discard bay leaf, ladle into bowls and serve. Enjoy!

Nutrition: calories 198, fat 3, fiber 2, carbs 6, protein 8

Tomato Soup

Preparation time: 10 minutes
Cooking time: 20 minutes
Servings: 3

Ingredients:

- 4 medium tomatoes, grated
- 1 green bell pepper, chopped
- 1 garlic clove, minced
- 1 tablespoon olive oil
- ¼ cup white rice
- ½ teaspoon sweet paprika
- ½ tablespoon peppercorns
- Salt and black pepper to the taste
- 3 cups hot water
- ½ bunch parsley, chopped

Directions:

Heat up a pot with the olive oil over medium heat, add bell pepper and garlic, stir and cook for 5 minutes. Add paprika, stir and cook for 1 minute. Add tomatoes, bring to a boil, cover and boil for 10 minutes. Add water, rice, salt, pepper and peppercorns, stir and boil until the rice is done. Add parsley, stir, ladle into bowls and serve. Enjoy!

Nutrition: calories 200, fat 2, fiber 3, carbs 5, protein 7

Greek Eggplant Soup

Preparation time: 15 minutes
Cooking time: 1 hour and 30 minutes
Servings: 4

Ingredients:
- 1 big eggplant, sliced lengthwise
- 3 tomatoes, halved
- 1 yellow onion, halved
- 2 tablespoons olive oil
- 6 garlic cloves
- 4 cups chicken stock
- 1 tablespoon thyme, chopped
- 1 cup heavy cream
- Salt and black pepper to the taste
- 3 and ½ ounces goat cheese, crumbled

Directions:

Arrange tomatoes, eggplant, garlic and onion on a lined baking sheet. Brush with oil, introduce in the oven at 400 degrees F and bake for 45 minutes. Scoop out pulp from veggies, transfer to a pan and heat up over medium heat. Add chicken stock and thyme, stir, bring to a simmer and cook for 45 minutes. Transfer soup to a blender, pulse well, return the cream to pot, bring to a simmer, add salt and pepper and cream, stir, ladle into bowls and serve with goat cheese sprinkled on top. Enjoy!

Nutrition: calories 200, fat 3, fiber 3, carbs 5, protein 8

Greek Tomato And Fish Soup

Preparation time: 10 minutes
Cooking time: 35 minutes
Servings: 6

Ingredients:
- 6 big tomatoes, peeled and chopped
- 2 tablespoons olive oil
- 1 yellow onion, chopped
- 2 celery stalks, chopped
- 1 carrot, chopped
- 1 jalapeno, chopped
- 1 green bell pepper, chopped
- 2 garlic cloves, minced
- 3 fish fillets, cubed
- 4 cups chicken stock
- Salt and black pepper to the taste
- A splash of balsamic vinegar
- A handful of basil leaves, chopped

Directions:

Heat up a pot with the oil over medium high heat, add onion, celery, bell pepper, jalapeno, carrot and garlic, stir and cook for 10 minutes. Add stock, tomatoes, vinegar, salt and pepper to the taste, bring to a boil, reduce heat to medium and simmer for 15 minutes. Add fish cubes, stir and cook for 10 minutes more. Ladle into bowls, sprinkle basil on top and serve. Enjoy!

Nutrition: calories 198, fat 3, fiber 1, carbs 7, protein 10

Broccoli Delight

Preparation time: 30 minutes
Cooking time: 0 minutes
Servings: 2

Ingredients:

- 10 ounces mushrooms, chopped
- 1 broccoli head, florets separated and chopped
- 1 garlic clove, minced
- 1 tablespoon agave nectar
- 1 tablespoon balsamic vinegar
- 1 yellow onion, chopped
- 1 tablespoon olive oil
- A pinch of sea salt and black pepper
- 1 teaspoon basil, dried
- 1 avocado, peeled and pitted
- A pinch of red pepper flakes
- 1 and ½ cups water

Directions:

In a bowl, mix mushrooms with broccoli, onion, garlic and avocado. In another bowl, mix agave with vinegar, oil, salt, pepper and basil and whisk well. Pour this over veggies, toss to coat and leave aside for 30 minutes. Transfer this to your blender, add water, more salt and pepper and pulse until you obtain cream. Divide into bowls, sprinkle pepper flakes on top and serve. Enjoy!

Nutrition: calories 182, fat 3, fiber 3, carbs 5, protein 8

Unique Mushroom Soup

Preparation time: 3 hours and 10 minutes
Cooking time: 0 minutes
Servings: 3

Ingredients:

- 1 yellow onion
- 1 tablespoon agave
- 1 tablespoon balsamic vinegar
- 4 tablespoons olive oil+ 1 teaspoon
- 12 ounces mushrooms, roughly chopped
- 1 tomato, chopped
- 1 avocado, pitted, peeled and roughly chopped
- 1 garlic clove, minced
- A pinch of salt and black pepper
- 1 and ½ cups water

Directions:

In a bowl, mix mushrooms with agave, vinegar, garlic, salt, pepper and 3 tablespoons olive oil and stir. Transfer mushrooms mix to your dehydrator and dehydrate them for 3 hours. Pour this mix into your blender, add onion, 1 tablespoon oil, tomato, avocado, some more salt and pepper and the water and pulse very well. Divide into soup bowls, drizzle 1 teaspoon oil on top and serve. Enjoy!

Nutrition: calories 183, fat 3, fiber 2, carbs 5, protein 8

Corn Soup

Preparation time: 10 minutes
Cooking time: 0 minutes
Servings: 3

Ingredients:

- 1 small avocado, pitted and peeled
- 1 cup corn
- ½ zucchini, chopped
- 2 cups water
- A pinch of sea salt and black pepper
- 1 tablespoon white vinegar
- 1 tablespoon olive oil
- 1 teaspoon saffron

Directions:

In your blender, mix avocado with corn, zucchini, salt, pepper and oil and blend well. Add water and pulse a few more times. Add saffron, stir once again, divide into bowls and serve. Enjoy!

Nutrition: calories 200, fat 2, fiber 3, carbs 5, protein 8

Simple Greek Cucumber Soup

Preparation time: 10 minutes
Cooking time: 0 minutes
Servings: 2

Ingredients:

- 2 cucumbers, peeled
- 2 green onions, chopped
- 1/3 cup dill, chopped
- 1 tablespoon lemon juice
- 1 teaspoon lemon juice
- A pinch of sea salt
- ½ cup water
- ½ cup hemp seeds
- A drizzle of olive oil

Directions:

In your blender, mix cucumber with green onions, dill, 1 tablespoon lemon juice, salt, hemp seeds and pulse really well. Add the oil gradually and pulse again well. Divide into soup bowls, add the rest of the lemon juice on top and serve. Enjoy!

Nutrition: calories 187, fat 3, fiber 2, carbs 6, protein 4

Cold Mint Soup

Preparation time: 10 minutes
Cooking time: 0 minutes
Servings: 2

Ingredients:
- 2 cups water
- ½ cups peanuts
- 1 cup spinach
- 1 cup broccoli florets
- A handful leek, chopped
- 1 teaspoon ginger, grated
- 1 garlic clove, minced
- A handful basil, chopped
- Juice of ½ lemon
- A pinch of sea salt and black pepper to the taste

Directions:
Put peanuts in your blender, pulse until you obtain a powder and then mix with the water. Pulse again and then mix with spinach, broccoli, leek, ginger, garlic, salt, pepper, lemon juice and basil. Blend everything well again, divide into bowls and serve. Enjoy!

Greek Garlic Soup

Preparation time: 10 minutes
Cooking time: 0 minutes
Servings: 3

Ingredients:
- 1 tablespoon olive oil
- 1 and ½ cups low fat milk
- 3 garlic cloves, grated
- A pinch of sea salt and white pepper
- ½ teaspoon apple cider vinegar
- A drizzle of olive oil for serving
- 1 tablespoon coriander, chopped

Directions:
In your blender, mix olive oil with almond milk, garlic, salt, pepper and vinegar and blend well. Divide into bowls, drizzle some olive oil on top and sprinkle coriander at the end. Enjoy!

Delicious Mediterranean Rolls

Preparation time: 6 hours and 10 minutes
Cooking time: 10 minutes
Servings: 8

Ingredients:

- 4 carrots, grated
- ½ pound mushrooms, chopped
- 1 and ¼ cups snow peas, trimmed
- 1 and ¼ cup bean sprouts

For the sauce:

- 6 green tea bags
- ½ cup hot water
- 3 tablespoons soy sauce
- ½ cup lime juice
- 1 tablespoon honey

- 16 rice wrappers
- 16 basil leaves
- 3 cups hot water
- 10 green tea bags

- 1 tablespoon chili sauce
- 1 teaspoon ginger, grated
- 2 garlic cloves, minced
- 2 green onions, chopped

Directions:

Put mushrooms, peas, carrots and bean sprouts in a pot, add some water to cover, bring to a simmer over medium high heat, blanch them or 1 minutes, drain, pat dry them and put them in a bowl. Put 3 cups hot water in a bowl, add 10 tea bags, cover, leave aside for 5 minutes, discard tea bags and transfer tea to another bowl. Soak rice wrappers in tea for 1 minute, pat dry, leave aside for 2 minutes and arrange them on a working surface. Divide mushrooms, carrots, peas and sprouts on each wrapper, add basil leaves as well, roll them and keep all rolls in the fridge for 6 hours. Meanwhile, in a bowl, mix ½ cup hot water with 6 tea bags, cover and leave aside for 5 minutes. Discard tea bags, transfer tea to another bowl and mix with honey, chili sauce, ginger, green onions, garlic, soy sauce and lime juice and whisk really well. Serve your rolls with the sauce on the side. Enjoy!

Nutrition: calories 150, fat 2, fiber 3, carbs 5, protein 4

Godley Quinoa Salad

Preparation time: 10 minutes
Cooking time: 12 minutes
Servings: 6

Ingredients:

- 8 green tea bags
- 2 cups hot water
- 1 cup red quinoa
- ½ cup almonds, roasted and chopped
- ½ cup cherries, pitted

- ½ cup parsley, chopped
- A pinch of sea salt
- Black pepper to the taste
- 2 tablespoons olive oil

Directions:

Put tea bags in a bowl, add hot water, cover and leave aside for 10 minutes. Discard tea bags and transfer tea to pot. Bring to a simmer over medium heat, add quinoa, stir, cover and cook for 12 minutes. Transfer quinoa to a bowl, fluff with a fork and then mix with cherries, parsley, almonds, salt, pepper and the oil. Toss to coat and serve warm. Enjoy!

Nutrition: calories 150, fat 2, fiber 3, carbs 5, protein 2

Crazy And Tasty Pasta Salad

Preparation time: 10 minutes
Cooking time: 6 minutes
Servings: 8

Ingredients:
- 2 quarts water
- 12 ounces fusilli pasta
- A pinch of salt
- 1 avocado, pitted, peeled and chopped
- 1 cup red bell pepper, chopped
- 1 small cucumber, chopped
- 2 mangos, peeled and cubed
- Some black sesame seeds
- 1/3 cup olive oil
- 1 garlic clove, minced
- 2 tablespoons lime juice
- 1 teaspoon mustard
- Black pepper to the taste

Directions:

Put the water in a pot, bring to a boil over medium high heat, add pasta, cook according to instructions and drain them well. In a salad bowl, mix pasta with avocado, red bell pepper, cucumber and mango. In a small bowl, mix oil with lime juice, garlic, mustard, salt and pepper and whisk well. Add this to your pasta salad, toss to coat and serve with black sesame seeds on top. Enjoy!

Nutrition: calories 243, fat 4, fiber 12, carbs 22, protein 6

Fresh Zucchini Soup

Preparation time: 2 hours and 10 minutes
Cooking time: 25 minutes
Servings: 6

Ingredients:
- ½ cup fennel bulb, chopped
- ½ cup sweet onion, chopped
- 1 tablespoon olive oil
- 3 garlic cloves, minced
- 5 cups zucchini, chopped
- 1 cup water
- 2 cups veggie stock
- Salt to the taste
- 2 teaspoons white wine vinegar
- 1 teaspoon lemon juice
- 1 teaspoon lemon zest, grated

Directions:

Heat up a Dutch oven with the oil over medium heat, add onion, garlic and fennel, stir and cook for 5 minutes. Add zucchini, stir and cook for 3 more minutes. Add water, veggie stock, stir, bring to a simmer and cook for 15 minutes. Transfer to your food processor and blend for 4 minutes. Add salt, vinegar, lemon juice and zest and blend again. Leave the soup to cool down, cover and introduce in the fridge for 2 hours. Ladle into bowls and enjoy! Enjoy!

Nutrition: calories 200, fat 1, fiber 3, carbs 5, protein 8

Bell Peppers And Goat Cheese

Preparation time: 10 minutes
Cooking time: 10 minutes
Servings: 6

Ingredients:

- 2 big green bell peppers, cut into 6 wedges
- 2 tablespoons olive oil
- 1 garlic clove finely chopped
- 1 tablespoon lemon pepper
- ½ cup goat cheese

Directions:

In a bowl, mix bell peppers with garlic, drizzle oil, seal, toss to coat and leave aside for 10 minutes. Place peppers on preheated grill over medium high heat and cook for 3 minutes. In a bowl, mix goat cheese with lemon pepper and whisk well. Stuff peppers with goat cheese, place on the preheated grill again and cook for 3 more minutes. Serve right away! Enjoy!

Nutrition: calories 186, fat 4, fiber 2, carbs 7, protein 9

Mediterranean Zucchini And Penne

Preparation time: 10 minutes
Cooking time: 20 minutes
Servings: 4

Ingredients:

- 8 prosciutto slices, cut into thin strips
- Salt and black pepper to the taste
- 5 tablespoons olive oil
- 2 zucchinis, quartered and chopped
- 1 yellow onion, chopped
- 1 cup corn kernels
- 1 pound penne
- 3 tablespoons mint, chopped
- ½ cup pecorino cheese, grated
- 2 teaspoons cider vinegar

Directions:

Put water in a pot, add salt, bring to a boil, add penne, cook according to instructions, drain, reserve ½ cup cooking liquid and leave pasta aside for now. Heat up a pan with 2 tablespoons oil over medium heat, add prosciutto, stir, cook for 5 minutes, transfer to paper towels, drain fat and also leave aside for now. Heat up the pan with 1 more tablespoon oil over medium heat, add onion and some salt, stir and cook for 6 minutes. Add zucchini, corn, more salt and some pepper, stir and cook for 5 minutes. Take off heat, add mint and half of the pecorino and stir well. Heat up the pan with the rest of the oil over medium heat, add pasta, reserved cooking liquid, zucchini mix, vinegar, more salt and pepper, stir and cook for 1 minute. Divide between plates and serve with the rest of the cheese sprinkled all over and with the prosciutto on top. Enjoy!

Special Beans Salad

Preparation time: 1 hour and 10 minutes
Cooking time: 0 minutes
Servings: 8

Ingredients:

- 15 ounces canned cannellini beans, drained
- 15 ounces canned kidney beans, drained
- 15 ounces canned black beans, drained
- 1 green bell pepper, chopped
- 1 red bell pepper, chopped
- Salt and black pepper to the taste
- 1 garlic clove, minced
- 10 ounces corn kernels
- ½ cup olive oil
- 1 red onion, chopped
- 2 tablespoons lime juice
- ½ cup red wine vinegar
- 1 tablespoon lemon juice
- 2 tablespoons sugar
- ½ tablespoon cumin, ground
- ¼ cup cilantro, chopped
- A dash of hot sauce
- ½ teaspoon chili powder

Directions:

In a bowl, mix cannellini, kidney and black beans with bell peppers, red onion and corn. In another bowl, mix oil with lime juice, garlic, vinegar, lemon juice, sugar, cumin, cilantro, hot sauce and chili powder and whisk well. Pour this over the salad, add salt and pepper, toss to coat and keep in the fridge for 1 hour before serving. Enjoy!

Nutrition: calories 200, fat 4, fiber 2, carbs 6, protein 8

Surprising Veggie Salad

Preparation time: 10 minutes
Cooking time: 0 minutes
Servings: 8

Ingredients:

For the salad dressing:

- 2 tablespoons honey
- ¼ cup lime juice
- ½ teaspoon cumin
- 1 garlic clove, minced

For the salad:

- 1 bell pepper, chopped
- 1 head lettuce, chopped
- 1 small red onion, chopped
- 1 zucchini, chopped

- Salt and black pepper to the taste
- 2 tablespoons canola oil
- 2 tablespoons olive oil

- 1 and ½ cups corn
- 4 tomatoes, chopped
- ½ cup cilantro, chopped
- 1 and ½ cups canned black beans, drained

Directions:

In a bowl, mix cumin with honey, lime juice, garlic, salt and pepper. Add 2 tablespoons canola oil and 2 tablespoons olive oil gradually, stir very well and leave aside. In a salad bowl, mix lettuce with bell pepper, red onion, zucchini, tomatoes, corn, beans and cilantro. Add the honey salad dressing you've made at the beginning, toss to coat and serve. Enjoy!

Nutrition: calories 201, fat 4, fiber 3, carbs 7, protein 9

Amazing Veggie And Fish Salad

Preparation time: 10 minutes
Cooking time: 30 minutes
Servings: 2

Ingredients:
- 1 cup water
- ¾ cup quinoa, rinsed
- 1 red capsicum, chopped
- 3 yellow pan squash, chopped
- 1 baby eggplant, chopped
- 1 zucchini, chopped
- ½ sweet potato, chopped
- 1 tablespoon olive oil

For the salad dressing:
- 2 tablespoons coriander, chopped
- ¼ cup lime juice

- 1 red onion, cut into wedges
- 1 teaspoon hot paprika
- 2 teaspoons cumin, ground
- Salt and black pepper to the taste
- 2 medium snapper fillets, boneless and skinless
- 4 cups baby spinach

- ¼ cup olive oil

Directions:

Put quinoa in a small pot, add the water, leave aside for 15 minutes, bring to a boil over medium heat, cook for 15 minutes, take off heat, leave aside for another 10 minutes and fluff with a fork. Place capsicum, squash, eggplant, zucchini, spinach, sweet potato and red onion on a baking tray. Add 1 tablespoon oil, toss to coat, introduce in the oven at 400 degrees F, bake for 15 minutes and leave aside. Place fish in another baking tray, season with salt, pepper, hot paprika and cumin, introduce in the oven at 400 degrees F, bake for 10 minutes, take out of the oven and flake it. Meanwhile, in a small bowl, mix coriander with salt, pepper, ¼ cup oil and lime juice and whisk very well. In a salad bowl, mix quinoa with roasted veggies and fish. Add salad dressing, more salt and pepper, toss to coat and serve. Enjoy!

Nutrition: calories 185, fat 4, fiber 2, carbs 6, protein 8

Different And Delicious Beans Soup

Preparation time: 10 minutes
Cooking time: 1 hour
Servings: 4

Ingredients:
- 1 tomato, chopped
- 1 garlic clove, minced
- 2 cups fava beans, dried
- 4 cups water
- 1 small yellow onion, chopped

- 1 tablespoon olive oil
- Salt and black pepper to the taste
- ¼ teaspoon cumin, ground
- ¼ teaspoon saffron threads, crushed

Directions:

Put beans in a pot, add the water, bring to a boil over high heat, reduce temperature to medium low, cover and cook for 40 minutes. In your food processor, mix garlic with salt, pepper, tomato and onion and pulse well. Heat up another pot with the oil over medium high heat, add tomato mix, stir and cook for 5 minutes. Add beans and their liquid, cumin and saffron, stir and cook for 10 more minutes. Add more salt and pepper, stir, ladle into bowls and serve. Enjoy!

Nutrition: calories 213, fat 3, fiber 2, carbs 3, protein 8

Delicious Roasted Mushrooms

Preparation time: 10 minutes
Cooking time: 25 minutes
Servings: 4

Ingredients:

- 2 tablespoons olive oil
- Salt and black pepper to the taste
- 16 ounces mushrooms
- 1 cup quinoa
- 2 cups water
- ½ cup parmesan, grated
- ¼ cup parsley, chopped
- ¼ cup green onions, chopped
- 1 garlic clove, minced
- 3 teaspoons lemon juice
- 2 tablespoons pepitas, toasted

Directions:

Spread mushrooms on a lined baking sheet, add 1 tablespoon oil, salt and pepper and toss to coat. Introduce in the oven at 425 degrees F and bake for 18 minutes. Put water and quinoa in a pan, bring to a boil over medium high heat, reduce temperature, cook for 20 minutes, take off heat, cover, leave aside for 5 minutes and fluff with a fork. Add parmesan, parsley, salt, pepper, green onions and the rest of the oil and toss to coat. Add lemon juice and stir again. Divide quinoa on plates, add mushrooms on top, sprinkle pepitas all over and serve. Enjoy!

Nutrition: calories 132, fat 6, fiber 3, carbs 10, protein 7

Tasty Stuffed Peppers

Preparation time: 10 minutes
Cooking time: 20 minutes
Servings: 4

Ingredients:

- 1 courgette, chopped
- 4 red peppers, cut in halves
- 2 tablespoons olive oil
- 17 ounces already cooked quinoa
- 3 ounces feta cheese, crumbled
- Salt and black pepper to the taste
- A handful parsley, finely chopped

Directions:

Place peppers on a lined baking sheet, drizzle 1 tablespoon oil, season with salt and pepper, introduce in the oven at 350 degrees F and cook for 15 minutes. Heat up a pan with the rest of the oil over medium heat, add courgette, cook for 5 minutes, take off heat and mix with quinoa, salt, pepper, cheese and parsley and stir. Take peppers out of the oven, divide quinoa mix between them, introduce in the oven again and cook for 5 minutes more. Serve hot. Enjoy!

Nutrition: calories 245, fat 8, fiber 11, carbs 33, protein 11

Broad Bean Toasts

Preparation time: 15 minutes
Cooking time: 5 minutes
Servings: 2

Ingredients:

- 12 ounces broad bean
- 3.5 ounces feta cheese, crumbled
- 1 tablespoon olive oil
- 2 tablespoons mint leaves, chopped
- Salt and black pepper to the taste
- 2 ounces mixed salad leaves
- 10 cherry tomatoes, cut in halves
- 1 teaspoon lemon juice
- 4 baguette slices

Directions:

Put some water in a pot, bring to a boil over medium high heat, add beans, cook for 4 minutes, drain and put into a bowl. Add feta and mint, salt and pepper to the taste and half of the oil and toss to coat. In another bowl, mix tomatoes with salad leaves, some salt, pepper, lemon juice and the rest of the oil and toss to coat. Divide this on serving plates, add toasted bread slices and top them with beans mix. Serve right away. Enjoy!

Nutrition: calories 354, fat 12, fiber 11, carbs 23, protein 20

Tasty Spinach with Chili

Preparation time: 10 minutes
Cooking time: 5 minutes
Servings: 4

Ingredients:

- 1 tablespoon butter
- Zest from 1 lemon
- 3 tablespoons bread crumbs
- 2 garlic cloves, minced
- 17 ounces spinach
- 1 red chili, chopped
- Salt and black pepper to the taste

Directions:

Heat up a pan with the butter over medium high heat, add breadcrumbs, garlic, chili and lemon zest, cook for 3 minutes, take off heat, transfer to a bowl and season with salt and pepper. Heat up the pan again over medium heat, add spinach, stir and cook for 2 minutes. Divide spinach on plates, top with bread crumbs mix and serve. Enjoy!

Nutrition: calories 160, fat 7, fiber 3, carbs 20, protein 7

Roasted Peppers And Tomatoes

Preparation time: 10 minutes
Cooking time: 1 hour and 10 minutes
Servings: 4

Ingredients:

- 2 ounces canned anchovy, sliced
- 4 red bell peppers, deseeded and cut in halves
- 8 cherry tomatoes cut in halves
- 2 rosemary sprigs
- 2 garlic cloves, minced
- Salt and black pepper to the taste
- 2 tablespoon olive oil

Directions:

Place peppers in a baking dish, add some oil, salt and pepper, toss to coat, introduce in the oven at 300 degrees F and cook for 40 minutes. Take peppers out of the oven, divide tomatoes, anchovies, garlic and rosemary in each half, drizzle the rest of the oil, introduce in the oven again and cook for 30 minutes more. Serve them warm. Enjoy!

Nutrition: calories 156, fat 11, fiber 3, carbs 13, protein 4

Delicious Roasted Asparagus

Preparation time: 10 minutes
Cooking time: 15 minutes
Servings: 4

Ingredients:

- 2 pounds fresh asparagus, trimmed
- ¼ cup olive oil
- Salt and black pepper to the taste
- 1 teaspoon lemon zest
- 4 garlic cloves, minced
- ½ teaspoon oregano, dried
- ¼ teaspoon red pepper flakes
- 4 ounces feta cheese, crumbled
- 2 tablespoons parsley, finely chopped
- Juice of 1 lemon

Directions:

Heat up a pan with the oil over medium high heat, add lemon zest, garlic, pepper flakes and oregano, stir and cook for 2 minutes. Place asparagus on a lined baking sheet, add oil mix from the pan and toss to coat. Add cheese, salt and pepper, introduce in the oven at 400 degrees F and roast for 13 minutes. Take asparagus out of the oven, add lemon juice and parsley, toss to coat again, divide between plates and serve hot. Enjoy!

Nutrition: calories 300, fat 23, fiber 5, carbs 12, protein 12

Delicious Stuffed Eggplants

Preparation time: 10 minutes
Cooking time: 1 hour
Servings: 4

Ingredients:

- 4 small eggplants cut into halves lengthwise
- Salt and black pepper to the taste
- 10 tablespoons olive oil
- 2 and ½ pounds tomatoes, cut in halves and grated
- 1 green bell pepper, chopped
- 1 yellow onion, chopped
- 1 tablespoon garlic, minced
- ½ cup cauliflower, chopped
- 1 teaspoon oregano, chopped
- ½ cup parsley, chopped
- 3 ounces feta cheese, crumbled

Directions:

Place eggplant halves on a lined baking sheet, add salt, pepper and 4 tablespoons oil, introduce them in the oven at 375 degrees F and roast for 35 minutes. Heat up a pan with 3 tablespoons oil over medium high heat, add onion, stir and cook for 5 minutes. Add bell pepper, garlic and cauliflower, stir and cook for 5 minutes. Take the pan off the heat, add parsley, tomato, salt, pepper, oregano and cheese and stir well. Take eggplant halves out of the oven, divide tomato mix in each half, drizzle the rest of the oil over them, introduce in the oven again and roast for 10 minutes more. Serve hot. Enjoy!

Nutrition: calories 240, fat 4, fiber, 2, carbs 19, protein 2

Delicious Spaghetti With Grilled Veggies

Preparation time: 10 minutes
Cooking time: 15 minutes
Servings: 4

Ingredients:

- 2 zucchinis cut in rounds
- 1 pound plum tomatoes cut in halves
- Salt and black pepper to the taste
- 2 small eggplants cut into rounds
- 1 red onion, sliced
- 1 red bell pepper, roughly chopped
- 1 garlic head
- ¼ cup olive oil
- 1 teaspoon herbs de Provence
- ¾ cup kalamata olives, pitted and chopped
- 2 tablespoons basil, chopped
- 12 ounces spaghetti
- 2 teaspoons marjoram, chopped
- ½ cup feta cheese, crumbled

Directions:

In a bowl, mix tomatoes with eggplant, red pepper, zucchini, garlic and onion with herbs, salt, pepper and 3 tablespoons oil and toss to coat. Place all veggies on the preheated grill, cook for 8 minutes and transfer them to a bowl. Chop veggies, except garlic, return them to the bowl and mix with half of the olives. Put garlic in your food processor, add the rest of the olives and the oil and blend well. Put water in a pot, bring to a boil over medium high heat, add salt, add spaghetti, cook according to instructions, drain and reserve ½ cup of cooking water. In a bowl, mix veggies with half of the garlic sauce, basil and marjoram. Add pasta, stir and transfer everything to a pan. Heat up over medium heat, add reserved cooking liquid and the rest of the garlic sauce, stir and divide between plates. Sprinkle cheese on top and serve. Enjoy!

Nutrition: calories 340, fat 23, fiber 11, carbs 32, protein 13

Delicious Grilled Eggplant

Preparation time: 10 minutes
Cooking time: 10 minutes
Servings: 4

Ingredients:

- ½ tablespoon balsamic vinegar
- ½ tablespoon red wine vinegar
- 1 tablespoon currants, dried
- 1 garlic clove
- Salt and black pepper to the taste
- 2 tablespoons pine nuts, toasted and chopped
- 1 red bell pepper
- 1 and ½ tablespoons olive oil
- 1 tablespoon marjoram, chopped
- 3 tablespoons parsley, chopped
- A pinch of cayenne pepper
- For the eggplants:
- 1 eggplant, cut into rounds
- 3 tablespoons olive oil
- Salt and black pepper to the taste

Directions:

In a bowl, mix wine vinegar with balsamic one and currants and stir. In a mortar and pestle mix garlic with salt and pepper and pound until you obtain a paste. Grill bell pepper on your kitchen grill, transfer to a bowl, cover, leave aside for a few minutes, peel and chop it. Add bell pepper to the bowl with the currants. Also add garlic paste, 1 and ½ tablespoons oil, cayenne pepper, marjoram, nuts and parsley, stir and leave aside. Heat up your kitchen grill over medium high heat, brush eggplant pieces with 3 tablespoons oil, season with salt and pepper, place them on the grill and cook for 4 minutes. Flip, cook for another 4 minutes and transfer to plates. Spread relish you've made earlier and serve. Enjoy!

Nutrition: calories 140, fat 12, fiber 4, carbs 7, protein 2

Eggplant Caviar

Preparation time: 10 minutes
Cooking time: 35 minutes
Servings: 12

Ingredients:

- 2 big eggplants cut in halves
- 30 garlic cloves
- 2 tablespoons lemon juice
- 1 teaspoon lemon zest, grated
- 4 tablespoons olive oil
- 1 tablespoon parsley, chopped
- Salt and black pepper to the taste

Directions:

Put eggplant halves on a lined baking sheet, also spread garlic cloves, drizzle 2 tablespoons oil over them, season with salt and pepper, introduce in the oven at 350 degrees F and roast for 35 minutes. Take eggplants and garlic out of the oven and leave aside to cool down. Peel eggplants, chop flesh well and put in a bowl. Also chop garlic very finely and add to the same bowl. Add salt, pepper, lemon zest, lemon juice, oil and parsley, stir well and keep in the fridge until you serve it. Enjoy!

Nutrition: calories 20, fat 3, fiber 1, carbs 3, protein 0

Delicious Stuffed Avocado

Preparation time: 10 minutes
Cooking time: 7 minutes
Servings: 4

Ingredients:

- 1 and ½ teaspoons paprika
- 1 teaspoon cayenne pepper
- Salt and black pepper to the taste
- ½ teaspoon garlic powder
- ½ teaspoon onion powder
- ½ teaspoon thyme
- ½ teaspoon basil
- 1 tablespoon hot sauce
- Juice from 2 limes
- 2 tablespoons olive oil
- 3 tablespoons cilantro, chopped
- 2 avocados, cut in halves and pitted
- 20 shrimp, peeled and deveined
- ¼ cup red onion, chopped
- 1 tomato, chopped
- 1 red chili pepper, chopped

Directions:

Drizzle juice from 1 lime over avocado halves, brush them with 1 tablespoon oil and leave aside for now. In a bowl, mix the rest of the lime juice with 1 tablespoon oil, hot sauce, cilantro, salt, pepper and tomato and stir. In another bowl, mix paprika with salt, pepper, onion and garlic powder, cayenne, basil and thyme and stir. Arrange shrimp on skewers, place them on preheated grill over medium high heat, add seasoning mix you've just made, drizzle some oil, cook for 3 minutes on each side, transfer to a cutting board, discard skewers, chop shrimp and add to the bowl with the veggies. Add avocado halves on the grill, cook for a few minutes and transfer to a platter. Spoon veggies and shrimp mixture into each half and serve. Enjoy!

Nutrition: calories 234, fat 12, fiber 4, carbs 12, protein 22

Beets With Garlic

Preparation time: 10 minutes
Cooking time: 1 hour
Servings: 4

Ingredients:

- 2 garlic cloves, minced
- 2 pounds beets
- Salt and black pepper to the taste
- 2 tablespoons extra virgin olive oil
- A handful cilantro, chopped

Directions:

Put beets on a lined baking sheet, introduce in the oven at 400 degrees F and bake for 1 hour. Take beets out of the oven, leave them to cool down, peel, chop and put them in a bowl. Add salt, pepper, garlic, oil and cilantro, stir, divide on plates and serve. Enjoy!

Nutrition: calories 150, fat 4, fiber 7, carbs 22, protein 4

Delicious Beets Patties

Preparation time: 10 minutes
Cooking time: 35 minutes
Servings: 6

Ingredients:

- 3 beets
- 4 tablespoons olive oil
- Salt and black pepper to the taste
- 1 yellow onion, chopped
- 2 teaspoons cumin, ground
- ¼ teaspoon allspice, ground
- 1 cup milk
- 1 cup chickpea flour
- 3 tablespoons already cooked chickpeas
- Vegetable oil for frying
- 2 tablespoons lemon juice

Directions:

Heat up a pan with 1 tablespoon olive oil over medium high heat, add onion, allspice and cumin, stir, cook for 4 minutes, take off heat and transfer to a bowl. Put beets in a pot, add water to cover, bring to a boil over medium heat, cook for 20 minutes, drain, cool down, peel and grate. Put milk in a pot, bring to a boil over medium heat, add chickpea flour and whisk well until you obtain a paste. Add salt and pepper to the taste and the rest of the olive oil, stir, reduce heat to low and cook for 8 minutes stirring often. Take paste off heat, cool it down and mix with grated beets, sautéed onions, lemon juice and chickpeas. Stir well, shape small balls from this mix, arrange them on a lined baking sheet and keep in the fridge for a while. Heat up a pan with the vegetable oil over medium high heat, add beets balls, cook for 4 minutes, transfer to paper towels, drain grease and arrange them on a platter. Serve with Greek yogurt on the side. Enjoy!

Nutrition: calories 140, fat 4, fiber 6, carbs 20, protein 4

Beet Hummus

Preparation time: 30 minutes
Cooking time: 1 hour
Servings: 6

Ingredients:

- 3 beets
- 3 tablespoons tahini
- 3 tablespoons olive oil
- 1 teaspoon cumin, ground
- 1 tablespoon apple cider vinegar
- 3 garlic cloves, roasted
- Salt and black pepper to the taste
- Sesame seeds, toasted for serving

Directions:

Put beet in a baking dish, add 1 tablespoon oil, rub them, cover with tin foil, introduce in the oven at 425 degrees F and bake for 1 hour. Take beets out of the oven, leave them to cool down, peel and chop them. Put beets in your food processor, add the rest of the oil, salt, pepper, tahini, garlic, vinegar and cumin and pulse well. Transfer to a bowl, keep in the fridge for 30 minutes, sprinkle sesame seeds on top and serve. Enjoy!

Nutrition: calories 50, fat 3, fiber 1, carbs 4, protein 2

ous Roasted Broccoli

Preparation time: 10 minutes
Cooking time: 10 minutes
Servings: 4

Ingredients:

- 12 ounces broccoli, cut into small florets
- 1 tablespoon olive oil
- Salt and black pepper to the taste
- 1 cup cherry tomatoes cut in halves
- 2 garlic cloves, minced
- ½ teaspoon lemon zest, grated
- 10 black olives, pitted and chopped
- 1 tablespoon lemon juice
- 1 teaspoon oregano, dried
- 2 teaspoons capers, drained

Directions:

In a bowl, mix broccoli with salt, pepper, tomatoes, garlic and oil and toss to coat. Transfer this to a baking sheet, introduce in the oven at 450 degrees F and bake for 13 minutes. In a bowl, mix capers with lemon zest, lemon juice, oregano and olives and stir gently. Divide roasted broccoli mix on plates, add capers and olives mix on top and serve. Enjoy!

Nutrition: calories 90, fat 7, fiber 3, carbs 6, protein 4

Simple Pasta With Broccoli

Preparation time: 10 minutes
Cooking time: 12 minutes
Servings: 4

Ingredients:

- 1 and ½ pounds broccoli, stalks and florets chopped
- ¼ cup olive oil
- Salt and black pepper to the taste
- ¾ pound macaroni
- 3 garlic cloves, minced
- ½ cup walnuts, chopped
- 4 anchovy fillets, drained
- ¼ cup parmesan, grated

Directions:

Put water and some salt in a pot, bring to a boil over medium high heat, add broccoli stalks, stir and cook for 3 minutes. Add macaroni stir and cook for 5 minutes. Add broccoli florets, stir, cook for 3 minutes more and drain everything. Heat up a pan with the oil over medium high heat, add walnuts, stir and cook for 2 minutes. Add anchovies and garlic, stir and cook for 2 minutes. Add pasta, broccoli florets and stalks, salt, pepper and parmesan, stir well for 1 minute, take off heat and divide between plates. Enjoy!

Nutrition: calories 256, fat 7, fiber 5, carbs 42, protein 14

Broccoli Delight

Preparation time: 10 minutes
Cooking time: 10 minutes
Servings: 4

Ingredients:

- 1 broccoli head, florets separated and roughly chopped
- 1 tablespoon extra-virgin olive oil
- 1 yellow onion, chopped
- 1 garlic clove, minced
- ½ pound tomatoes, chopped
- ¼ pint chicken stock
- 8 stuffed olives
- 1 tablespoon oregano, chopped
- 1 tablespoon parsley, chopped
- Salt and black pepper to the taste

Directions:

Heat up a pan with the oil over medium high heat, add garlic and onion, stir and cook for 3 minutes. Add tomatoes, chicken stock and oregano, stir, bring to a boil and cook for 3 minutes. Add olives, broccoli, salt, pepper and parsley, stir, cover and cook for 6 minutes more. Divide between plates and serve hot. Enjoy!

Nutrition: calories 100, fat 1, fiber 3, carbs 3, protein 5

Delicious Brussels Sprouts

Preparation time: 10 minutes
Cooking time: 10 minutes
Servings: 4

Ingredients:

- 1 pound Brussels sprouts
- 2 teaspoons lemon juice
- 3 tablespoons olive oil
- Salt and black pepper to the taste
- 1 tablespoon mustard
- 2 garlic cloves, minced
- 1 tablespoon lemon zest
- 1 tablespoon parsley, chopped
- 2 tablespoons parmesan, grated

Directions:

Put Brussels sprouts in a steamer basket and place it in a pot. Add water to the pot, bring to a boil over medium high heat, cover, steam for 10 minutes and transfer sprouts to a bowl. In a bowl, mix oil with, salt, pepper, lemon juice, garlic, parsley, mustard and lemon zest and whisk well. Add this over Brussels sprouts, toss to coat and divide among plates. Sprinkle parmesan on top and serve. Enjoy!

Nutrition: calories 145, fat 11, fiber 3.3, carbs 9, protein 5

Caramelized Brussels Sprouts

Preparation time: 10 minutes
Cooking time: 20 minutes
Servings: 4

Ingredients:

- 2 tablespoons balsamic vinegar
- 1 and ½ pounds Brussels sprouts
- Salt and black pepper to the taste
- 3 tablespoons olive oil
- 2 teaspoons honey

Directions:

In a bowl, mix Brussels sprouts with 2 tablespoons oil, salt and pepper and toss to coat. Spread Brussels sprouts on a lined baking sheet, introduce in the oven at 425 degrees F and bake for 20 minutes. Take sprouts out of the oven and transfer to a bowl. Add the rest of the oil, balsamic vinegar, honey, salt and pepper, toss to coat, divide into bowls and serve. Enjoy!

Nutrition: calories 200, fat 8, fiber 3, carbs 7, protein 5

Delicious Summer Squash

Preparation time: 10 minutes
Cooking time: 10 minutes
Servings: 4

Ingredients:

- 1 tablespoon extra-virgin olive oil
- ¼ cup yellow onion, chopped
- 1 summer squash, sliced
- 1 garlic clove, minced
- 1 zucchini, thinly sliced
- ½ teaspoon oregano, dried
- Salt and black pepper to the taste
- 1 plum tomato, chopped
- ¼ cup feta cheese, crumbled

Directions:

Heat up a pan with the oil over medium high heat, add onion, stir and cook for 2 minutes. Add squash and zucchini, stir and cook for 8 minutes. Add garlic, stir and cook for 1 minute more. Add tomato, oregano, salt, pepper and cheese, stir well, take off heat and divide between plates. Enjoy!

Nutrition: calories 70, fat 5, fiber 2, carbs 4, protein 4

Mediterranean Diet Salad Recipes

Chickpeas And Avocado Salad
Preparation time: 10 minutes
Cooking time: 30 minutes
Servings: 4

Ingredients:

- 15 ounces canned chickpeas, drained
- Salt and black pepper to the taste
- 1 tablespoon extra-virgin olive oil
- 1 avocado, pitted, peeled and chopped
- ½ teaspoon lime juice
- 2 ounces feta cheese, crumbled
- 2 scallions, chopped

Directions:

Place chickpeas on a lined baking sheet, add salt, pepper and oil, toss to coat, introduce in the oven at 400 degrees F and bake for 30 minutes. In a bowl mix avocado with lime juice and mash well. Divide this between plates, add roasted chickpeas on top, salt, pepper, cheese and scallions and serve. Enjoy!

Nutrition: calories 230, fat 12, fiber 12, carbs 34, protein 13

Fresh And Delicious Salad
Preparation time: 10 minutes
Cooking time: 0 minutes
Servings: 4

Ingredients:

- 1 and ½ teaspoons orange zest, grated
- ¼ cup orange juice
- 2 oranges, peeled and sliced
- 3 tablespoons white wine vinegar
- ¾ teaspoon thyme, chopped
- 2 teaspoons rosemary, chopped
- ¼ cup olive oil
- Salt and black pepper to the taste
- 10 ounces baby romaine lettuce, chopped
- 1 pear, cored and cut into medium wedges
- 4 ounces mozzarella, cut into medium pieces
- 1/3 cup red onion, chopped
- 4 dates, pitted and chopped

Directions:

In a bowl, mix orange juice with zest, vinegar, thyme, rosemary, oil, salt and pepper and whisk well. Divide orange slices on serving plates, add lettuce leaves, pear wedges, dates, mozzarella, onion, salt, pepper and toss. Add vinaigrette, toss to coat and serve. Enjoy!

Nutrition: calories 230, fat 12, fiber 7, carbs 32, protein 8

Tasty Halloumi And Arugula Salad

Preparation time: 15 minutes
Cooking time: 4 minutes
Servings: 4

Ingredients:

- 8 ounces halloumi cheese, cubed
- 1 tablespoon capers, drained and chopped
- 1 and ½ tablespoons red wine vinegar
- 1 teaspoon honey
- 1 teaspoon lemon zest, grated
- 1 teaspoon parsley, chopped
- ½ teaspoon garlic, minced
- Salt and black pepper to the taste
- 5 ounces arugula
- 5 tablespoons olive oil
- ¼ cup pistachios, chopped

Directions:

Put halloumi in a bowl, add hot water to cover, leave aside for 15 minutes, drain and pat dry well. Heat up a pan with 2 tablespoons oil over medium high heat, add halloumi, stir, cook for 4 minutes, transfer to paper towels, drain excess grease and put in a salad bowl. Add arugula and pistachios and toss. In a small bowl, mix capers with vinegar, lemon zest, parsley, garlic, honey, salt, pepper and the rest of the oil and whisk well. Add this to halloumi salad, toss to coat and serve. Enjoy!

Nutrition: calories 230, fat 23, fiber 3, carbs 8, protein 16

Simple Herbs Salad

Preparation time: 30 minutes
Cooking time: 0 minutes
Servings: 4

Ingredients:

- 5 tablespoons olive oil
- 1/3 cup tahini
- ½ cup raisins
- 4 tablespoons lemon juice
- 1 tablespoon water
- ¼ cup chives, chopped
- ¾ cup parsley, chopped
- ¼ cup cilantro, chopped
- Salt and black pepper to the taste
- ¼ cup fennel, chopped
- ¼ cup dill, chopped
- ¼ cup mint leaves, torn
- 3 radishes, cut into matchsticks
- ¼ cup pistachios, toasted
- ¼ cup tarragon, chopped
- 1 tablespoon sesame seeds, toasted

Directions:

Put raisins in a bowl, add warm water to cover, leave aside for 30 minutes, drain and put in a bowl. In a small bowl, mix tahini with 3 tablespoons lemon juice, 3 tablespoons oil, salt, pepper and 1 tablespoon water and whisk well. Spread this on serving plates and leave them aside for now. In a salad bowl, mix parsley with cilantro, chives, fennel, mint, dill, tarragon, the rest of the oil, the rest of the lemon juice, salt and pepper and toss to coat. Divide this on tahini mix, top with raisins, pistachios, radishes and sesame seeds and serve. Enjoy!

Nutrition: calories 240, fat 22, fiber 2, carbs 18, protein 4

Delicious Chicken Salad

Preparation time: 10 minutes
Cooking time: 5 minutes
Servings: 4

Ingredients:

For the chicken:
- 1 tablespoon oregano, chopped
- 2 garlic cloves, minced
- 5 chicken breast halves, skinless and boneless
- 1 tablespoons lemon zest
- ¼ teaspoon water

For the salad:
- 2 pints cherry tomatoes cut in halves
- 1 small red onion, thinly sliced
- 1 cucumber, sliced
- 1 and ½ tablespoons olive oil
- 1/3 cup black olives, pitted and cut in halves
- Salt and black pepper to the taste
- 2 tablespoons parsley, chopped
- A drizzle of olive oil
- 6 lemon wedges

- 1 cup tzatziki sauce
- Salt and black pepper to the taste
- 1 teaspoon oregano, chopped
- 4 pitas, toasted

Directions:

In a mortar, mix garlic with water, salt, pepper 1 teaspoon lemon zest and 1 tablespoon oregano and stir well. Rub chicken pieces with this mix, drizzle them with some oil, put them on preheated grill over medium high heat, cook for 4 minutes, flip, cook for 1 minutes more, transfer to a plate, squeeze 2 lemon wedges over them, sprinkle parsley and leave aside for now. In a salad bowl, mix tomatoes with olives, onion and cucumber. Add salt, pepper, 1 and ½ tablespoons oil and 1 teaspoon oregano, toss to coat and divide on serving plates. Cut chicken breasts into strips and add on top of salad. Drizzle tzatziki all over and serve with pitas and the remaining lemon wedges. Enjoy!

Nutrition: calories 400, fat 22, fiber 4, carbs 34, protein 34

Simple Spinach And Steak Salad

Preparation time: 5 hours
Cooking time: 10 minutes
Servings: 4

Ingredients:

- 3 garlic cloves, minced
- 5 and ½ tablespoons olive oil
- 2 teaspoons red wine vinegar
- 1 tablespoons oregano, chopped
- Salt and black pepper to the taste
- 2 tablespoons parsley, chopped
- 1 pound beef meat, sliced
- 1 tablespoon lemon juice
- 1 tablespoon capers, chopped
-
- 1 teaspoon thyme, chopped
- 7 ounces feta cheese, cubed
- ¼ teaspoon red chili flakes
- 5 ounces baby spinach
- 2 cucumbers, thinly sliced
- 1 and ½ cups cherry tomatoes cut in halves
- ½ cup kalamata olives, pitted and cut in halves

Directions:

In a bowl, mix 3 tablespoons oil with vinegar, oregano, garlic, salt and pepper and whisk. Add beef meat, cover and keep in the fridge for 4 hours. In another bowl, mix the rest of the oil with thyme, parsley, capers, lemon juice and chili flakes and whisk. Add feta, toss to coat and leave aside for 1 hour. Heat up your kitchen grill over medium high heat, add beef pieces, grill for 8 minutes, turning every 2 minutes, transfer them to a cutting board, leave aside for cool down, thinly slice and season with salt and pepper to the taste. In a salad bowl, mix spinach with tomatoes, cucumber and olives. Add feta and its marinade, salt and pepper to the taste, toss to coat and divide on serving plates. Top with steak pieces and serve. Enjoy!

Nutrition: calories 340, fat 32, fiber 4, carbs 11, protein 34

Grilled Potato Salad

Cooking time: 50 minutes
Servings: 6

Ingredients:

- 4 sweet potatoes
- 3 tablespoons olive oil
- ¼ cup olive oil
- 1/3 cup orange juice
- 1 tablespoon orange juice
- 2 tablespoons pomegranate molasses
- ½ teaspoon sumac, ground
- 1 tablespoon red wine vinegar
- ½ teaspoon sugar
- Salt and black pepper to the taste
- 1 tablespoon orange zest, grated
- 3 tablespoons honey
- 2 tablespoons mint, chopped
- 1/3 cup pistachios, chopped
- 1 cup Greek yogurt
- 1/3 cup pomegranate seeds

Directions:

Put potatoes on a lined baking sheet, introduce in the oven at 350 degrees F, bake for 40 minutes, leave them aside for 1 hour to cool down, peel them, cut into wedges and put on a cutting board. In a bowl, mix ¼ cup oil with 1 tablespoon orange juice, sugar, vinegar, pomegranate molasses, sumac, salt and pepper and whisk. In another bowl, mix the rest of the orange juice with orange zest, honey, salt, pepper and the rest of the oil and whisk well again. In a third bowl mix yogurt with some salt and pepper and with the mint and whisk. Brush potato wedges with the honey mix, add some salt, place pieces on your kitchen grill heated over medium high heat, cook for 3 minutes and transfer to serving plates. Sprinkle pistachios, pomegranate seeds, drizzle the vinaigrette you've made earlier, and serve with the yogurt sauce on top. Enjoy!

Nutrition: calories 240, fat 14, fiber 3, carbs 32, protein 5

Cucumber Salad

Preparation time: 5 minutes
Cooking time: 0 minutes
Servings: 4

Ingredients:

- 2 tablespoons olive oil
- 3 tablespoons red wine vinegar
- 1 teaspoon oregano, dried
- 3 cucumbers, peeled and thinly sliced
- Salt and black pepper to the taste
- 1 small red onion, chopped
- ¼ cup feta cheese, crumbled
- 1 tablespoon dill, chopped

Directions:

In a bowl, mix oil with vinegar, oregano, salt and pepper and whisk well. In a salad bowl, mix cucumber slices with onion, cheese and dill. Add salad dressing, toss to coat and serve. Enjoy!

Nutrition: calories 53, fat 0.3, fiber 0.5, carbs 11, protein 1

Incredible Cabbage Salad

Preparation time: 10 minutes
Cooking time: 2 minutes
Servings: 4

Ingredients:

- 1 teaspoon cumin, ground
- 1 small red onion, chopped
- 1 tablespoon olive oil
- 1 teaspoon coriander, ground
- 2 tablespoons lemon juice
- 2 teaspoons honey
- 1 tablespoon lemon zest, grated
- Salt and black pepper to the taste
- 1 cup Greek yogurt
- 1 cabbage head, cut into halves and thinly sliced
- ½ cup mint, chopped
- 2 carrots, cut into thin strips
- ¼ cup pistachios, chopped

Directions:

Put the onion in a bowl, add water to cover, leave aside for 20 minutes, drain and put in a bowl. Heat up a pan over medium high heat, add oil cumin and coriander, stir, cook for 2 minutes, take off heat and leave aside to cool down. Add salt, pepper, lemon juice, lemon zest, honey and yogurt and stir well. In a salad bowl, mix cabbage with onion, mint and carrots. Add salad dressing, sprinkle pistachios, toss to coat and leave aside for 10 minutes before serving. Add more salt and pepper to the taste and serve. Enjoy!

Nutrition: calories 139, fat 5, fiber 5, carbs 13, protein 5

Carrot And Raisins Salad

Preparation time: 10 minutes
Cooking time: 0 minutes
Servings: 6

Ingredients:

- Juice of 1 lemon
- 5 tablespoons olive oil
- 1 teaspoon ginger, grated
- 1 tablespoon apple cider vinegar
- 8 carrots, peeled and grated
- Salt and black pepper to the taste
- ½ cup almonds, toasted and sliced
- ¼ cup black raisins
- 1/3 cup pistachios, toasted
- 1 red chili pepper, chopped
- ½ cup mint, chopped
- 1 tablespoon sumac, ground
- ½ cup parsley, chopped

Directions:

In a bowl, mix vinegar with ginger, oil, lemon juice, salt and pepper to the taste and whisk well. In a salad bowl, mix carrots with almonds, raisins, pistachios, chili pepper, salt and pepper and stir. Add vinaigrette, sumac, mint and parsley, toss to coat and serve. Enjoy!

Nutrition: calories 100, fat 4, fiber 4, carbs 1, protein 4

Delicious Bread Salad

Preparation time: 10 minutes
Cooking time: 7 minutes
Servings: 4

Ingredients:

- 1 shallot, chopped
- ¼ cup lemon juice
- 5 ounces lavash
- ½ teaspoon sugar
- 7 tablespoons olive oil
- Salt and black pepper to the taste
- 15 ounces canned chickpeas, drained
- 1/3 cup mint, chopped
- 8 ounces cherry tomatoes cut in halves
- 6 ounces feta cheese, crumbled
- 6 ounces snap peas, cut in quarters
- 3 ounces baby arugula

Directions:

Introduce lavash in the oven at 350 degrees F and bake for 7 minutes. Take out of the oven and leave aside to cool down. In a bowl, mix sugar with shallot, lemon juice, salt and pepper, stir and leave aside for 10 minutes. Add the oil and mint and whisk again very well. In a salad bowl, mix tomatoes with snap peas, chickpeas and the vinaigrette and toss to coat. Add arugula, feta cheese, crumbled lavash, toss again to coat and serve right away. Enjoy!

Nutrition: calories 340, fat 23, fiber 12, carbs 23, protein 25

Tasty Fennel Salad

Preparation time: 10 minutes
Cooking time: 0 minutes
Servings: 4

Ingredients:

- ½ cup almonds, toasted and sliced
- 3 tablespoons lemon juice
- 2 fennel bulbs, trimmed, cut in halves, cored and shaved crosswise
- Salt and black pepper to the taste
- ¼ cup mint, torn
- ¼ cup olive oil

Directions:

In a bowl, mix fennel shavings with lemon juice, salt and pepper, stir and leave aside for 10 minutes. Add the oil and half of the almonds, toss to coat and spread on a platter. Add mint, the rest of the almonds, more salt and pepper and serve. Enjoy!

Nutrition: calories 200, fat 12, fiber 9, carbs 19, protein 4

Delicious Mixed Greens Salad

Preparation time: 10 minutes
Cooking time: 8 minutes
Servings: 4

Ingredients:

- ½ loaf sourdough bread, cubed
- ¼ teaspoon paprika
- 2 tablespoons Manchego, grated
- 9 tablespoons olive oil
- 1 and ½ tablespoons sherry vinegar
- Salt and black pepper to the taste
- 1 teaspoon mustard
- 5 cups baby greens
- ¾ cup green olives, pitted and chopped
- 12 thin slices ham, torn

Directions:

In a bowl, mix 6 tablespoons oil with Manchego, paprika and bread cubes, toss to coat, spread on a lined baking sheet, introduce in the oven at 400 degrees F and bake for 8 minutes. In a bowl, mix mustard with salt, pepper, the rest of the oil and the vinegar and whisk well. Put greens in a salad bowl, add baked bread cubes, olives, ham and the vinaigrette you've just made, toss to coat and serve. Enjoy!

Nutrition: calories 250, fat 14, fiber 2, carbs 15, protein 9

Tomato And Watermelon Salad

Preparation time: 10 minutes
Cooking time: 0 minutes
Servings: 4

Ingredients:

- 2 cups cherry tomatoes cut in halves
- 1 and ½ cups watermelon, chopped
- 2 cups baby arugula
- 3 small cucumbers, chopped
- ¼ cup basil, torn
- ¾ cup feta cheese, cubed
- 1 tablespoon lemon juice
- Salt and black pepper to the taste
- 1 tablespoon olive oil

Directions:

In a salad bowl, mix cucumber with arugula, tomatoes, watermelon, basil and feta. In another bowl, mix oil with salt, pepper and lemon juice and whisk well. Pour this over salad, toss to coat and serve. Enjoy!

Nutrition: calories 140, fat 4, fiber 2, carbs 10, protein 5

Simple Farro Salad

Preparation time: 10 minutes
Cooking time: 35 minutes
Servings: 8

Ingredients:

- 7 cups water
- 3 cups pearled farro
- Salt and black pepper to the taste
- ½ cup black olives, pitted and chopped
- 1/3 cup red wine vinegar
- ½ cup olive oil
- 1 tablespoons olive oil
- 1 teaspoon lemon zest, grated
- 1 cup fennel, chopped
- 1 cup jarred artichoke hearts, drained
- 1 cup already cooked cannellini beans
- 1 cup radicchio, shredded
- ¼ cup basil leaves, chopped
- ¾ cup pine nuts, toasted

Directions:

Put the water in a pot, bring to a boil over high heat, add salt and farro, stir, reduce heat to medium-low and cook for 35 minutes. Drain, rinse and transfer farro to a baking sheet. Spread farro, add 1 tablespoon oil, salt and pepper, toss to coat and leave aside to cool down. In a bowl, mix the rest of the oil with the vinegar, lemon zest, olives, salt and pepper and whisk well. Transfer farro to a salad bowl, add fennel, artichokes, cannellini beans, radicchio, basil, nuts, salt and pepper and toss. Add the vinaigrette, toss to coat and keep in the fridge until you serve it. Enjoy!

Nutrition: calories 340, fat 21, fiber 9, carbs 45, protein 11

Delicious Asparagus Salad

Preparation time: 10 minutes
Cooking time: 0 minutes
Servings: 4

Ingredients:

- 8 slices of prosciutto, chopped
- 2 oranges, peeled, cut into segments
- 1 tablespoon orange juice
- 1 pound asparagus, trimmed
- ½ cup water
- 5 tablespoons olive oil
- ½ cup pistachios, roasted and chopped
- Salt and black pepper to the taste
- 1-ounce parmesan cheese, grated

Directions:

Put asparagus in a heatproof dish, add the water, salt, pepper and 1 tablespoon olive oil, toss to coat, introduce in your microwave and cook on High for 5 minutes. Divide asparagus on serving plates; add prosciutto and oranges on top. Divide pistachios, the rest of the oil and the orange juice on each serving plate. Season with more salt and pepper if needed, sprinkle parmesan at the end and serve. Enjoy!

Nutrition: calories 230, fat 12, fiber 4, carbs 12, protein 14

Simple Quince Salad

Preparation time: 10 minutes
Cooking time: 45 minutes
Servings: 4

Ingredients:

- 2 tablespoons honey
- 2 lemon zest strips
- 1 pound quinces, peeled, cored and cut into quarters
- 4 cups baby arugula
- 2 tablespoons olive oil
- Salt and black pepper to the taste
- 4 ounces prosciutto, cut into strips
- 2 ounces manchego, shaved
- 4 teaspoons balsamic vinegar
- 1/3 cup almonds, toasted and chopped

Directions:

Put quinces in a pot. Add lemon zest, honey and some water to cover them, bring to a boil over medium high heat, cover, simmer for 45 minutes, take off heat and leave aside to cool down. In a salad bowl, mix arugula with ham, oil, salt and pepper. Slice quince quarters and add to salad bowl. Add almonds, and manchego, drizzle balsamic vinegar all over and serve. Enjoy!

Nutrition: calories 240, fat 12, fiber 3, carbs 18, protein 13

Different Potato Salad

Preparation time: 10 minutes
Cooking time: 20 minutes
Servings: 8

Ingredients:

- ¼ cup lemon juice
- Salt and black pepper to the taste
- 2 teaspoons Dijon mustard
- ¼ cup olive oil
- 2 garlic cloves, minced and mashed
- ½ teaspoon red pepper flakes
- 2 teaspoons marjoram, chopped
- For the salad:
- ¼ cup rice vinegar
- 1 tablespoon olive oil
- 3 and ¼ pounds baby red potatoes
- 2 cup frozen artichoke hearts
- Salt and black pepper to the taste
- ¾ cup mint, chopped
- 1 cup black olives, pitted and chopped

Directions:

In a bowl, mix lemon juice with salt, pepper, mustard, ¼ cup oil, 2 garlic cloves, marjoram and pepper flakes and whisk well. In a bowl, mix vinegar with salt and whisk well. Put potatoes in a pot, add salt and water to cover, bring to a boil over high heat, reduce temperature, cook for 10 minutes, take off heat, drain, cool them down, peel and cut them into chunks. Put potatoes in a salad bowl, add rice vinegar mixed with salt and toss to coat. Heat up a pan with 1 tablespoon oil over medium high heat, add artichoke hearts and some salt and brown on both sides. Add these over potatoes, also add mint and olives. Add salt and pepper to the taste and the vinaigrette you've made at the beginning, toss to coat and serve. Enjoy!

Nutrition: calories 145, fat 4, fiber 3, carbs 11, protein 4

Bulgur And Grape Salad

Preparation time: 10 minutes
Cooking time: 1 hour
Servings: 6

Ingredients:

- 1 cup red grapes, cut in quarters
- 1 cup bulgur
- 1 cup celery, chopped
- 3 tablespoons dried currants
- ¼ cup parsley, chopped
- 1/3 cup walnuts, toasted and chopped
- 3 tablespoons walnut oil
- 3 tablespoons balsamic vinegar
- Salt and black pepper to the taste
- 2 tablespoons shallot, minced
- 1 cup water

Directions:

Put the water in a pot, bring to a boil over medium high heat, add bulgur, take off heat and leave aside for 1 hour. Fluff bulgur and transfer to a bowl. Add celery, grapes, parsley, walnuts, walnut oil, currants, shallot, salt, pepper and vinegar, toss to coat and serve. Enjoy!

Nutrition: calories 220, fat 11, fiber 6, carbs 24, protein 5

Chickpeas Salad

Preparation time: 10 minutes
Cooking time: 1 hour and 30 minutes
Servings: 4

Ingredients:

- 3 cups canned chickpeas, drained
- 2 bay leaves
- ¼ teaspoon turmeric
- Salt and black pepper to the taste
- 1 yellow onion, cut in half
- 3 potatoes
- 1 cup yogurt
- ¼ cup sour cream
- 1 tablespoon ginger, grated
- 1 teaspoon fennel seeds, toasted and ground
- 1and ½ teaspoons cumin, toasted and ground
- 1 cucumber, chopped
- 1 hot green chili pepper, chopped
- 1 red onion, chopped
- ¼ cup mint, chopped
- ¼ cup cilantro, chopped
- 8 cups water

Directions:

Put beans in a pot, add the water over them, bring to a boil over medium high heat, add bay leaves, yellow onion, salt, pepper and turmeric, stir, reduce to medium and cook for 1 hour and 30 minutes, take off heat and leave aside to cool down. Meanwhile, put potatoes in another pot, add salt, bring to a boil over high heat, cook for 20 minutes, drain, leave aside to cool down, peel and cut them into small cubes. In a bowl, mix yogurt with sour cream, cumin, ginger, chili pepper and fennel and whisk well. In a bowl mix chickpeas with red onion, potatoes and cucumber. Add mint, cilantro, more salt and pepper to the taste and the yogurt dressing. Toss to coat and serve after 15 minutes. Enjoy!

Nutrition: calories 210, fat 4, fiber 8, carbs 32, protein 8

Mediterranean Diet Dessert Recipes

Easy Chocolate Shake

Preparation time: 5 minutes
Cooking time: 0 minutes
Servings: 2

Ingredients:
- 2 medium bananas, peeled
- 2 teaspoons cocoa powder
- ½ big avocado, mashed
- ¾ cup low fat milk
- A pinch of salt

Directions:
Put bananas in your blender and pulse a few times. Add cocoa powder, avocado and a pinch of salt and pulse again. Add milk, pulse a few more seconds, divide into 2 glass and serve right away. Enjoy!

Nutrition: calories 185, fat 3, fiber 4, carbs 6, protein 7

Lemon And Banana Bars

Preparation time: 30 minutes
Cooking time: 0 minutes
Servings: 4
-

Ingredients:
- 1 cup olive oil
- 1 and ½ bananas, peeled and chopped
- A pinch of salt
- 1/3 cup agave syrup
- ¼ cup lemon juice
- A pinch of lemon zest, grated
- 3 kiwis, peeled and chopped
- Raw hemp seeds for the crust

Directions:
In your food processor, mix bananas with kiwis, almost all the oil, a pinch of salt, agave syrup, lemon juice and a pinch of lemon zest and pulse well. Grease a pan with the remaining oil, spread hemp seeds on the bottom, pour mix, spread, introduce in the fridge for 30 minutes, slice and serve bars. Enjoy!

Nutrition: calories 187, fat 3, fiber 3, carbs 4, protein 4

Mediterranean Strawberry Cobbler

Preparation time: 10 minutes
Cooking time: 30 minutes
Servings: 6

Ingredients:

- ¾ cup sugar
- 6 cups strawberries, halved
- 1/8 teaspoon baking powder
- 1 tablespoon lemon juice
- ½ cup spelled flour
- 1/8 teaspoon baking soda
- A pinch of salt
- ½ cup water
- 3 and ½ tablespoon olive oil
- Cooking spray

Directions:

Spray a baking dish with some cooking spray and leave aside. In a bowl, mix strawberries with half of palm sugar, sprinkle some flour and add lemon juice, whisk and pour into the baking dish. In another bowl, mix flour with the rest of the sugar, a pinch of salt, baking powder and soda and stir well. Add the olive oil and mix until the whole thing with your hands. Add ½ cup water and spread over strawberries. Introduce in the oven at 375 degrees F and bake for 30 minutes. Take cobbler out of the oven, leave aside for 10 minutes and then serve. Enjoy!

Nutrition: calories 221, fat 3, fiber 3, carbs 6, protein 9

Divine Greek Cake

Preparation time: 10 minutes
Cooking time: 35 minutes
Servings: 12

Ingredients:

- 6 tablespoons black tea powder
- 2 cups low fat milk
- ½ cup butter
- 2 cups sugar
- 4 eggs

For the cream:

- 6 tablespoons honey
- 4 cups sugar
- 2 teaspoons vanilla extract
- ½ cup olive oil
- 3 and ½ cups flour
- 1 teaspoon baking soda
- 3 teaspoons baking powder

- 1 cup butter, soft

Directions:

Put the milk in a pot and warm it up over medium heat. Add tea, stir well, take off heat and leave aside until it's cold enough. In a bowl, mix ½ cup butter with 2 cups sugar and stir well. Add eggs, vegetable oil, vanilla extract, baking powder, baking soda and 3 and ½ cups flour and stir everything really well. Pour this into 2 greased round pans, introduce in the oven at 350 degrees F and bake for 30 minutes. Leave cakes to cool down. In a bowl, mix 1 cup butter with honey and 4 cups sugar and stir really well. Arrange one cake on a platter, spread the cream all over, top with the other cake and keep in the fridge until you serve it. Enjoy!

Nutrition: calories 200, fat 4, fiber 4, carbs 6, protein 2

Green Tea Pudding

Preparation time: 2 hours and 10 minutes
Cooking time: 5 minutes
Servings: 6

Ingredients:

- 14 ounces milk
- 2 tablespoons green tea powder
- 14 ounces heavy cream
- 3 tablespoons sugar
- 1 teaspoon gelatin powder

Directions:

Put the milk in a pan, add sugar, gelatin and green tea powder, stir, bring to a simmer and cook for 2 minutes. Take off heat, leave aside to cool down, add heavy cream, stir, divide into cups and keep in the fridge for 2 hours before serving. Enjoy!

Nutrition: calories 120, fat 3, fiber 3, carbs 7, protein 4

Easy Apple Pie

Preparation time: 10 minutes
Cooking time: 1 hour and 5 minutes
Servings: 8

Ingredients:

- ½ cup sugar
- 4 apples, peeled, cored and cut into chunks
- 1 cup flour
- 3 eggs

Directions:

Spread apple pieces on the bottom of a lined spring form. In a bowl, mix eggs with sugar and stir well. Add flour and stir well again. Pour this over apples, introduce in the oven at 375 digress F and bake for 1 hour. Flip pie upside down when it's done, slice and serve. Enjoy!

Nutrition: calories 200, fat 4, fiber 3, carbs 6, protein 8

Apricot Cream

Preparation time: 2 hours and 10 minutes
Cooking time: 0 minutes
Servings: 4

Ingredients:
- ¾ cup apricot pulp
- 1 cup low fat milk
- ½ cup whipping cream
- 3 eggs, whites and yolks separated
- 1/3 cup sugar
- 1 teaspoon lemon juice
- ½ teaspoon vanilla
- 1 package gelatin
- 1 tablespoon warm water

Directions:

In a bowl, mix warm water with gelatin and whisk well. In another bowl, mix sugar with egg yolks and milk and also whisk well. Introduce this in preheated broiler and cook until it thickens. Add gelatin to this mix, stir and leave aside to cool down. In your food processor, mix the apricot pulp with lemon juice and vanilla and pulse well. Add this to gelatin mix and stir well. In a bowl, beat egg white using your mixer. Add this to gelatin mix as well and stir everything. Divide this into molds and serve after you've kept in the fridge for 2 hours. Enjoy!

Nutrition: calories 129, fat 4, fiber 6, carbs 8, protein 9

Mediterranean Cherry Delight

Preparation time: 10 minutes
Cooking time: 30 minutes
Servings: 4

Ingredients:
- ½ cup sugar+ 2 tablespoons sugar
- 2 pounds cherries, pitted
- 4 cups water
- 1 vanilla bean
- 1 tablespoon cornstarch, mixed with ½ tablespoon water
- 1 cinnamon stick
- 1 cup low fat milk
- Zest from 1 lemon, grated
- 1/3 cup cream of wheat
- 3 egg yolks
- 3 tablespoons rum

Directions:

Heat up a pan with the water over medium heat, add ½ cup sugar, vanilla bean, cinnamon stick and cherries, stir and boil for 10 minutes. Add cornstarch, stir and bring to a boil again. Heat up another pot over medium heat, add milk, lemon zest and 2 tablespoons sugar, stir and bring to a simmer. Add cream of wheat, stir and cook for 5 minutes. In a bowl, mix egg yolks with some of the cream of the wheat mix, stir well and add to the mix in the pot. Shape small dumplings from this mix and drop them into cherry soup, stir gently, take off heat and leave aside to cool down before serving.

Nutrition: calories 200, fat 3, fiber 2, carbs 5, protein 8

Easy Plum Cake

Preparation time: 1 hour and 20 minutes
Cooking time: 40 minutes
Servings: 8

Ingredients:

- 7 ounces flour
- 1 package dried yeast
- 1 ounce butter, soft
- A pinch of salt
- 1 egg, whisked
- 5 tablespoons sugar
- 3 ounces warm milk
- 1 and ¾ pounds plums, pitted and cut in quarters
- Zest from 1 lemon, grated
- 1 ounce almond flakes

Directions:

In a bowl, mix yeast with butter, flour, a pinch of salt and 3 tablespoons sugar and stir well. Add milk and egg and whisk for 4 minutes until you obtain a dough. Arrange the dough in a spring form pan which you've greased with some of the butter earlier, cover and leave aside for 1 hour. Arrange plums on top of the butter, sprinkle the rest of the sugar, introduce in the oven at 350 degrees F, bake for 40 minutes, cool down, sprinkle almond flakes and lemon zest on top, slice and serve. Enjoy!

Nutrition: calories 192, fat 4, fiber 2, carbs 6, protein 7

Special Lentils Cookies

Preparation time: 10 minutes
Cooking time: 25 minutes
Servings: 36

Ingredients:

- 1 cup water
- 1 cup lentils, cooked, drained and rinsed
- 1 cup white flour
- 1 teaspoon cinnamon
- 1 cup whole wheat flour
- 1 teaspoon baking powder
- ½ teaspoon nutmeg, ground
- A pinch of salt
- 1 cup butter, soft
- ½ cup brown sugar
- ½ cup white sugar
- 1 egg
- 2 teaspoons almond extract
- 1 cup raisins
- 1 cup rolled oats
- 1 cup coconut, unsweetened and shredded

Directions:

Put lentils in a pot, add the water, bring to a boil over medium heat , cook for 15 minutes, take off heat, leave aside to cool down and mash them to create a paste. In a bowl, mix white and whole wheat flour with salt, cinnamon, baking powder and nutmeg and stir. In a bowl, mix butter with white and brown sugar and stir using your kitchen mixer for 2 minutes. Add egg, almond extract and lentils mix and mix again. Add flour mixture and stir until you obtain a dough. Add oats, raisins and coconut and stir gently. Scoop tablespoons of dough on 2 lined baking sheets, introduce them in the oven at 350 degrees F and bake for 18 minutes. Leave them to cool down for a few minutes, arrange on a serving platter and serve. Enjoy!

Nutrition: calories 154, fat 2, fiber 2, carbs 4, protein 7

Special Mediterranean Brownies

Preparation time: 10 minutes
Cooking time: 15 minutes
Servings: 8

Ingredients:
- 28 ounces canned lentils, rinsed and drained
- 12 dates
- 1 tablespoon honey
- 1 banana, peeled and chopped
- ½ teaspoon baking soda
- 4 tablespoons almond butter
- 2 tablespoons cocoa powder

Directions:

Put lentils in your food processor and blend well. Add butter, banana, cocoa, baking soda and honey and blend again well. Add dates and pulse a few more times. Pour this into a greased pan, spread evenly, introduce in the oven at 375 degrees F and bake for 15 minutes. Take brownies out of the oven, cut, arrange on a platter and serve them cold. Enjoy!

Nutrition: calories 162, fat 4, fiber 2, carbs 3, protein 4

Red Lentils Ice Cream

Preparation time: 30 minutes
Cooking time: 1 hour and 20 minutes
Servings: 4

Ingredients:
- ½ cup red lentils, rinsed
- Juice of ½ lemon
- ½ cup sugar
- 1 and ½ cups water
- A pinch of salt
- 3 cups almond milk
- ½ cup honey
- Juice from 2 limes
- 2 teaspoons cardamom, ground
- 1 teaspoon rose water
- 3 drops vanilla extract

Directions:

Heat up a pan over medium high heat with the water, sugar, some salt and lemon juice. Stir until sugar melts and bring to a boil. Add lentils, stir, reduce heat to low and simmer for 1 hour and 20 minutes. Drain lentils, transfer them to a bowl, add coconut milk, honey, limes juice, cardamom, rosewater and vanilla extract and whisk very well everything. Transfer this to your ice cream machine and process for 30 minutes. Serve in dessert cups. Enjoy!

Nutrition: calories 114, fat 4, fiber 3, carbs 5, protein 4

Maple Cupcakes

Preparation time: 10 minutes
Cooking time: 20 minutes
Servings: 4

Ingredients:
- 4 tablespoons butter
- 4 eggs
- ½ cup pure applesauce
- 2 teaspoons cinnamon powder
- 1 teaspoon vanilla extract
- ½ apple, cored and sliced
- 4 teaspoons maple syrup
- ¾ cup almond flour
- ½ teaspoon baking powder
- Cinnamon powder for serving
- A pinch of salt

Directions:

Heat up a pan with the butter over medium heat, add applesauce, vanilla, eggs and maple syrup, stir, take off heat and leave aside to cool down. Add almond flour, cinnamon, baking powder and a pinch of salt, whisk, pour in a cupcake pan, introduce in the oven at 350 degrees F and bake for 20 minutes. Take out of the oven, leave them to cool down, transfer to a platter, top with apple slices and cinnamon and serve! Enjoy!

Nutrition: calories 150, fat 3, fiber 1, carbs 5, protein 4

Delicious Rhubarb Pie

Preparation time: 30 minutes
Cooking time: 1 hour
Servings: 6

Ingredients:
- 1 and ¼ cups almond flour
- 8 tablespoons butter
- A pinch of salt

For the filling:
- 3 cups rhubarb, chopped
- 3 tablespoons almond flour
- 1 and ½ cups sugar
- 2 eggs

- 5 tablespoons cold water
- 1 teaspoon sugar

- A pinch of salt
- ½ teaspoon nutmeg, ground
- 1 tablespoon butter
- 2 tablespoons low fat milk

Directions:

In a bowl, mix 1 and ¼ cups flour with salt and 1 teaspoon sugar and stir. Add 8 tablespoons of butter and the cold water and knead until you obtain a dough. Transfer dough to a floured working surface, shape a disk, flatten, wrap in plastic and keep in the fridge for about 30 minutes. Take dough, roll and transfer to a pie plate. In a bowl, mix rhubarb with a pinch of salt, 1 and ½ cups sugar, nutmeg, 3 tablespoons flour and whisk. In a second bowl, whisk eggs with milk. Add this to rhubarb mix, stir well, pour into pie crust and bake in the oven for 50 minutes at 400 degrees F. Cut and serve it cold. Enjoy!

Nutrition: calories 200, fat 2, fiber 1, carbs 6, protein 3

Couscous Dessert

Preparation time: 15 minutes
Cooking time: 2 minutes
Servings: 4

Ingredients:
- 1 cup couscous
- 2 tablespoons rose water
- 2 cups fruit juice
- 3 tablespoons butter
- ¼ cup pistachio, grated
- ¼ cup almonds, blanched
- ½ cup sugar
- 1 tablespoon cinnamon powder
- ½ cup pomegranate seeds

Directions:

In a pot, mix fruit juice with rose water and couscous, bring to a boil over medium heat, cover, take off heat, leave aside for 15 minutes and fluff with a fork. Add melted butter and stir well. Also add almonds and pistachios and whisk. Divide on small dessert plates, sprinkle sugar, cinnamon and pomegranate seeds on top and serve. Enjoy!

Nutrition: calories 200, fat 2, fiber 2, carbs 4, protein 7

The Most Amazing Apricot Sorbet

Preparation time: 2 hours and 10 minutes
Cooking time: 10 minutes
Servings: 4

Ingredients:
- 2 cups sparkling wine
- 1 cup palm sugar
- 2 strips lemon peel
- A pinch of salt
- 1 and ½ pounds apricots pitted and cut in halves

Directions:

Heat up a saucepan over medium heat, add sugar, wine, apricots, lemon peel and a pinch of salt, stir bring to a simmer, cook for 10 minutes, take off heat and discard lemon peel. Transfer this cold to a food processor and pulse very well. Put this in a casserole, introduce in the freezer and leave there for 2 hours. Take out of the freezer and serve! Enjoy!

Nutrition: calories 172, fat 4, fiber 3, carbs 6, protein 6

Greek Apple Crisp

Preparation time: 10 minutes
Cooking time: 40 minutes
Servings: 4

Ingredients:
- 2 cup cranberries
- 3 cups apple, cubed
- A drizzle of olive oil
- ½ cup sugar
- 1/3 cup almond flour
- 1 cup oats
- ¼ canola oil
- ½ cup palm sugar

Directions:

In a bowl, mix apples with cranberries and ½ cup sugar and stir well. In another bowl, mix flour with oats, canola oil and ½ cup sugar and stir well. Pour apple mixture into a baking dish which you've greased with some olive oil, sprinkle flour mix on top, introduce in the oven at 350 degrees F and bake for 40 minutes. Take apple crisp out of the oven, leave aside to cool down and serve! Enjoy!

Nutrition: calories 202, fat 2, fiber 3, carbs 4, protein 2

Fresh Lemon Tart

Preparation time: 1 hour
Cooking time: 45 minutes
Servings: 6

Ingredients:
For the crust:
- 2 tablespoons sugar
- 2 cups white flour
- A pinch of salt

For the filling:
- 2 eggs, whisked
- 1 and ¼ cup sugar
- 10 tablespoons melted and chilled butter
- 3 tablespoons ice water
- 12 tablespoons cold butter

- Juice from 2 lemons
- Zest of 2 lemons, grated

Directions:

In a bowl, mix 2 cups flour with a pinch of salt and 2 tablespoons sugar and whisk. Add 12 tablespoons butter and the water, knead until you obtain a firm dough, shape a ball, wrap in plastic and keep in the fridge for 1 hour. Transfer dough to a floured working surface, flatten it, arrange on the bottom of a tart pan, prick with a fork, cover with tin foil and keep in the fridge for 20 minutes. Fill this with pie weights, introduce in the oven at 375 degrees F and bake shell for 15 minutes. Get rid of the pie weights, bake 5 more minutes and leave aside for now. In a bowl, mix 1 and ¼ cup sugar with eggs, 10 tablespoons butter, lemon juice and lemon zest and whisk very well. Pour this into pie crust, spread evenly, introduce in the oven and bake for 25 minutes. Cut and serve it. Enjoy!

Nutrition: calories 182, fat 4, fiber 1, carbs 2, protein 3

Summer Berry Dessert

Preparation time: 10 minutes
Cooking time: 5 minutes
Servings: 8

Ingredients:

- 1 and ½ cups blueberries
- 1 and ½ cups strawberries, cut in quarters
- 2 tablespoons cornstarch
- 3 tablespoons sugar
- 1 and ½ cups pure apple juice
- Vanilla Greek yogurt for serving

Directions:

In a heat proof dish, mix blueberries with strawberries and 2 tablespoons sugar. Heat up apple juice in a pot over medium high heat, add cornstarch, stir and boil for 2 minutes. Allow sauce to cool down for 10 minutes, pour over fruit mix, add the rest of the sugar, cover dish and keep in the fridge until it's cold enough. Spoon fruit mix in small bowl, top with Greek yogurt and serve! Enjoy!

Nutrition: calories 174, fat 3, fiber 3, carbs 3, protein 5

The Most Delicious Almond Pudding

Preparation time: 20 minutes
Cooking time: 2 hours and 35 minutes
Servings: 8

Ingredients:

- 1 mandarin, peeled and sliced
- Juice from 2 mandarins
- 2 tablespoons brown sugar
- 4 ounces butter, soft
- 2 eggs, whisked
- ¾ cup sugar
- ¾ cup white flour
- ¾ cup almonds, ground
- Honey for serving

Directions:

Grease a loaf pan with some butter and sprinkle the brown sugar on the bottom. Arrange slices from 1 mandarin over the sugar and leave aside. In a bowl, mix butter with sugar and eggs and whisk using your mixer. Add almonds, flour and the mandarin juice and stir. Spoon mix over mandarin slices, place pan in your slow cooker, cover and cook on High for 2 hours and 30 minutes. Uncover, leave aside for a few minutes, transfer to a plate and serve with honey on top. Enjoy!

Nutrition: calories 162, fat 3, fiber 2, carbs 3, protein 6

Strawberry Shortcakes

Preparation time: 20 minutes
Cooking time: 1 hour and 30 minutes
Servings: 6

Ingredients:
- Olive oil cooking spray
- ¼ cup sugar+ 4 tablespoons
- 1 and ½ cup almond flour
- 1 teaspoon baking powder
- A pinch of salt
- ¼ teaspoon baking soda
- 1/3 cup butter
- 1 cup low fat buttermilk
- 1 egg, whisked
- 2 cups strawberries, sliced
- 1 tablespoon rum
- 1 tablespoon mint, chopped
- 1 teaspoon lime zest, grated
- ½ cup whipping cream

Directions:
Grease 6 small jars with olive oil cooking spray and leave them aside for now. In a bowl, mix flour with ¼ cup sugar, baking powder, salt and baking soda and stir. In another bowl, mix buttermilk with egg, stir, add to flour mixture and whisk. Spoon this dough into jars, cover with tin foil, arrange them in your slow cooker, add some water to the bottom, cover and cook on High for 1 hour and 30 minutes. Meanwhile, in a bowl, mix strawberries with 3 tablespoons sugar and rum and toss to coat. Add mint, lime zest, stir and leave aside in a cold place. In another bowl, mix whipping cream with 1 tablespoon sugar and stir Uncover slow cooker, take jars out, divide strawberry mix and whipped cream on top and serve. Enjoy!

Nutrition: calories 164, fat 2, fiber 3, carbs 5, protein 2

Mediterranean Sponge Cake

Preparation time: 10 minutes
Cooking time: 20 minutes
Servings: 12

Ingredients:
- 3 cups almond flour
- 3 teaspoons baking powder
- ½ cup cornstarch
- 1 teaspoon baking soda
- 1 cup olive oil
- 1 and ½ cup low fat milk
- 1 and 2/3 cup sugar
- 2 cups water
- ¼ cup lemon juice
- 2 teaspoons vanilla extract

Directions:
In a bowl, mix flour with cornstarch, baking powder, baking soda and sugar and whisk well. In another bowl, mix oil with milk, water, vanilla and lemon juice and whisk. Combine the two mixtures, stir, pour into a greased baking dish, introduce in the oven at 357 degrees F and bake for 20 minutes. Leave cake to cool down, cut and serve! Enjoy!

Nutrition: calories 246, fat 3, fiber 1, carbs 6, protein 2

Apple Dessert

Preparation time: 3 minutes
Cooking time: 4 minutes
Servings: 1

Ingredients:
- 1 apple, peeled, cored and chopped
- ¼ cup canned pumpkin flesh
- 2 tablespoons water
- A pinch of pumpkin spice

Directions:

In a bowl, mix some apple slices with some of the pumpkin flesh. Sprinkle pumpkin spice, layer the rest of the apples and pumpkin flesh and top with pumpkin spice again. Add water, introduce in the microwave and heat up for 4 minutes. Serve right away! Enjoy!

Nutrition: calories 99, fat 0.4, fiber 3, carbs 5, protein 1

Special Mediterranean Smoothie

Preparation time: 5 minutes
Cooking time: 0 minutes
Servings: 2

Ingredients:
- 1 and ½ cup low fat milk
- 1 cup blueberries
- 4 big strawberries, chopped
- ½ banana, peeled
- 2 tablespoons hemp seeds
- 1 and ½ tablespoons chia seeds
- A handful spinach
- 1 teaspoon cinnamon

Directions:

Put blueberries in your blender and mix well. Add milk and stir again. Add banana, strawberries and spinach and blend some more. Add hemp and chia seeds and mix a few more times. Add cinnamon at the end, stir, pour into a glass and serve. Enjoy!

Nutrition: calories 121, fat 2, fiber 3, carbs 6, protein 5

Strawberry Summer Smoothie

Preparation time: 6 minutes
Cooking time: 0 minutes
Servings: 2

Ingredients:
- ½ banana, peeled
- 2 cups strawberries, halved
- 3 tablespoons spearmint
- 1 and ½ cups coconut water
- ½ avocado, pitted and peeled
- 1 date, chopped
- Ice cubes for serving

Directions:

Put banana in your blender and pulse a few times. Add strawberries, coconut water and avocado and blend again. Add spearmint and date and blend some more. Pour into a glass and enjoy!

Nutrition: calories 100, fat 0, fiber 1, carbs 2, protein 3

Mediterranean Melon Delight

Preparation time: 15 minutes
Cooking time: 0 minutes
Servings: 2

Ingredients:
- 2 ripe melons, peeled and cubed
- Equal parts lime juice and pure maple syrup
- Ice for serving

Directions:
Place melon cubes in a bowl add lime juice and maple syrup. Cover and keep in the fridge until you serve. Divide into bowl and serve with ice. Enjoy!

Nutrition: calories 78, fat 0, fiber 0, carbs 0, protein 2

Red Grape Cake

Preparation time: 10 minutes
Cooking time: 40 minutes
Servings: 8

Ingredients:
- 1 cup whole wheat flour
- 1 and ½ teaspoon baking powder
- ½ cup cornmeal
- A pinch of salt
- 2 eggs
- 2/3 cup sugar
- ½ cup extra virgin olive oil
- 1/3 cup low fat milk
- 1 teaspoon vanilla extract
- 1 teaspoon lemon zest, grated
- 1 and ¾ cup red grapes, halved

Directions:
In a bowl, mix flour with cornmeal, a pinch of salt and baking powder, stir and leave aside. In another bowl, mix eggs with sugar and blend using your kitchen mixer for 5 minutes. Add oil and beat for 1 more minute. Add milk, vanilla and lemon zest and stir again. Add flour to this mix and half of the grapes and stir. Grease a baking pan, pour the batter in it, introduce in the oven at 35 degrees F for 10 minutes. Arrange the rest of the grapes on top, introduce in the oven again and bake for about 30 more minutes. Take out of the oven, cool down a bit, slice and serve it. Enjoy!

Nutrition: calories 120, fat 2, fiber 2, carbs 4, protein 4

Cherry Sorbet

Preparation time: 2 hours and 20 minutes
Cooking time: 0 minutes
Servings: 7

Ingredients:

- ½ cup cocoa powder
- ¾ cup red cherry jam
- ¼ cup sugar

For the compote:

- ¼ cup sugar

- 2 cups water
- A pinch of salt

- 1 pound cherries, pitted and halved

Directions:

In a pan, mix cherry jam with cocoa, sugar and a pinch of salt, stir, bring to a boil over medium heat, add the water, stir again, remove from heat and leave aside to cool down completely. Whisk this sorbet again, pour in a casserole and keep in the freezer for 1 hour. In a bowl, mix ¼ cup sugar with cherries, toss to coat and leave aside for 1 hour. Serve this cherries compote with the sorbet. Enjoy!

Nutrition: calories 197, fat 1, fiber 3, carbs 5, protein 1

Rice Pudding

Preparation time: 15 minutes
Cooking time: 45 minutes
Servings: 6

Ingredients:

- ½ cup basmati rice
- 4 cups milk
- ¼ cup raisins
- 3 tablespoons sugar
- ½ teaspoon cardamom
- ¼ teaspoon cinnamon powder
- ½ teaspoon rose water
- ¼ cup almonds, chopped
- 1 tablespoon orange zest, grated

Directions:

Soak rice in some water for 10 minutes, drain and leave aside. In a pan, mix sugar with milk, stir and bring to a boil at a medium high temperature. Add rice, cardamom, cinnamon, raisins, reduce heat to low and cook for 45 minutes stirring all the time. Add rose water, take off heat and leave aside for a few minutes. In a bowl, mix orange zest with almonds. Pour rice pudding into bowls, sprinkle almond mix on top and serve cold. Enjoy!

Nutrition: calories 120, fat 1, fiber 2, carbs 2, protein 3

Tasty And Easy Cake

Preparation time: 10 minutes
Cooking time: 1 hour and 10 minutes
Servings: 4

Ingredients:

- 8 eggs, whisked
- 3 pounds ricotta cheese
- ½ pound sugar
- Zest from 1 lemon, grated
- Zest from 1 orange, grated
- Butter for the pan

Directions:

In a bowl, mix eggs with sugar, cheese, lemon and orange zest and stir very well. Grease a baking pan with some butter, pour the eggs mixture, introduce in the oven at 425 degrees F and bake for 30 minutes. Reduce heat to 380 degrees F and bake for 40 more minutes. Take out of the oven, leave the cake to cool down and serve! Enjoy!

Nutrition: calories 110, fat 3, fiber 2, carbs 3, protein 4

Fruit Cream

Preparation time: 10 minutes
Cooking time: 0 minutes
Servings: 4

Ingredients:

- 1 cup apples, chopped
- 1 cup pineapple, chopped
- 1 cup banana, peeled and chopped
- 1 cup melon, peeled and chopped
- 1 cup papaya, peeled and chopped
- ½ teaspoon vanilla powder
- ¾ cup cashews, soaked for 6 hours and drained
- Stevia to the taste
- Some cold water

Directions:

Put cashews in your food processor, add stevia and vanilla, blend, transfer to a bowl and keep in the fridge for now. In a bowl, arrange a layer of mixed apples with bananas, pineapples, melon and papaya. Add a layer of cold cashew paste, another layer of fruits, another one of cashew paste and top with a layer of fruits. Serve right away! Enjoy!

Nutrition: calories 140, fat 1, fiber 1, carbs 3, protein 2

Poppy Seed Delight

Preparation time: 10 minutes
Cooking time: 5 minutes
Servings: 4

Ingredients:

- 1 tablespoon lemon juice
- Zest of 2 lemons, grated
- 2 cups milk
- 1 teaspoon almond extract
- 1 teaspoon vanilla extract
- 1 cup whole wheat flour
- 1/3 cup oat bran
- 2/3 cups all-purpose flour
- 1 and ½ teaspoon baking powder
- 2 tablespoons sugar
- A pinch of salt
- ¼ cup olive oil
- ½ cup silver almonds, chopped

Directions:

In a bowl, mix almond milk with lemon zest, lemon juice, vanilla extract, poppy seeds and almond extract and stir very well. Add oil and whisk well again. In another bowl, mix all purpose flour with whole wheat flour, sugar, a pinch of salt, oat bran and baking powder and stir well. Combine the 2 mixtures and stir. Add almonds and stir again. Heat up a pan over medium high heat, grease with some olive oil, drop 1/3 cup pancakes batter, spread evenly, cook for 2 minutes, flip and cook another 2 minutes, transfer to a plate and leave aside. Repeat this with the rest of the batter and serve pancakes right away. Enjoy!

Nutrition: calories 80, fat 1, fiber 2, carbs 5, protein 3

Butter Cups

Preparation time: 2 hours and 10 minutes
Cooking time: 0 minutes
Servings: 6

Ingredients:
- 5 tablespoons almond flour
- ½ cup soft butter
- 1 cup, chocolate, chopped
- 1 teaspoon matcha powder+ some more for the topping
- 3 tablespoons sugar
- 1 teaspoon coconut oil
- A pinch of salt
- Cocoa nibs

Directions:

In a bowl, mix butter with almond flour, sugar and matcha powder, stir, cover and keep in the fridge for 10 minutes. Put chocolate in a bowl, place it over another bowl filled with boiling water, stir until it melts and mix with the oil. Spoon 2 teaspoons of this melted mix in an each cup of a muffin liner. Take 1 tablespoon matcha mix, shape a ball, place in a muffin liner, press to flatten it and repeat this with the rest of the mix. Top each with 1 tablespoon melted chocolate and spread evenly. In a small bowl, mix a pinch of sea salt with a pinch of matcha powder, stir and sprinkle all over muffins. Add cocoa nibs on top, introduce them in the freezer and keep there until they are firm. Enjoy!

Nutrition: calories 230, fat 2, fiber 1, carbs 4, protein 3

Summer Mango Surprise

Preparation time: 30 minutes
Cooking time: 0 minutes
Servings: 4

Ingredients:
- 3 cups mango, cut into medium chunks
- ½ cup low fat milk
- ¼ cup sugar

Directions:

Put mango pieces in your blender and pulse a few times. Add sugar and pulse again. Add milk, blend for 15 seconds, transfer to bowls and keep in the freezer for 20 minutes before serving. Enjoy!

Nutrition: calories 160, fat 2, fiber 2, carbs 3, protein 1

Fresh Chocolate Delight

Preparation time: 10 minutes
Cooking time: 5 minutes
Servings: 4

Ingredients:

- 2 cups water
- 1/3 cup brown sugar
- 2/3 cup white sugar
- A pinch of salt
- ¾ cup cocoa powder
- 6 ounces dark chocolate, chopped
- Zest and juice from 1 lemon

Directions:

Put 1 and ½ cups water in a pot, heat up over medium heat, add brown and white sugar, a pinch of salt and cocoa powder, stir, bring to a boil and simmer for 1 minute. Take pot off the heat, add chocolate and stir until it melts. Add the rest of the water, lemon zest and juice and whisk again very well. Leave aside to cool down, transfer to your ice cream maker process. Serve when it's done! Enjoy!

Nutrition: calories 160, fat 3, fiber 3, carbs 7, protein 10

Pineapple Cake

Preparation time: 10 minutes
Cooking time: 40 minutes
Servings: 8

Ingredients:

- 3 cups white flour
- ¼ cup olive oil
- 1 and ½ cup butter
- 1 teaspoon vanilla extract
- 2 and ¼ cups sugar
- 1 and ¼ cup natural apple sauce
- 2 teaspoons baking powder
- 1 and ¼ cups low fat milk
- A pinch of salt
- 2 tablespoons white vinegar
- 1 and ½ cups brown sugar
- 16 pecans
- 16 pineapple slices

Directions:

Grease 2 cake pans with olive oil, sprinkle some flour and brown sugar and coat well. Pour ½ cup melted butter and spread evenly. Put 1 pineapple slice in the middle of each pan, then divide rest of the slices in a circle around the edges of cake pans. Add 1 pecan in the middle of each pineapple slice and leave pans aside for now. In a bowl, mix milk with white vinegar, whisk and leave aside as well. Put the rest of the butter in a bowl, add white sugar, apple sauce and vanilla and whisk using your hand mixer. In a bowl, mix flour with a pinch of salt and baking powder. Add this to milk mixture and whisk again. Pour this over pineapples, spread, introduce pans in the oven at 350 degrees F and bake for 40 minutes. Take cakes out of the oven, leave them aside for 10 minutes, invert them on platters, cut and serve. Enjoy!

Nutrition: calories 200, fat 1, fiber 2, carbs 6, protein 4

Fresh Lemon Fudge

Preparation time: 3 hours and 10 minutes
Cooking time: 0 minutes
Servings: 6

Ingredients:
- 1/3 cup natural cashew butter
- 1 and ½ tablespoons olive oil
- 2 tablespoons butter
- 5 tablespoons lemon juice
- ½ teaspoon lemon zest, grated
- A pinch of salt
- 1 tablespoons maple syrup

Directions:

In a bowl, mix cashew butter with butter, oil, lemon juice, lemon zest, a pinch of salt and maple syrup and whisk until you obtain a creamy mix. Line a muffin tray with parchment paper, scoop 1 tablespoon of lemon fudge mix in each of the muffin tins and keep in the freezer for 3 hours before serving. Enjoy!

Nutrition: calories 72, fat 4, fiber 1, carbs 3, protein 1

Summer Tart

Preparation time: 2 hours and 10 minutes
Cooking time: 15 minutes
Servings: 6

Ingredients:
For the crust:
- 2 cups graham cracker crumbs

For the filling:
- ¼ cup maple syrup
- 14 ounces low fat milk

For the topping:
- ½ pint blueberries
- ½ pint cherries
- 7 tablespoons olive oil
- Zest from 1 lemon
- Juice of 1 lemon
- 1-pint strawberries, halved

Directions:

Put crackers in your blender and pulse a few times. Heat up a pan with the oil over medium high heat, add crumbled graham crackers and stir well. Press well on the bottom of a tart pan, introduce in the oven at 350 degrees F and bake for 10 minutes. Put the milk in a bowl, add maple syrup, lemon zest and lemon juice and stir well. Take tart crust out of the oven, leave aside to completely cool down, pour this coconut milk mixture into it, spread evenly and introduce in the freezer for 2 hours. Spread blueberries, cherries and strawberries on top and keep in the fridge until you serve it. Enjoy!

Nutrition: calories 130, fat 4, fiber 1, carbs 6, protein 9

Mediterranean Tangerine Cake

Preparation time: 10 minutes
Cooking time: 20 minutes
Servings: 8

Ingredients:
- ¾ cup sugar
- 2 cups almond flour
- ¼ cup olive oil
- ½ cup low fat milk
- 1 teaspoon cider vinegar
- ½ teaspoon vanilla extract
- Juice and zest of 2 lemons
- Juice and zest from 1 tangerine
- Tangerine segments, for serving

Directions:

Put flour in a bowl, mix with salt and sugar and stir. In another bowl, mix oil with coconut milk, vinegar, vanilla extract, lemon juice and zest and zest from the tangerine and whisk very well. Mix flour with wet ingredients, stir until you obtain a batter, pour into a greased cake pan, introduce in the oven at 375 degrees F and bake for 20 minutes. Transfer cake to a platter, cut and pour the tangerine juice all over it. Serve right away with tangerine segments on top. Enjoy!

Nutrition: calories 190, fat 1, fiber 1, carbs 4, protein 4

Blueberry And Rosemary Dessert

Preparation time: 10 minutes
Cooking time: 30 minutes
Servings: 6

Ingredients:
- 2 cups garbanzo bean flour
- 2 cups rolled oats
- 8 cups blueberries
- 1 stick butter
- 1 cup walnuts, chopped
- 3 tablespoons maple syrup
- A pinch of salt
- 2 tablespoons rosemary, chopped

Directions:

Spread blueberries in a greased baking pan and leave aside. Meanwhile, in your food processor, mix rolled oats with bean flour, walnuts, vegan butter, maple syrup, a pinch of salt and rosemary and blend well. Layer this mix over blueberries, introduce everything in the oven at 350 degrees F and bake for 30 minutes. Take dessert out of the oven, leave aside to cool down, cut and serve. Enjoy!

Nutrition: calories 150, fat 3, fiber 2, carbs 7, protein 4

Delicious Yogourt Mousse

Preparation time: 8 hours
Cooking time: 3 minutes
Servings: 4

Ingredients:

- 2 cups yogurt
- ¼ cup honey
- A pinch of salt
- ½ vanilla bean
- ¾ cup heavy cream
- 2 tablespoons water
- For the berries:
- 1 tablespoon honey
- ¼ cup balsamic vinegar
- A pinch of black pepper
- 2 cups mixed blueberries and raspberries
- 4 amaretto cookies, crushed

Directions:

Strain yogurt, spoon into a cheesecloth, press, cover and keep in the fridge for 4 hours. Heat up a pan with the water and a pinch of salt over medium high heat, add ¼ cup honey, vanilla seeds and the bean, stir, bring to a boil, cook for 2 minutes, take off heat, leave aside to cool down for 10 minutes and discard vanilla bean. Mix cream with a mixer, add yogurt and whisk for 3 minutes. Divide this into dessert glasses, cover and keep in the fridge for 4 hours. Before serving the mousse, heat up a pan over medium heat, add vinegar, a pinch of pepper and 1 tablespoon honey, stir, bring to a boil and simmer for 2 minutes. Take off heat, add berries, stir and pour over yogurt mousse. Garnish each glass with crumbled amaretto cookies. Enjoy!

Nutrition: calories 340, fat 21, fiber 3, carbs 43, protein 6

Simple Grilled Peaches

Preparation time: 10 minutes
Cooking time: 5 minutes
Servings: 4

Ingredients:

- 1/3 cup almonds, toasted
- 1/3 cup pistachios, toasted
- 1 tablespoon cumin seeds
- 1 tablespoon caraway seeds
- 1 tablespoon cumin seeds
- 1 teaspoon crushed pepper
- 2 teaspoons salt
- 3 tablespoons sesame seeds, toasted
- 1 teaspoon mint
- 1 teaspoon nigella seeds
- ½ teaspoon marjoram, dried
- 1 teaspoon lemon zest, grated
- 4 peaches, halved
- A drizzle of olive oil
- Whipped cream
- Blueberries

Directions:

In your food processor, mix pistachios with almonds, coriander, cumin, caraway, crushed pepper, sesame seeds, salt, nigella seeds, mint, marjoram and lemon zest and ground everything well. Heat up your grill over medium high heat, add peach halves, brush them with some oil, grill for 4 minutes and divide between plates. Add some of the nuts mix you've made and serve with blueberries and whipped cream. Enjoy!

Nutrition: calories 70, fat 1, fiber 4, carbs 17, protein 1

Almond Cake

Preparation time: 10 minutes
Cooking time: 40 minutes
Servings: 10

Ingredients:

- ½ pound almonds, blanched and ground
- Zest from 1 lemon, grated
- Zest from 1 orange, grated
- 1 and ¼ cups sugar
- 6 eggs, whites and yolks separated
- 4 drops almond extract
- Confectioner's sugar

Directions:

Beat egg yolks with your mixer very well. Add sugar, almond extract, orange and lemon zest and almonds and stir well. Beat egg whites in another bowl with your mixer. Add egg yolks mix and stir everything. Pour this into a greased baking dish, introduce in the oven at 350 degrees F and bake for 40 minutes. Take cake out of the oven, leave it to cool down, slice, dust confectioners' sugar on top and serve. Enjoy!

Nutrition: calories 200, fat 0, fiber 0, carbs 23, protein 6

Orange And Hazelnut Cake

Preparation time: 10 minutes
Cooking time: 40 minutes
Servings: 10

Ingredients:

For the syrup:
- 1 and ¼ cups sugar
- 2/3 cup water
- 2 and ½ tablespoons orange water

For the cake:
- 2 and ¼ cups hazelnut flour
- 5 eggs, whites and yolks separated
- 1 cup sugar
- 2 and ½ tablespoons orange juice
- Zest from 1 orange, grated
- 2 tablespoons confectioners' sugar for serving
- 1 and 1/3 cups Greek yogurt for serving
- Pulp from 4 passion fruits

Directions:

Put the water in a pot and bring to a boil over medium high heat. Add orange juice and 1 and ¼ cups sugar, stir and boil for 10 minutes. Take off heat, add orange zest and orange water, stir and leave aside. In a bowl, beat egg yolks with 1 cup sugar and hazelnut flour using your mixer. In another bowl, beat egg whites using your mixer as well. Combine the 2 mixtures and stir well. Pour this batter into a greased and lined baking form, introduce in the oven at 350 degrees F and bake for 30 minutes. Take cake out of the oven, leave it to cool down a bit, slice and serve with the orange sauce you've made, with yogurt, confectioners' sugar dusted on top and passion fruit pulp on the side. Enjoy!

Nutrition: calories 234, fat 1, fiber 2, carbs 4, protein 7

Semolina Pudding

Preparation time: 10 minutes
Cooking time: 7 minutes
Servings: 18

Ingredients:

- 2 cups semolina, ground
- 1 cup olive oil
- 4 cups hot water
- 2 and ½ cups water
- 1 cup raisins
- 1 teaspoon cinnamon powder

Directions:

Heat up a pan with the oil over medium high heat, add semolina and brown it for 3 minutes stirring often. Add sugar, stir and cook for 4 minutes more. Add hot, water, stir, reduce heat and simmer for a few more minutes until it thickens. Divide into bowls, sprinkle raisins and cinnamon and serve. Enjoy!

Nutrition: calories 240, fat 12, fiber 1, carbs 32, protein 3

Delicious Greek Ice Cream

Preparation time: 2 hours
Cooking time: 0
Servings: 8

Ingredients:

- 2/3 cup heavy cream
- 4 and ¼ cups Greek yogurt
- 2/3 cup sugar
- 6 tablespoons lemon juice

Directions:

In your ice cream maker, mix yogurt with cream, sugar and lemon juice, stir, introduce in your freezer for 2 hours and then serve. Enjoy!

Nutrition: calories 134, fat 7, fiber 0, carbs 16, protein 1

Honey Baked Nectarines

Preparation time: 10 minutes
Cooking time: 30 minutes
Servings: 3

Ingredients:

- 3 teaspoons brown sugar
- 3 nectarines, cut into halves and stones removed
- 1 teaspoon vanilla extract
- 6 tablespoons yogurt
- 3 tablespoons honey

Directions:

Place nectarines on a lined baking sheet, add brown sugar, honey and vanilla, introduce in the oven at 350 degrees F and bake for 15 minutes. Take nectarines out of the oven, toss them a bit in the pan, introduce in the oven again and bake for 15 minutes more. Serve them with Greek yogurt on top. Enjoy!

Nutrition: calories 221, fat 7, fiber 3, carbs 55, protein 2

Tasty Yogurt Pudding

Preparation time: 10 minutes
Cooking time: 0 minutes
Servings: 1

Ingredients:

- 1 tablespoon cocoa powder
- ¾ cup Greek yogurt
- 5 drops vanilla stevia
- 4 tablespoons strawberry jam

Directions:

In a bowl, mix yogurt with cocoa powder and stir. Add vanilla stevia and stir again. Top with strawberry jam and keep in the fridge until you serve. Enjoy!

Nutrition: calories 113, fat 4, fiber 2, carbs 14, protein 12

Simple Bread Pudding

Preparation time: 10 minutes
Cooking time: 40 minutes
Servings: 6

Ingredients:

- 12 ounces bread, sliced
- 1.5-ounce sultanas
- 2 tablespoons lemon marmalade
- 4 eggs
- 1.5 ounces sugar
- 1-pint milk
- 3 tablespoons brandy
- 4 allspice berries, crushed
- ¼ teaspoon nutmeg, grated

Directions:

Place half of the bread slices in a baking dish and spread marmalade over them. Sprinkle sultanas and add the rest of the bread slices. In a bowl, mix eggs with milk, nutmeg, allspice, sugar and brandy and whisk well. Pour this over bread pudding, introduce in the oven at 350 degrees F and bake for 40 minutes. Take bread pudding out of the oven, leave it aside to cool down, slice, arrange on plates and serve. Enjoy!

Nutrition: calories 300, fat 12, fiber 1, carbs 32, protein 24

Lemon Pudding

Preparation time: 10 minutes
Cooking time: 5 minutes
Servings: 4

Ingredients:

- ¾ cup sugar
- 2 and ½ cups milk
- ¼ cup cornstarch
- 3 egg yolks, whisked
- Juice from 2 lemons
- A pinch of salt
- Zest of 2 lemons, grated
- 2 tablespoons butter
- Whipped cream

Directions:

In a bowl, mix cornstarch with sugar, milk, egg yolks, salt and zest and whisk well. Pour this into a pan, heat up over medium heat, stir and cook until it thickens. Take off heat, add butter and lemon juice and stir. Divide into 4 dishes, leave pudding aside to cool down and serve with whipped cream on top. Enjoy!

Nutrition: calories 200, fat 2, fiber 1, carbs 4, protein 1

Conclusion

Make an important step and change your lifestyle. Live a healthier life by choosing a healthy diet: the Mediterranean one! You will be surprised to find out that this diet doesn't mean you should deprive yourself of eating tasty dishes! it only means eating healthy ones, full of amazing ingredients!

The Mediterranean diet is such an amazing life option! It can make you a healthier person and you will be able to live a long and happy life!

If you made the decision and if you've chosen this wonderful diet, then all you need is this amazing cooking journal to help you get started.
Get your hands on this great recipe collection and start cooking the Mediterranean way!
Have fun and enjoy the best meals of your life!

Recipe Index

Made in the USA
Lexington, KY
22 March 2018